PÂTÉS
AND
TERRINES

PÂTÉS
AND
TERRINES

Friedrich W. Ehlert · Edouard Longue · Michael Raffael · Frank Wesel

HAMLYN
London · New York · Sydney · Toronto

This edition published in 1984 by
The Hamlyn Publishing Group Limited
London · New York · Sydney · Toronto
Astronaut House, Feltham, Middlesex, England
© Copyright The Hamlyn Publishing Group Limited 1984

First published under the title
Das Grosse Buch der Pasteten
© Copyright by Teubner Edition

ISBN 0 600 32375 7

Phototypeset in 9½ on 10½pt Monophoto Times by
Tameside Filmsetting Limited, Lancashire

Printed in Spain

Front cover photograph by James Jackson

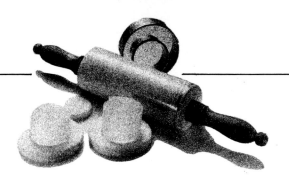

Contents

Introduction

We are happy to be able to bring you a book unique in both content and format, a book on one of the most interesting aspects of the art of cookery. The emphasis is firmly on the word 'art', for in fact its subject is more than mere cookery, pâté and terrine making having a long and complex culinary history. Without doubt it is a fascinating, many-faceted subject. The fascination, and to some extent the air of mystery, which surrounds pâté making was one of the main reasons behind this book.

The number of pâté and related recipes from around the world is legion and it would have been impossible to include them all in this book. It was more a case of having to choose from a host of recipes those that truly justified the term pâtés and terrines, and those that closely resemble them in their methods of preparation. Here we had to define our terms of reference exactly because the 'pâtés and terrines' which have come down to us from the past include terrines, galantines, ballotines, etc. The differences between these dishes are often confused, not only when transposed from one country to another, but even on a national level. Terrines are called pâtés, or vice versa, and terrines are often referred to as parfaits or galantines. We have tried to bring a little order into this confusion by setting out certain basic criteria for each type of pâté or terrine, to help you identify them with more certainty. In this we have taken into account historical development as well as the opinions of experts both at home and abroad. In each separate chapter we have attempted to explain the individual characteristics of each type.

In choosing the recipes for inclusion in this book we have selected the most representative examples of each group of pâtés. A typical recipe, which we have called a basic recipe, is explained in every chapter with both text and photographs. These are both recipes in their own right, which you should be able to follow without difficulty, and at the same time they provide all the information you need to create imaginative new dishes of your own. That is why we have devoted a lot of space to these basic recipes. Regardless of whether it is pastry making, fillings, or how to stuff a galantine that worries you, you will find all these explained in both photographs and text with all the essential information.

Pâtés and terrines have continued to grow in popularity in recent years. Our book celebrates this renaissance and will certainly be indispensable for all cooks intent on scaling the heights of this culinary art, but it will also appeal to those who prefer simpler dishes, such as country terrines with all their honest goodness. We have tried to produce a book that will satisfy all the requirements of the professional chef, and at the same time provide the enthusiastic cook at home with a book that is easy to follow. It is to be hoped that we have achieved these aims, that the reader will enjoy the book and find inspiration in it, develop the skill of pâté making and at the same time derive all possible pleasure from a classic work of this kind and from the pâtés and terrines which it contains.

Christian Teubner

Pastries

Long ago, the inventive Ancient Greeks were already encasing meat, fish and all kinds of vegetables in pastry and they are thus credited with inventing the pie. It is also an established fact that the ancient Romans followed their example. But no-one knows exactly who invented pastry, that crisp crust which encloses the choicest foods, protecting them, preserving their juices and enhancing their flavour. It seems certain however that the first pastries were made simply with flour and water and resembled our eggless pasta dough. This has led to the conjecture that the ancient Greeks and Romans left their pastry uneaten out of consideration for their teeth, and indeed it would have required considerable force to bite through this primitive form of pastry to reach the filling.

Easy-to-work pastry

It is clear that early pastry cooks were not slow to discover the advantages of adding fat and eggs to give their pastry a more edible, lighter consistency. But pastry was not always intended for eating. In the Middle Ages it was used to make attractive table decorations, designed to stimulate the appetite. While these could be extremely artistic constructions, sometimes the designs were very simple. However, simple or extravagant, to be eaten or not, a pastry crust has always been an important part of pie making and justifiably so. Pastry was, and still is, an easy-to-work material. The simpler the pastry (that is, the less fat it contains) the more complex the constructions that can be made with it. This is obvious from the exotic pastry constructions of the Middle Ages, the Renaissance, the Baroque and Rococo periods, described in the literature of the time.

The first great pastry cooks were the Italians, who were later imitated by the French. It was they who first improved the flavour of pies by leaving out the pastry altogether, thus inventing the terrine and galantine.

It must be light, and rich in fat

The most important pastry, and the first in the history of pie making, is the shortcrust or kneading pastry, known in grandmother's day and even earlier as rub-in pastry, after the process of rubbing the fat into the flour with the hands to form crumbs before adding the other ingredients. It is still made in the same way today, or alternatively all the ingredients can be worked quickly together to give a good pastry which is rich in fat. Most pies intended to be eaten cold, and some small pies to be eaten hot, are made with shortcrust. It can also be used for old-fashioned English pies, even though suet pastry is more often used – and for good reason, for beef suet makes pastry flaky and light.

Piecrusts to be eaten hot

Puff pastry piecrusts are invariably eaten hot, as in the case of bouchées à la reine, vol-au-vents and patties. There are, of course, sweet cakes made with puff pastry which are eaten cold, but in the case of savoury pies puff pastry is, without exception, eaten hot, for the pastry loses its flaky consistency when it cools; then the moist filling makes the pastry heavy. This pushes puff pastry into second place in the order of importance of piecrusts, it is a delight to eat when it has been expertly prepared. Although there are several ways of making it, the principle remains the same: the thinnest and finest possible layers of a water-based dough and butter give this pastry its airy consistency. Contrary to general opinion, puff pastry is not particularly difficult to make, but it is extremely time-consuming. To save time you can use one of the frozen varieties on the market, for these are generally excellent, but if you particularly want a puff pastry made with butter you will have to make your own.

We still have not mentioned the third type of pastry used for pâté making: yeast or brioche pastry. This plays only a minor part in classic pâtés, but some chefs, such as the famous Maître Haeberlin of Alsace, make a superb foie gras in yeast pastry. Yeast dough is better known, however, in connection with Russian *pirozhki*, Galician and South American *empanadas* and a number of speciality dishes.

As far as pâté making is concerned you can forget about pasta and choux pastry, although there are a few specialities in which they are used.

Shortcrust pastry (piecrust)

Shortcrust pastry is usually associated with sweet tarts, but shortcrust for savoury pies naturally contains no sugar. In France and Switzerland the term shortcrust or pâte brisée refers exclusively to piecrust which contains salt rather than sugar.

Of all the pastries used for piemaking shortcrust comes top of the list, for almost all savoury pies are made with it. The quantities of its basic ingredients – namely flour, fat and liquid – vary according to the type of pie. More fat and less fluid gives an extremely crumbly pastry which is quite difficult to handle. It does not cling well together and falls apart easily when rolled. If the liquid content is increased the pastry holds together better and is easier to handle. The quality and quantity of flour is also crucial, the most important thing being for the flour to be fresh with a pleasant wheaty smell.

Flour that has been stored for a long time becomes more elastic in use and can make for brittle pastry. The quality of the flour also influences the amount of water needed, so if you are making a pastry crust for the first time, don't add all the flour initially, but keep some back to work into the pastry if it does not hold together well. If the pastry is too firm you will have to work in a little more water. It is essential for the pastry to hold together if it is to line the tin properly. It is better to use a firmer pastry for cutting into decorations.

Don't think you are restricted solely to salt for seasoning pastry. You can use other seasonings too, sprinkling them into the pastry once you have decided on the character of the filling; a country-style filling, heavily flavoured with garlic, for example, goes well with a sprinkling of pepper and nutmeg. For fish and veal pâtés a touch of ginger will complement the flavour. After mixing, the dough must be left to stand in the refrigerator for at least an hour. This will allow it to settle and to take on a slightly softer consistency (a point to bear in mind when mixing the pastry) and easier to roll. To work together any leftover pastry, knead it as little as possible on as little flour as possible and reroll. Overworking the pastry can easily make it brittle so that it shrinks during cooking.

The following recipe for a good all-round pastry should give excellent results:

450 g/1 lb flour
225 g/8 oz butter
1 teaspoon salt
5 tablespoons water
1 egg

Pastry made with lard is also recommended. It is easy to work and gives a crisp result.

Sample recipe:

450 g/1 lb flour
175 g/6 oz lard
1 scant teaspoon salt
75 to 150 ml/⅛ to ¼ pint

1 **Sieve the flour onto the worktop.** Make a well in the centre, cut the butter into cubes and place it in the well. Sprinkle with the salt. Professional chefs can estimate the quantity by eye, but it is advisable to weigh it if you are unsure.

2 **Pour the water onto the butter.** You can add all the water at once, or add it gradually if you prefer. The latter method would be easier for beginners for if the water is added gradually it binds easier and quicker with the butter (or other fat).

3 **Add the egg.** Make sure that it is the same temperature as the butter, otherwise it will be difficult to work in. It is a good idea to break the egg into a cup initially to test for freshness. Mix the butter, egg and water together.

4 **Gradually work in the flour.** Work the butter with one hand, adding small amounts of flour with a pastry scraper in the other hand. Work as quickly and carefully as possible, mixing the ingredients thoroughly together.

5 **Knead the pastry together as quickly as possible.** The faster you work, the better the pastry will hold together; it may nevertheless become dry and cracked, but you can remedy this by adding a little more cold water.

Evenly rolled

Pastry is easy if you place a strip of wood of the required thickness either side. 3 to 4 mm/⅛ in is the right thickness for lining tins, but for bouchées, for example, roll to 6 to 7 mm/scant ¼ in.

A second method: rubbing in

Whichever method you choose, the end result will be the same. Rubbed-in pastry takes its name from the method of preparation. Here the fat and flour are rubbed in with the fingertips into crumbs. The same method is used to make a crumble, for example. This is an old method which is still very popular.

1 **For the rubbed-in method, sieve the flour** onto the worktop. Add the butter in small pieces. Rub in carefully with the fingers, working the butter into the flour to form a crumbly mixture.

2 **Make a well in the mixture.** Sprinkle with the salt and pour in the water. Then add the egg. Work the liquid into part of the flour-and-fat mixture, then blend in the remaining mixture working from the outside inwards.

3 **Using both hands, shape the mixture quickly** into a ball and knead firmly, so that the mixture clings together well. Like pastry made by the previous method, rubbed-in pastry also needs to be covered and left to stand in the refrigerator for 1 hour.

How much pastry do you need?

Recipes are sometimes extremely comprehensive and this can make them appear complicated. To avoid this the recipes in this book have been kept as simple as possible. For pâtés, the quantity of pastry required is given in grammes and ounces. This may be confusing to anyone who is not used to baking, so, to avoid any problems, we have compiled the table on the right: this tells you what ingredients you require to make a given weight of pastry. It may also tempt you to try variations of your own on any given recipe. By altering the egg or fat content, or the quantities of flour, many such experiments have inspired new ideas which have been successful enough to become standard recipes. In the same way

you can experiment with the kind and quantity of seasoning, thus creating your own individual recipes.

It is always advisable to make more pastry than you actually need, for it is easier to roll out a larger sheet of pastry and cut it to size than to try to roll the pastry to fit the

dish exactly. You can use any leftovers to make decorations or make them into savoury sticks sprinkled with poppy seeds and caraway.

For about 675 g/1½ lb pastry	For about 1 kg/2¼ lb pastry	For about 1.5 kg/3½ lb pastry	For about 1.75 kg/3¾ lb pastry
450 g/1 lb plain flour 225 g/8 oz butter 1 teaspoon salt 1 egg white 5–8 tablespoons water	575 g/1¼ lb plain flour 275 g/10 oz butter 1½ teaspoons salt 1 egg 6–9 tablespoons water	800 g/1¾ lb plain flour 400 g/14 oz butter 2 teaspoons salt 1 egg 1 egg white 150–275 ml/5–9 fl oz water	1 kg/2¼ lb plain flour 500 g/18 oz butter 2½ teaspoons salt 2 eggs 250–325 ml/8–11 fl oz water

Suet pastry

There is no need to turn up your nose at the thought of pastry made with beef fat, i.e. suet, especially if it is best beef fat, kidney suet.

Suet makes pastry rise well and gives a consistency like that of puff pastry, but it should only be used for pies that are to be served hot.

225 g/8 oz beef suet (kidney fat)
450 g/1 lb flour
1 teaspoon salt
200–300 ml/7–10 fl oz water

1 Prepare the suet. If you leave it to stand in the refrigerator for a while it will come out of the skin easily. You can also buy suet skinned and chopped, but the best kidney suet is only available in the piece.

2 Finely chop the suet. This is easiest with a large, sharp knife held in both hands like a chopping knife. Sprinkle lightly with flour to prevent the suet sticking together.

3 Initial mixing. With the fingertips thoroughly mix the flour, fat and salt in a bowl, crumbling the suet as you mix. Do not completely crush the pieces of fat or the pastry will not rise so well.

4 Add the water a little at a time – 200 ml/7 fl oz will usually be enough. Add more only if necessary. Stir briskly while adding water to bind the flour and fat well together.

5 Knead the pastry, as quickly and firmly as possible. Fat, flour and water must form a homogenous mixture. Suet pastry does not keep, but should also be left to stand or chilled for a while before baking.

Yeast pastry

Yeast pastry is seldom used in pâté making, but it is worth a mention as it is used in a few speciality dishes, in Russian *pirozhki*, or Spanish *empañadas*, for example. It is important to use fresh yeast if you can, because of its pure yeast cells which multiply rapidly in the right environment. And the right environment for yeast consists of food and moisture – provided by the dough – together with warmth. By a process of fermentation the yeast cells change the starches present in the flour into glucose, which in turn changes into alcohol and carbon dioxide. It is this gas which makes yeast pastry so light, quite apart from the typically fresh and pleasant taste which the yeast gives. There are two ways of making yeast pastry. The first method, the one illustrated in the photographs, is the warmth method. The second method, the cold method, consists of dissolving the yeast in milk and mixing the pastry without allowing time for fermentation. This sort of dough is particularly suitable for fillings which are extremely sensitive to heat. Whichever method you choose, yeast pastry is much easier to make than many people think.

Basic recipe:

450 g/1 lb plain flour
25 g/1 oz fresh yeast or 15 g/½ oz dried
225 ml/8 fl oz lukewarm milk
40 g/1½ oz butter
2 eggs
1 teaspoon salt

1 **Sieve the flour into a bowl.** Make a well in the centre. Crumble the fresh yeast into the well or sprinkle over the dried. Pour on the lukewarm milk. Stir to dissolve the yeast in the milk. Sprinkle a fine layer of flour over this mixture.

2 **Cover the bowl and leave the mixture to rise** for 15 minutes in a warm, draught-free room. Cracks on the surface of the yeast mixture appear in the covering flour and are a sign that the mixture has risen sufficiently.

3 **While the mixture is rising,** melt the butter in a saucepan. Add the eggs and beat them into the butter. Stir in the salt and leave to cool slightly until lukewarm.

4 **Pour the egg and butter mixture over the yeast mixture** in the bowl. Stir all the ingredients together with a spoon and beat for a time until the dough becomes lighter and the ingredients are thoroughly mixed.

5 **Knead the dough with your hands** until dry and smooth. This stage can be done with a spoon, but you will get better results if you do it by hand. If the dough is too soft you can add a little more flour at this stage.

6 **The dry, kneaded dough** is now shaped into a ball. Place in the bowl, sprinkle with flour and cover the bowl. Leave to rise for 15 to 20 minutes to give the yeast cells sufficient time to ferment fully.

7 **When fully risen the dough** should at least have doubled in volume. Then it has risen fully. To give a finer texture, knead through once more, and leave to rise for a further 15 to 20 minutes in a covered bowl.

Puff pastry

This is the lightest pastry of all, and is particularly suitable for cases which are to be baked blind and filled later with a hot filling. It takes some time to make, but is quite easy if you stick to the rules. Alternate fine layers of flour-and-water pastry and butter cause the pastry to rise during baking. There are two methods of preparation; you can either wrap the butter in the water pastry, or instead work the butter with a little flour, roll it out and wrap the water pastry in the butter.

800 g/1¾ lb plain flour
400 ml/14 fl oz water
2½ teaspoons salt
1 kg/2¼ lb butter
200 g/7 oz flour

1 **To make the flour-and-water pastry,** sieve the flour onto a pastry board and make a well in the centre. Add the cold water and salt and work together quickly with your hands, working from the centre outwards.

2 **Knead the pastry** until the surface is smooth and shiny. Shape into a ball, cover and leave in the refrigerator for at least 15 minutes. A cross cut in the top will help the pastry to settle.

3 **Next prepare the butter** The butter should be as cold as possible. Cut up the butter, place on the pastry board, sift flour over and work them together. Shape into a ball, cover and again leave to stand in the refrigerator.

4 **Roll out the butter.** It should not stick to the board if it is thoroughly chilled and the board liberally sprinkled with flour. Roll the butter into a rectangle about 45 × 75 cm/18 × 30 in.

5 **The flour-and-water pastry goes inside the butter.** The pastry should be rolled to 40 × 35 cm/16 × 14 in and placed over one half of the butter. Fold over the other half of the butter sheet.

6 **Place the edges together** and press firmly together with the fingers to seal the pastry completely inside the butter. Sprinkle the work surface lightly with flour.

7 **Roll from bottom to top.** It is essential to maintain an even pressure with the rolling pin to get even layers of pastry. Then roll alternately from left to right.

8 **Roll from left to right.** By continually changing direction you will keep the layers even as the pastry becomes thinner and thinner. Roll the pastry to about 45 × 75 cm/18 × 30 in and chill for 15 to 20 minutes.

Puff pastry
an alternative method

Experts could spend many happy hours discussing which of the two methods of making puff pastry is the correct one – or whether perhaps a combination of the two would give the best results. In fact the results are almost identical. The pastry described in the photographs is made with an outer layer of butter and flour. The advantage of this method is that it will not dry out and can be stored for a few days before use. It has a tendency to stick to the work surface during rolling out, but you can usually prevent sticking by sprinkling the surface generously with flour.

The second method also has its advantages: with the pastry on the outside you can use unadulterated butter, that is without flour, whereas in a warm room you will have to add up to 10 per cent flour to the butter to make it easy to handle by the first method. But it soon dries out and then cracks during rolling, allowing the butter to escape. You can avoid this by wrapping the pastry in foil before standing it in the refrigerator.

1 kg/2¼ lb plain flour
500 ml/17 fl oz water
15 g/½ oz salt
1 kg/2¼ lb butter

or

900 g/2 lb plain flour
450 ml/16 fl oz water
15 g/½ oz salt
1 kg/2¼ lb butter
100 g/4 oz plain flour

Cut a cross in the top of the flour-and-water pastry. Work it into a smooth dough in the usual way, shape into a ball, flatten slightly and cut the top. Cream the butter until smooth and shape into a slab, or work in with the flour.

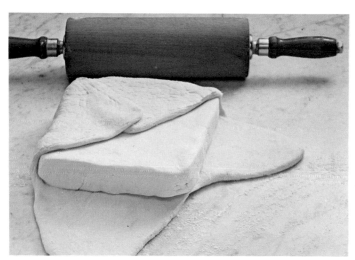

Wrap the butter in the pastry. The cross in the top will make it easy to roll four pieces outwards from the centre. Place the slab of butter in the centre and fold over the four corners of pastry, sealing the edges. You will get a better seal if you first brush the edges with water. Roll and make your turns as described for the first method.

9 **To make a single turn,** fold one third of the pastry into the centre and fold the remaining third over it like an envelope. You now have three layers of pastry one on top of the other. Wrap in greaseproof paper and leave in the refrigerator for 15 to 20 minutes.

10 **To make a double turn,** fold the left and right edges into the centre, so that they meet. Then fold the pastry over again lengthways to give four layers one on top of the other. Again, leave to stand.

11 **How many turns was that?** A simple way of remembering is after each turn to make the appropriate number of fingerprints in the pastry. You will need four turns altogether, two single and two double.

Seasonings

It is difficult for us to imagine the immense variety of seasonings used by cooks in the past, but literature provides us with several examples.

We tend to forget that a knowledge of seasonings was indispensable to the medieval cook. In the days before refrigerators they were used liberally to hide the taste and smell of foods which were no longer fresh. Pepper, for example, not only masked such flavours – it also delayed the process of decay by up to 24 hours. Pies, however, required a profusion of seasonings for other quite special reasons. Seasonings were both rare and expensive: pepper for example was worth its weight in gold and some businesses made their profits in dealing in spices alone. One pound of nutmeg cost as much as seven fatted oxen, according to a price list of 1393. So spices became a status symbol and were most used where they created the maximum impression – that is, in pies, the most showy of all the dishes brought to the table. At the wedding banquet of a sixteenth-century Burgundian nobleman 190 pounds of pepper alone were used.

Explorers like Columbus, Magellan and Vasco da Gama had a lot to thank the cookery business for: when they landed on foreign soil they did not only look for gold, for astronomically expensive spices were even more in demand in Europe. It was at this time that the special association of individual herbs and spices with a particular geographical area was established: cloves from the Moluccas, ginger from India, chilli from America, allspice from Jamaica and Cuba. You can see from this small sample of countries which produce the spices used in pâté and terrine making that you can almost imagine yourself following in Columbus's footsteps. You can imagine too the amount of international wheeling and dealing which went into producing a good meal – and it was a long time before spices became any cheaper. To keep prices high the Dutch restricted planting of nutmeg trees in their spice islands to the few that they needed for their own requirements. And finally, there were also those herbs and spices which were native to Europe. The more inventive cooks replaced foreign spices with imaginative combinations of fresh or dried herbs, a form of economy which was to appear over and over again in times of need.

But less imagination is required in today's commercial world where you can buy mixtures of pâté seasonings. No-one could object to them on the grounds of their quality, but what a comedown from the time when seasonings were an opportunity for creativity and a means of self-expression! Ready-mixed herbs take away the greatest pleasure in pâté and terrine making: the chance to give these culinary works of art their own, quite individual flavour.

The art of mixing herbs and spices

It is not as difficult to use herbs successfully as is often thought. With 15 ingredients, which you probably already have in the kitchen cupboard, you can make a 'basic seasoning' with which to experiment. You can use these ingredients to mix enough seasoning to keep some in stock, but no more than you are likely to use within six months, for herbs soon lose their aroma, especially when mixed with other herbs. That is why it is important to stick to the quantities given in the recipe, or to what you think you can use. This mixture forms a basis on which you can experiment. You may make mistakes – but you may also make the most delicious discoveries.

While you can give your imagination free rein, do not totally ignore the experience of generations of cooks who have learnt what goes well with what – and what does not. Wild boar and juniper, for example: these bitter berries can be added to the basic seasoning to complement any game dish. A little marjoram and garlic also bring out the flavour of game very well. But avoid strongly flavoured herbs with a delicate venison pâté, where grated orange or lemon peel are better than marjoram. Rosemary and sage go well with poultry, and concentrated fresh orange juice goes well with duck. Another idea for duck is to add coarsely chopped green peppercorns, as in one variation on foie gras. You can see that there are no limits to the possible variations. But you need to feel your way carefully to avoid gross and possibly expensive errors of judgement: a goose liver pâté seasoned with garlic might make your dinner guests beat an immediate, hasty retreat.

Alcoholic flavourings

Labels such as 'cooking wine' or 'hotel quality', which are synonymous with second-rate, should serve as a warning. Despite the assertions made in many cookery books, you should use only the best for cooking, the wine with the best bouquet, the brandy with the best aroma. Alcohol content is unimportant, only the flavour counts. The alcohol evaporates of course and you can't get drunk from eating pâté.

Alcohol should never be mixed directly into the filling, for it expands and could cause the pastry to crack during baking. So it is best to use liquor in food in the following way: use it to dilute the juices left in the pan after cooking the main ingredients and reduce it, where possible adding a little stock made with leftover bits of the meat used for the pâté. The sauce obtained can be added to the filling or used to moisten the other ingredients. It is obvious that a sauce of this kind is always better than barbarically sprinkling a filling with some kind of cheap spirits.

Allspice

Pimenta officinalis

Often called Jamaican pepper, allspice is the dried berries of the Jamaican pepper tree, from the myrtle family. Its name exactly describes its flavour, which combines those of several spices. Allspice is particularly good in meat, poultry, and even fish, fillings and is included in most spice mixtures for pâtés. Its flavour is not overpowering so it is seldom used as an individual seasoning.

Aniseed

Pimpinella anisum

A spice known for thousands of year from the *umbelliferae* family. The drie seeds taste and smell extremely spicy a fresh. Aniseed is typical of the spices be used in isolation and should be used very small quantities in mixtures. Yea dough *pirozhki* can be sprinkled wi whole seeds. The flavour goes well wi hot-and-sweet meat fillings.

Star aniseed *Illicum verum* is unrelat botanically to *Pimpinella anisum*, it nonetheless very similar in flavour.

Cardamom

Elettaria cardamomum

This is the dried fruit of the Indian cardamom plant. The three-sectioned seed pods range in colour from white (bleached) to brown-black, depending on the degree of drying. The most common is the light brown, bought ground or as whole seeds. It smells and tastes pleasantly spicy, is slightly hot and is ideal for spice mixtures. It is a must in a variety of curry powders or pâté seasonings for a truly spicy flavour.

Chillies, Cayenne pepper

Capsicum frutescens

This, the hottest of all spices, is grown in its South American homeland in various sizes, colours and strengths. The name cayenne pepper is confusing, for botanically the plant belongs to the paprika, and not the pepper, family.

In its dried, ground form it is the ideal seasoning to give hotness with neutral flavour, best used in small quantities with fish and shellfish and in more generous quantities in hot meat fillings and stews.

Coriander

Coriandrum sativum

A spice dating from the time of the Old Testament. The dried seeds have a pleasant, mildly spicy taste. Its main use is in combination with other spices, which makes it one of the main ingredients of curry. It goes well in spice mixtures for coarse pâtés.

The green leaves of the coriander (ciliantro) are an aromatic herb, although the flavour is oily and pungent, for which reason most books warn against their use.

Cumin

Cuminum cyminum

This is not to be confused with *Car carvi*, a member of the Mediterran parsley family. The golden brown se look very much like caraway and hav highly aromatic and slightly bitter fl our. Cumin is a spice long neglected northern climes, although it makes ideal seasoning for strongly flavou meat and is suitable for inclusion in s mixtures – use it in spice mixtures pâtés or curries. Excellent too chutneys and other accompaniments. sauces.

Ginger

Zingiber officinale

Ginger is the rhizome root of the reed-like ginger plant of the spice lily family. Whole roots keep their flavour over long periods and, freshly grated, are always preferable to ground ginger. They have a burning hot, slightly sweet flavour and will go excellently as part of a mixture of seasonings for meat fillings, game, poultry and fish.

Fresh ginger roots are usually one of the milder varieties and should be used more generously.

Green peppercorns

Piper nigrum

This is a newcomer from the pepper family, used freeze-dried or available preserved in its raw state. Both varieties have a mild, aromatic pepper flavour, which is excellent where pepper is used as the only seasoning. The dried form is stronger, but still relatively mild. Despite accepted practice, the green variety should never be used as whole seeds. Its full aroma comes out only when crushed.

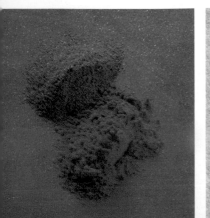

Paprika

Capsicum annuum

The most widely used types of paprika are mild paprika, sweet paprika, which is medium-hot, and rose paprika, the hottest of the three. All three come from pimentoes. The degree of hotness is determined by the amount of capsaicin, found in the dividing walls of the pod. The more of this section of the plant included in the powder, the hotter it will be. It is best in stews, sauces and highly flavoured meat mixtures.

Pepper

Piper nigrum

Pepper only retains its full spiciness hotness when freshly ground. White black pepper come from the same p Black pepper is originally green, bec ing brown-black and shrivelled d drying. It is hot and quite direct in t For white pepper the fully ripe seed used; they are soaked, the skins remo and then dried. It is less hot and mild flavour. When buying whole peppero remember: the larger the corns, the b the aroma.

Bay

Laurus nobilis

This is a pâté seasoning par excellence, and often used as a decoration for terrines. The leaves of the evergreen bay tree can be used fresh or dried. Fresh leaves are more aromatic, but have a slightly bitter taste, which disappears after drying for 2–3 hours. Chopped or crumbled bay leaves give an appropriately spicy flavour to meat fillings, and are especially good in liver and poultry pâtés.

Caraway

Carum carvi

Caraway, the dried dehiscent fruit of the caraway plant, grows wild throughout Europe and is also widely cultivated. An unusual spice with an indefinable flavour, used in all types of recipes from bread to baked cabbage. Its strong taste makes it a spice best used on its own with meat, cheese, cabbage or bread. Nevertheless it can be blended with other spices, in curries for example, or in mixed seasonings for country-style pâtés.

Cinnamon, Cassia

Cinnamomum zeylanicum/cassia

here are two types of cinnamon, which e rarely available separately in the ops. Cinnamon and cassia are both the ied inner bark of the cinnamon tree, t their flavours are quite different. ylon cinnamon is aromatically spicy, eet and mild and light in colour. The inner the bark the better the cinnamon. ssia has a highly spiced flavour, is eetly hot, and darker, and the bark nsiderably thicker. Cassia is suitable strongly-flavoured fillings, cinnamon more delicate ones.

Cloves

Caryophyllus aromaticus

The clove is the dried flower bud of the clove tree. Its unmistakable taste is highly spiced, almost burning. Although a typical spice for individual use, it can also be combined successfully with other spices. Cloves are essential in most spice mixtures for sausage dishes and pâtés, but are also used on their own to season sauces and stews and, of course, fruit dishes. One point to watch: only buy cloves in small quantities for they quickly lose their aroma.

Curry powder

This is an asiatic mixture of spices, containing up to 30 separate spices. Curry – the word is an anglicisation of the Indian *kari* can be bought in powder or paste form and used with a wide range of curry dishes. Its main ingredients are coriander, pepper, chilli, cumin, cardamom, and turmeric which gives curry its distinctive yellowy-green colour. When buying spices for curry buy only the best quality, and store in small quantities in light-proof containers. It is an essential ingredient in the preparation of various curries and vol-au-vent fillings.

Fennel

Foeniculum vulgare

A spice from the umbelliferae family, like aniseed and caraway, ripe, dried fennel seeds have a highly aromatic, fairly sweet flavour, slightly reminiscent of aniseed. Native to Asia and the Mediterranean, it is used mainly in dishes from these areas. Used on its own as a flavouring for bread and cakes, it can also be used in spice mixtures in small quantities.

The tender leaves of the fennel plant can, like dill, be used for fish pâtés and terrines.

Juniper

Juniperus communis

niper berries – round in shape and mm/about ¼ inch in diameter, are the e berries of the juniper bush, native oughout Europe. They have a strong, htly bitter and resinous smell and our, which makes them the ideal spice spice mixtures for game. In pâté king they are occasionally used for ngs and sauces. The whole berries are en used to decorate game and country-e terrines. When stored be careful that y do not dry out.

Nutmeg and Mace

Myristica fragrans

Beneath the fleshy skin of the fruit of the nutmeg tree lies the hard (when ripe) nut. Within this shell lies the actual nut (nutmeg) surrounded by a seed covering (mace), often wrongly described as nutmeg blossom. Mace has a very pleasant, mildly spicy taste and is an ideal seasoning for any light spice mixture for pâtés and stews. The nutmeg, on the other hand, has a much stronger flavour and smell and should always be freshly grated.

Saffron

Crocus sativus

The name saffron comes from the Arabic *Za'fran*, meaning yellow. The spice is something of a hybrid as it is a spice and colouring at the same time. It is the dried stamens of a type of crocus, and it takes 80,000 stamens to produce 1 kg/2¼ lb saffron, which explains its high price. Its taste is unmistakably bitter-sweet. It is also highly coloured: 1 gram of saffron is sufficient to give 3 litres/5 pints water a deep yellow colour.

Yeast pastry coloured with saffron gives a beautiful golden-brown crust.

Vanilla

Vanilla planifolia

This is the fully ripe pod of a climbing orchid native to Mexico. By drying in the sun, soaking and fermentation the flavour is allowed to develop fully in the pod. Vanilla, actually a 'sweet seasoning' with an unmistakable scent and aroma, can also be used to vary spice mixtures for pâtés. It is particularly suitable for delicately-flavoured meat or poultry or fine liver pâtés. Vanilla should be stored in an airtight container, for it easily absorbs foreign smells.

Pâtés and Seasoning

These are two words which might cause a problem, for if we omit the 'and', we are left with the old, vague phrase 'pâté seasoning'. It is difficult to believe that this term has featured in cookery books for the last 300 years, with its constituent parts seldom listed. Even famous cooks used to refer in their recipes for lobster, sweetbreads and goose liver pâté to 'pâté seasoning'. When you attempted these recipes you were left to guess what such a mixture might contain. Now you can devise your secret formula, or simply buy mixture X made by company Y.

Your own basic mixture It is generally assumed that it is simpler and safer to use a bought pâté seasoning than to try and make your own with the limited selection of spices at your disposal. Nevertheless the inventive cook will welcome the opportunity to blend various seasonings to produce an individual, unmistakable flavour. Naturally the spices used should be fresh and of the best available quality. Whole seeds are preferable to the ground variety, as they will generally have more flavour. You can grind your spices in an electric coffee grinder or a food processor. The minute quantities of 8–10 separate spices required for one recipe cannot be weighed accurately even with the most expensive scales, so you should be prepared to make enough for several pâtés. This still leaves room for variation, for you can alter the flavour of the basic mixture by adding different spices, or even fresh herbs, each time you make a pâté.

Highly accurate scales are essential for weighing the minute quantities involved, if you want to guarantee the same flavour every time.

For delicately flavoured meat fillings

2 tablespoons white peppercorns
2 tablespoons ground coriander
25 g/1 oz fresh thyme
25 g/1 oz fresh basil
2 tablespoons ground cloves
3 tablespoons ground nutmeg
5 bay leaves
2 tablespoons ground allspice
2 tablespoons ground mace
25 g/1 oz dried mushrooms

An all-purpose spice mixture

2 tablespoons white peppercorns
2 tablespoons black peppercorns
2 tablespoons mild paprika
1 tablespoon hot paprika
1 sprig fresh marjoram
1 sprig fresh thyme
1 sprig fresh basil
1½ tablespoons ground nutmeg
1½ tablespoons ground mace
10 bay leaves
2 tablespoons ground cloves
1½ tablespoons ground ginger

For highly-flavoured country-style pâtés

20 g/¾ oz dried green peppercorns
1 tablespoon ground allspice
1 tablespoon ground mace
1 tablespoon mild paprika
1 tablespoon ground coriander
1 sprig fresh thyme
1 sprig fresh rosemary
1 sprig fresh basil
1 sprig fresh marjoram
1 heaped teaspoon ground cloves
6 bay leaves

Special seasoning for game

2 tablespoons white peppercorns
2 tablespoons black peppercorns
1 tablespoon mild paprika
1 tablespoon hot paprika
3 tablespoons fresh marjoram
2 sprigs fresh thyme
2 sprigs fresh basil
2 tablespoons ground nutmeg
2 tablespoons ground mace
10 bay leaves
2 tablespoons ground cloves
1 sprig fresh lovage
2 tablespoons ground ginger
25 g/1 oz juniper berries
50 g/2 oz dried mushrooms

Pâté salt, a mixture of pâté seasoning and salt, should not be made up without first checking for flavour. A mixture of this kind has two advantages: it stores well and involves only one lot of weighing. Depending on the mixture, you will need 20–40 g/¾–1½ oz spices to 500 g/18 oz salt, and 15–20 g/½–¾ oz pâté salt per 1 kg/2¼ lb filling.

Ready-made pâté seasoning

With all due respect to home-made seasonings, a really good (and here you will have to rely on the reputation of the manufacturer) bought pâté seasoning has several advantages, even for the most creative cooks.

The consumer cannot expect to be aware of the variable quality of individual spices, caused by variable harvests, but the manufacturer can balance out this factor. Commercial grinding techniques preserve more of the flavour than the kitchen coffee grinder and modern packaging guarantees freshness. This may be little compensation for uniformity of taste but, as with home-made mixtures, there is opportunity for a host of individual variations. You can use a bought mixture as a base and add a personal touch by adding fresh herbs or dried juniper berries, garlic, dried mushrooms or grated citrus fruit peel.

Testing your seasoning Regardless of whether you choose bought or homemade seasoning, you should always cook a trial sample before using your mixture for the first time (break off a small piece of the filling, shape into a ball and sauté for a minute or two). Only in this way can you ascertain the effect of your seasoning and salt. With bought seasonings quantities to use are sometimes indicated on the label or the ratio of salt to seasoning. This gives one further advantage when seasoning for it allows you to make larger quantities of salt seasoning in advance. If you always make the same quantity of filling for the same container, it is a good idea to wrap the pâté salt in individual foil packets, each containing enough for one pâté.

Other types of seasoning have an important part to play in the flavour of pâtés and terrines. Orange and lemon peel, for example, dried mushrooms, or the famous truffle. Finely chopped truffles give a wonderful flavour to pâtés.

Liquid seasonings, i.e. any alcohol, should be of top quality. Quality is particularly important with drinks of high alcoholic content, for alcohol should never be added directly to a filling, but slowly reduced with a stock to give a syrupy consistency. The alcohol evaporates during reducing, leaving only the flavour of the spirit. This is why you should use only the best. The same is true of wine which is often used to improve the flavour of the stock.

Quality is important, particularly with spirits whose alcohol content is evaporated off by reducing to leave only the basic flavour. It is clear that this makes it essential to use only the best brands. The quality of the wine used (Madeira, port or sherry for example) is an important factor in the flavour of an aspic jelly.

The onion – seasoning or vegetable?

There is no clear answer to this question when it comes to pâté making. In some types of gourmet pâté the rather ordinary flavour given by onion would be inappropriate, and garlic should never be used. The delicate flavour of shallots is better suited for such dishes. However it is quite a different matter with strongly-flavoured country-style pâtés and terrines. Here the strong flavour of the onion, and occasionally garlic, is quite suitable. But they are still a seasoning and should be used in relatively small quantities. In fillings for meat pies, and even puff pastry patties, onion is often an essential part.

1. White onions, usually hot and highly flavoured, are used where a strong flavour is required.

2. Red onions, ranging in colour from purple to violet, are milder and can be used in larger quantities.

3. Spring or leek onions are picked before reaching maturity, and are particularly mild and flavoursome.

4. The shallot, the mildest of the onion family, is a real seasoning onion, with a delicate, highly aromatic taste and little of the typical onion flavour.

5. Garlic, whose flavour is as popular as its smell is unpopular, is mainly used in highly-flavoured pork and lamb fillings.

Seasoning with herbs

Leaving aside Mediterranean cooking, which has always shown a predilection for herbs, the use of herbs has for centuries past tended to go in phases. People were inclined to turn to native herbs when times were hard and money in short supply. The reason for the present popularity of herbs is, hopefully, not a passing phase, but recognition of the fact that herbs (particularly fresh ones) can complement more exotic spices to give added variety to the number of possible seasonings.

Fresh herbs for pâtés and terrines

For a long time now ready made seasoning mixtures have included dried herbs. Replacing dried thyme with fresh when you make up your own mixture does not considerably alter the outcome. Fresh herbs should be used, however, where their qualities can be fully appreciated – in fish pâtés and terrines, for example, in aspics or the various sauces for hot pâtés. Indeed, you should try to experiment with the full range of herbs and not stick merely to parsley and chives. Fresh herbs have become so popular that they are now often sold in supermarkets and greengrocers', during the summer months at least. They will keep for up to a week in the refrigerator if you stand them in water, or sprinkle them with water and wrap them in a plastic bag.

The best thing of course is to have your own herb garden, but even a window box on a balcony can provide fresh herbs throughout the summer. Grown from seed or cuttings, you can always have a fresh supply of your favourite herbs. And if you grow more than you can use there are two ways of preserving herbs: the old-fashioned drying method (not all herbs can be dried however) and freezing, which preserves the qualities of the herbs excellently. It is worthwhile chopping herbs before freezing and freezing them in individual portions. But you can also freeze whole leaves (rosemary, basil and thyme are particularly suitable) and use them for decorating terrines.

1 Basil

Ocimum basilicum

Almost a universal herb, it has a strong, hot taste and should be used sparingly in delicately-flavoured dishes. Its slightly peppery taste goes with almost every type of meat, and also with vegetables and mushrooms.

2 Mugwort

Artemisia vulgaris

This is a traditional herb for poultry, especially duck and goose. Its pleasant but slightly bitter taste is similar to that of vermouth. Cut before flowering, it is milder and less bitter.

3 Savory

Satureja hortensis

Its German name *Pfefferkraut* (pepper herb) indicates this is a hot herb. Its true flavour is only brought out by boiling. Equally good fresh or dried.

4 Borage

Borago officinalis

Its individual flavour does not go well with all ingredients. Fresh, young leaves have a delicate flavour and go well with strongly-flavoured cold meat dishes, vegetables and sauces. It loses its flavour if dried.

5 Dill

Anethum graveolens

A real fresh herb, dill should never be cooked. Its refreshing flavour complements various salads and sauces, but it is best with fish. Ideal for freezing.

6 Tarragon

Artemisia dracunculus

This slightly bitter herb only retains its full flavour if used fresh. Recommended for hot and cold poultry and fish dishes, it also is very effective in combination with dill and lemon balm.

7 Lovage

Levisticum officinale

This herb is mainly used in strongly-flavoured pâtés or meat stews, but use sparingly to keep the rather strong celery-like taste in check.

8 Marjoram

Majorana hortensis

Too often associated with the more earthy dishes, in small quantities it is recommended for even the finest fish, game and poultry pâtés. It has the most flavour while in blossom and dries well.

9 Oregano

Origanum vulgare

Also known as wild marjoram, this is best known as a seasoning for pizza. It goes particularly well with strongly-flavoured fat meat. Cut it while still in blossom. Oregano is milder dried than fresh.

10 Parsley

Petroselinum crispum

Both the curly and flat-leaved varieties are used everywhere for seasoning and garnishing. Together with the root, it is an indispensable part of a bouquet garni. Use with meat dishes, mushrooms and vegetables. Parsley freezes well.

11 Mint

Mentha piperita

The leaves have a strong, refreshing smell, warming at first, and then cooling. Recommended for any dish where its refreshing flavour would be suitable, mint is also good dried, and freezes well.

12 Burnet

Pimpinella saxifraga

This aromatic little herb, with a slightly hot flavour, has a very pleasant taste and goes best with cold meat, poultry and fish. Burnet should not be boiled. It is unsuitable for drying.

13 Rosemary

Rosmarinus officinalis

This is a highly individual herb with a refreshing, camphor-like taste. Used in small quantities, rosemary goes well with meat, game, poultry and even fish. It loses none of its flavour when dried.

14 Sage

Salvia officinalis

Its strong, slightly bitter flavour goes equally well with all types of meat, poultry, game, and also eel or fish from the sea. It loses none of its flavour when dried.

15 Chives

Allium schoenoprasum

This is a herb from the onion family, with a similar taste. Chives are recommended whenever you want a fresh onion flavour. Cooking destroys most of its flavour.

16 Thyme

Thymus vulgaris

Its pleasant, slightly hot taste makes it an ideal partner for many types of meat, as well as fish and vegetables. It is equally good either fresh or dried.

17 Hyssop

Hyssopus officinalis

This is an extremely versatile, but little known, herb with a strong, slightly bitter smell and taste, but not an overpowering flavour. Recommended for strongly-flavoured meat pâtés, it loses flavour when dried.

18 Lemon balm

Melissa officinalis

The name says it all – it has a lemony taste and smell. Use this herb to flavour wherever lemon would be appropriate, particularly in fish dishes, but also with veal, game and poultry. It loses much of its flavour when dried.

Forcemeats

DELECTABLE FILLINGS FOR PÂTÉS

The French word *farce* (forcemeat) means 'practical joke, prank' and demonstrates the common origin of eating and display. At one time it was common to play a joke on the guests by filling a hen, fish or some other small animal with a *farce*. It was much later that forcemeat was improved and made more appetising to enhance the taste of the food that was stuffed. Eventually the preparation of stuffings became one of the highest achievements of the art of cooking.

Whereas the stuffing was only an interesting addition to stuffed meat dishes (galantines), the pâté was created to show off the filling, and finally the stuffing alone sufficed to form the terrine. These contain either the finest ingredients or alternatively simple, strongly-flavoured meats, as, for example, in the case of a homely liver pâté or a French country-style terrine.

There are many different methods of obtaining excellent results, but a good forcemeat must be light and airy; it must release its flavour as it melts on the tongue. This is equally true of a forcemeat made entirely with meat, or one which includes egg, bread, or even flour. Purists who make their pâtés and terrines strictly with meat alone, and only include pork fat where necessary, will no doubt stop reading at this point. But in some situations we all have to compromise, to save time maybe, or to make expensive ingredients go further, regardless of the fact that good home cooking will always be more welcome than a continual diet of gourmet specialities. This is in no way to detract from haute cuisine, but rather to underline the value of simple pâtés (and fillings).

The pure, classic forcemeat

This consists of three elements: firstly, the main flavouring ingredient, which gives the pâté its dominant flavour and usually its name too – for example, veal, game or poultry. Secondly, the pork, which is not absolutely essential, but which gives a good pâté its smoothness. Thirdly, the pork fat which, in the right quantities, makes the pâté light, gives it its individual, melting consistency, and is unrecognisable as fat. Added to these we have seasoning with possibly other meat, nuts or mushrooms. It is an extremely simple recipe.

Success in making forcemeat depends on the binding agents, which, in other types of forcemeat, would consist of eggs or breadcrumbs. In a pure meat forcemeat the binding agent is the meat's natural protein which holds the other ingredients together. But at high temperatures it tends to coagulate which makes it useless as a binding agent. As a result any preparation of fillings must be done at the lowest practical temperatures, and the mixture never allowed to reach room temperature. This would be enough to risk ruining the filling. Cold, cold and cold again must therefore be the watchword throughout the whole process of preparation, even though observing it may cause you a good deal of trouble, not to say discomfort!

Questions of quality

A point which is often disregarded in cookery becomes of the greatest importance in all fillings or pâtés: the finest meat, the freshest fish, the best-hung game, only these are good enough. There are few problems with game and game birds which live in their natural surroundings and feed from natural foods. There is more of a problem with fish. If you live on the coast fresh fish should prove no problem, but for anyone else, always buy from a reputable fishmonger where you can be sure the fish will have been properly refrigerated before it reaches him. It is quite a different matter with veal, pork and poultry. Modern production and feeding methods have made it difficult to find a good piece of pork in most industrialised countries. Some specialist butchers keep first quality meat but you will of course have to pay more. A firm, meaty joint from an animal fed by natural means is very different from 'commercially-reared' pork, which is usually of a good, light colour but poor texture.

To sum up: regardless of whether you are making a simple, country-style terrine, or an exotic quail pâté with truffles, pay attention to quality. It is sad that the wide choice in the shops today makes this more important than ever before, but there is a solution to the problem, organising your menu around foods available fresh on the market. This is not a new idea, but it guarantees quality and is essential to a good forcemeat.

One disadvantage of forcemeat is its richness, so do not eat excessive quantities of pies or pâtés: they should be eaten as carefully as they have been prepared.

Basic facts about forcemeats

There are just about as many forcemeats as there are different kinds of pâté, terrine or galantine. Every forcemeat is unique, if only by virtue of slight variations in composition or seasoning. Nevertheless there are only a limited number of very similar ways of making forcemeats, the main variations consisting primarily of the various binding agents.

A forcemeat should, as far as possible, hold together – bind – without any other help. The natural protein in the main

A triumph of the art of delicatessen. A selection of gourmet terrines in the chilled cabinet at Fauchon's, the famous Paris food store, which offers an unrivalled selection of pâtés and terrines, all made from the finest ingredients.

ingredient should bind sufficiently, thus retaining all the full flavour of meat or fish.

Protein binding is thus the only form of binding when lean meat and pork fat are used. Other binding agents which give a deliciously smooth filling when used correctly are: white bread with milk or cream, whole eggs, flour panada or rice.

Heat-sensitive protein

It is essential to release as much protein as possible from the meat by careful chopping. But heavy work, with any implement, produces heat and this in turn coagulates the protein and diminishes its binding qualities. This seems to be a vicious circle, but can be overcome easily if a few basic rules are observed.

1. Chill all ingredients thoroughly. Even the utensils, for example the mincer, should be cold.

2. Season the meat as you cut it: salt helps release the protein.

3. When chopping meat make sure your equipment is in perfect condition. The blade of the mincer, food processor or knife must be sharp, so that they actually cut the meat rather than crush it.

4. Chill the ingredients after each stage of the recipe, regardless of whether the forcemeat relies on natural protein for binding or includes some other binding agent.

5. Depending on the ingredients and method of preparation of the recipe, some ingredients such as fat or cream can be

frozen, and the frozen pieces of fat and frozen crushed cream will help keep the other ingredients cool during the chopping or mincing process.

In the end it is not half as difficult as it seems at first, when you consider the variety of utensils and the basic rules you must follow. But these rules *must* be followed if you are to get good results, no matter how small the quantities you are handling.

These basic points provide a framework within which you can give rein to your imagination when making pâtés, pies, galantines and terrines. A forcemeat offers unparalleled opportunities for experiment; different seasonings alone can provide a host of alternatives. You can devise new harmonies of taste by using the same filling in various forms. Binding agents can be varied by the use of either eggs, protein, white bread, flour panada or rice.

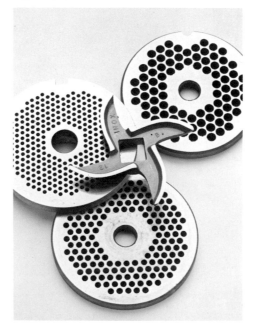

Sharp tools are essential if the ingredients for a forcemeat or stuffing are to be minced correctly. Regardless of whether you are using a simple hand-operated mincer or an electric machine, the blade must be sharp, to ensure that the meat or fish is cut rather than crushed. The same is equally true of the blades on domestic food processors. Since these work at very high speeds you might not notice that the blade is blunt, but it can have a particularly harmful effect, for the forcemeat or stuffing can overheat in a matter of seconds and rather than the protein being released it may coagulate.

Binding and lightening

1   **A pure forcemeat,** surely the simplest and finest of all. Binding is achieved through the meat's own protein, which is extremely sensitive to heat, so all stages of preparation should be carried out at the lowest possible temperatures. Use only fresh, best quality meat (with all fat and gristle removed) and firm, white pork fat.

2   **Bread, an easy way to make forcemeat light.** Together with egg white, milk or cream, soaked or – preferably – moist bread provides both lightness and binding at the same time. It is particularly recommended for fish, vegetable or meat stuffings, which are delicate and light.

3   **Egg in the forcemeat.** Eggs are both binding and lightening agents. In contrast to pure meat forcemeat, in which the pork fat is the lightening agent, the fat content can be considerably reduced if you include eggs. They act as a neutral-tasting binding agent for forcemeat with little meat content, or with a base other than meat, for example fish or vegetable.

4   **A flour panada can be used in any kind of forcemeat** with one proviso. If you add too much, or if the panada is incorrectly prepared, the forcemeat can take on a slightly sticky consistency. Two different methods of preparation should both give good results: the flour panada can be cooked in a saucepan like choux pastry, or boiled and diluted with milk, as for a béchamel sauce.

5   **Rice has a neutral taste,** even after boiling (in meat, fish or vegetable stock, or simply in water). Rice is a particularly good way of lightening delicate forcemeat, for example fish and fine vegetable. Take care not to add too much rice or the stuffing can take on a slightly greasy consistency.

Classic forcemeat made principally from game

This gourmet forcemeat is prepared according to a set of basic rules which should be followed whichever type you are preparing. Once this method is mastered you can devise a wide range of variations on the theme.

The flavour and success of a forcemeat or stuffing depends above all on the quality of its ingredients, particularly the main ingredient. The main ingredient gives it its dominant flavour and also determines the name of the pâté, galantine or terrine – as in venison pâté, for example. In the following example game, in this case venison, is the main ingredient. The same method also applies to poultry or meat.

A decisive factor in the smoothness and binding of the forcemeat is the temperature at which it is prepared. The protein which acts as binding agent soon coagulates at normal room temperatures and loses its binding qualities. Do not ignore any of the instructions on chilling if further stages are to be completed successfully and you are to get a good end result.

The main requirement for the classic forcemeat is that only fresh ingredients of best quality should be used. The second requirement is that the meat must be completely free from fat and gristle.

The third requirement is: cold, cold and cold again. The ingredients should be chilled after each stage, and your utensils should also be cold.

The ratio of ingredients for a classic forcemeat is:

$\frac{2}{5}$ main ingredient (game, poultry)
$\frac{1}{5}$ pork (moistening agent)
$\frac{2}{5}$ pork fat (lightening agent which also provides smoothness)

or

$\frac{2}{3}$ main ingredient (game, poultry) and moistening agent (pork) together
$\frac{1}{3}$ pork fat

1 **Skin the venison.** Wipe the joint of venison (in this case a haunch) with a damp cloth or kitchen paper. With a sharp knife lift away a strip of skin, 2–3 cm/1–1¼ in wide, then peel away the skin with the back of the knife.

2 **Bone the meat.** Cut out the joint bone. Cut off the skin and meat from the top of the joint. Loosen the knee bone at the joint and remove. Cut along the leg bone, dividing the meat along the natural joins in the skin.

3 **Remove the hollow bones.** Keep the bones and any trimmings (skin, gristle, small pieces of meat) to one side for the stock. Carefully cut out all veins and ligaments. Even after mincing these could cause the pâté to fall.

4 **Trim the pork** (remove skin and ligaments). For the forcemeat it is best to use loin of pork. Hold the bones firmly in the left hand and cut along the bone as far as the vertebrae. Turn the meat over and cut the bone free.

5 **Cut off the strip of meat** which runs along the outside of the loin – also known as the saddle – together with its fat. This is not used in a forcemeat or stuffing, but if chopped will make a good stew.

6 **Remove the ligaments.** With a very sharp knife cut off the fat from the back of the meat and any ligaments you can see. The meat should be completely free from fat and ligaments. A good butcher will of course bone the pork for you on request.

7 **The lean trimmed meat,** divided along the natural joins and with all skin and ligaments removed. Here we have the fillet from a pork loin, and venison flesh from the upper and lower leg.

8 **Cut the meat into strips.** Cut the meat into finger-length strips, about 1 cm/½ in thick. The spiral movement of a mincer works better with strips than cubes.

9 **Cut the pork fat into strips.** Use green pork fat (unsmoked, uncured). Cut off the rind cleanly and cut into strips as for the meat. Pork fat is easier to cut and handle if chilled in advance.

10 **Mix the salt and pâté seasoning.** The best way is to sieve them together. With bought pâté seasoning mix in the ratio given on the package. This will be given either in relation to the amount of salt or the quantity of forcemeat.

11 **The right time to season.** Sprinkle the seasoning evenly over the meat. Salt helps release the protein in the meat.

12 **Orange and lemon suits the flavour of game very well.** In the venison pâté recipe illustrated here grated orange and lemon peel and juniper berries are used as extra seasoning. They should be sprinkled over the strips of meat. Return the meat to the refrigerator and chill it thoroughly.

13 **Mince the meat.** Mince the chilled, seasoned meat – alternating between venison and pork – through the finest blade (1·5 mm/$\frac{1}{16}$ in) of the mincer. Chill the minced meat thoroughly once more.

14 **Repeat the process.** Mince the meat a second time. It is important that the mincer is in perfect working order so that the meat is minced rather than crushed.

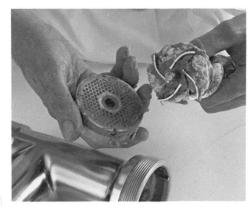

15 **Finally, mince the pork fat.** One tip: to get the last remnants of fat out of the mincer, run a piece of greaseproof paper through the mincer. It will not go right the way through and is easy to remove.

16 **Mix together the fat and meat** by hand. This is a rather messy method, but one that gives a particularly good texture. Place a bowl in a larger bowl filled with ice cubes. Place the chilled meat in the bowl and, with cool hands, work in the fat. NB: never allow the stuffing to become overwarm. A simpler way is to mince the fat with the meat. This will give excellent results, but not as good as by the first method.

17 **The final sieving of the pâté,** which is worthwhile, for even perfectly trimmed meat will leave a lot of fibre behind in the sieve. To push the pâté through use a metal scraper or, better still, a timbale mould.

Quick forcemeat made in the food processor

Experience has shown that the job is done much quicker with a food processor, with equally good results. This method does have its disadvantages however: you can only make small quantities (575–800 g/1¼–1¾ lb meat), otherwise the machine becomes too hot. In addition you must pay just as much attention to preparing the ingredients, trimming the meat just as thoroughly. But if the basic rules are followed, pâté making becomes easier and quicker. The food processor minces and mixes the ingredients in one process and this makes for considerable savings in both time and energy. Of course the food processor must be in excellent working order. The blade must be very sharp, so that the meat is minced and not crushed, releasing the important proteins which are to bind the pâté.

Effective cooling is essential. The food processor should be chilled in advance. The meat should be as cold as possible, but not frozen, and cut into cubes about 1 cm/½ inch in size. The pork fat should be frozen in advance and cut into similar cubes. This helps keep the meat cool during mincing. The ingredients should be salted and seasoned in advance. Keep your quantities small, between 75 and 150 g/3 and 5 oz depending on the size of the machine. When you make the first batch check how long it takes for the mixture to become smooth and of uniform consistency. To prevent overheating, never let the machine run for longer than necessary. If one batch feels warm in spite of these precautions, do not use it, for it could ruin the whole pâté. Chill the machine between batches.

You can improve the quality of forcemeat by passing it through a sieve to remove any bits of skin or ligament.

Meat and frozen pork fat are salted and seasoned in advance and minced together in one step. Mince small portions at a time; in this way the machine will run only for short periods and the pâté will remain cool.

The pâté should feel light, homogenous and cool. The food processor will make pâté in a matter of seconds, provided you obey to the letter the rules on chilling, no matter how exaggerated they may seem.

Forcemeat made with egg white and bread
Salmon pâté

A combination of egg white, cream and white bread makes an ideal binding and lightening in any pâté whose main ingredient is very light in flavour, for example fish, shellfish, veal or poultry.

As with all pâtés and pie fillings, freshness and quality are especially important with fish and shellfish. If possible, fish should always be used on the day it is caught; to exaggerate slightly, they should add a bit of fresh sea air to the pâté. Of course this is not always possible, for if you live inland it is difficult to buy freshly caught fish, although modern refrigeration and transport help preserve freshness. The best solution is to use freshly caught freshwater fish. Only as a

last resort should you use frozen fish, for only the very best is good enough for a pâté.

The white bread should be fresh, fine textured but not too soft. It is best to use a regular-shaped loaf because this makes for little wastage when you remove the crust. The bread is moistened with fresh single cream and egg white before mincing. Here again, as with any pâté, the ingredients should be chilled after each stage.

A decisive factor in how the pâté binds is the thorough stirring with a wooden spoon. The cream is stirred into the pâté mixture a spoonful at a time until it has a silky sheen. This gives the pâté its smoothness and helps it to bind. This stirring process will take as long as an hour, but a pâté can't be rushed if it is to turn out well.

The illustrations opposite show a salmon pâté in the making but are equally applicable to any fish or shellfish pâté.

Quantities given for fish or meat always refer to filleted fish and trimmed meat.

Basic recipe for fish pâté:

575 g/1¼ lb fish
150 g/5 oz white bread
150 ml/¼ pint single cream
500 ml/17 fl oz whipped cream
3 egg whites
100 g/4 oz sliced onion
seasoning

Only fresh fish should be used in pâtés. Filleting fish calls for quite a bit of skill and it is advisable to ask the fishmonger to do this for you. Don't forget that what the fishmonger sees as waste – the bones and head – will make a good fish stock. When you are ordering or buying your fillets of fish, ask him to set aside any bones or trimming. A fish stock is even more simply made than a meat one.

1 **Prepare the salmon.** Run your fingertips over the fish to check for bones, and where necessary remove with tweezers. Cut the fillet into long strips and leave to stand in a cool place.

2 **Remove the crusts from the bread.** Cut all the crust from a fresh, but not too soft, white loaf and then cut into $\frac{1}{2}$ cm/$\frac{1}{4}$ in slices. It is advisable to use an unsliced, regular shaped loaf.

3 **Moisten the bread.** Lay the sliced bread in a shallow dish. Pour the egg white over the bread and evenly spoon on the fresh single cream. Leave the bread to soak in a cool place.

4 **Season the ingredients.** Stir the bread into the egg white and cream then place it on a flat dish with the salmon strips. Soften the sliced onion in a little butter and sprinkle all the ingredients with pâté salt and seasoning.

5 **Mince the ingredients together.** After chilling once more, pass the ingredients alternately through the finest blade of the mincer (1–1$\frac{1}{2}$ mm/about $\frac{1}{16}$ in). Chill the pâté, mince a second time and chill again!

6 **Sieve the salmon pâté mixture.** Stand a stable fine metal sieve on a board and push through the pâté, using a metal scraper. This will remove any bones left in the pâté mixture.

7 **Stand the pâté over ice.** Transfer the chilled pâté mixture to a bowl and place this in a larger bowl filled with ice cubes. Stir with a wooden spoon until the ingredients are thoroughly mixed and the mixture takes on sheen.

8 **Work in the whipped cream.** Add 1 tablespoon whipped cream to the chilled pâté mixture and beat in well. Then add the next spoonful of cream. Repeat until you have incorporated all the cream.

9 **The finished, smooth pâté mixture.** The addition of whipped cream and a thorough beating makes the mixture as light and airy and smooth as silk. Sauté a small spoonful to test the seasoning.

Forcemeat with panada

Pheasant pâté A flour panada is an excellent way of making all fine forcemeats lighter. Its main use is with very tender meat, for example poultry, but also with fish and vegetables.

The whole quantity of flour panada is seldom required for a pâté. You can use the leftovers to make small dumplings for soup or small choux pastries for savoury fillings.

Basic recipe:

200 ml / 7 fl oz milk
40 g / 1½ oz butter
little salt, milled white pepper
and a dash nutmeg
100 g / 4 oz flour
2 eggs

1 **Bring the milk, butter and seasoning to the boil.** The method of preparing a flour panada is the same as for choux pastry. In a saucepan bring the milk, butter and seasoning to the boil over high heat.

2 **Add all the flour.** Fold a sheet of wrapping or greaseproof paper in half, open out and sieve the flour onto the paper. Tip the flour into the boiling milk and butter mixture all at once.

6 **Pass the flour panada through a fine sieve.** Using a pastry scraper, push the chilled panada through a sieve, to remove any lumps formed during the cooking process.

7 **Egg white for extra binding.** Whisk the egg white lightly to make it easier to add gradually. Add a little at a time to the meat. Again, the whole mixture should be kept very cold.

8 **Add the panada.** Flour panada is an excellent lightening agent for pâtés, for it rises better than bread during cooking. Stand the bowl in ice and gradually work the panada into the meat.

9 **Pass the pâté through a fine sieve.** When the panada is completely mixed in and the pâté mixture really cold, use a timbale mould or metal scraper to push it through the sieve to remove any ligaments. Chill.

10 **Add cream to give extra lightness.** Stir in the whipped cream a little at a time, making sure that each portion is thoroughly mixed before adding any more.

11 **The finished pâté mixture should be as smooth as silk.** When you have mixed in the cream beat the pâté over ice until it takes on a sheen. Beating makes it smooth and light, the hallmark of a good pâté.

3 **Cooking the panada.** Heat the mixture over a high flame until you have worked in all the flour. This is the most important stage in the whole process. Beat the panada vigorously and continuously.

4 **The finished panada.** The panada, which is soft at first, gradually becomes noticeably firmer. It has cooked sufficiently when it forms a ball which comes away easily from the base of the pan.

5 **Stir in the eggs.** Transfer the panada to a basin. Leave to cool slightly. Add an egg and beat it in thoroughly. Then add the second egg. Cover the bowl and leave the panada to stand in a cool place.

Essential test cooking

You should always cook a sample piece of any pâté mixture to avoid any nasty shocks when you come to eat it. By cooking a test spoonful you can check the seasoning, for experience has shown repeatedly that the flavour of uncooked pâté should always be slightly stronger than the flavour required in the finished pâté or terrine.

Test cooking also checks for binding. If the consistency is too firm and dry add a little more cream.

Place a small amount of pâté mixture in the palm of your hand and take off about half a teaspoon, drawing the spoon towards the ball of the hand.

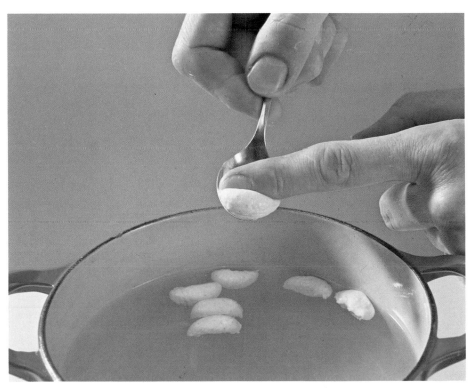

With the tip of your index finger push the ball of pâté off the spoon into the pan and cook for about 5 minutes. When cooked, the balls should be light and airy in consistency and not too firm. When pressed with the tongue against the roof of the mouth they should feel slightly firm before melting on the tongue.

Pâtés and Terrines

DIFFERENCES GREAT AND SMALL

'A pie is a French dish made from pastry, hollow inside and filled like a fritter.' The words of Sebastian Franck, alias Frank von Wörd, who was born in Donauwörth and is best remembered for his religious writings. But alongside his religious tracts he also published in 1534 'Weltbuch', the first popular work on cosmography. It is from this book that his definition of a pie is taken. His definition is more or less correct. Leaving aside several differences for the moment, the general term pie can also be applied to all kinds of terrines, galantines and bouchées. As regards his claim that the pie is a 'French dish', posterity has shown that Sebastian Franck was wrong. For we know now that even the ancient Greeks and Romans had pies, and that ancient cooks vied with each other to produce new variations on the theme. But it also seems equally clear that for our distant forbears the term pie included any kind of forcemeat, whether cooked in a dish, in pastry or as a stuffing for a joint of meat. Through the centuries, though, as pie making spread throughout Europe, people began to distinguish between these various dishes, introducing appropriate names to describe these different culinary masterpieces. That does not mean that the terms are not still confused even today – indeed they are, even in France and in England. But it is not so difficult to distinguish between the various concepts covered by the general term 'pie'.

With or without pastry

Basically it is quite simple: anything made from forcemeat and covered in pastry is a pie, whereas terrines are forcemeat alone without pastry, with nothing to detract from the pure flavour of the filling. This simple forcemeat is put into dishes lined with bacon or foil and they are baked in the oven, standing in a water bath. We should add that for centuries experts have been discussing the relative merits of pies and terrines. But since it is difficult to argue on matters of personal taste the question has never been resolved. Today, however, the trend seems to be towards the terrine. This is a pity, for richly decorated pies are a pleasure to behold and their attractive appearance stimulates the appetite admirably – not to mention their effect on the palate. In this respect it is pointless to talk about the higher calorie rating of pies over terrines. Neither pies nor terrines were invented with the slimmer in mind, nor should they be considered in this light today. And when nouvelle cuisine, which wholeheartedly adopted the terrine, chooses to do away with the traditional pork fat covering, it will be for reasons of flavour rather than nutritional value. Gourmets have never been inclined actually to eat the fat, yet it is a necessary part of the terrine, for it brings out the full flavour and keeps it moist. But even without fat many chefs of the nouvelle cuisine school produce pies and terrines which are real milestones in the history of cooking. One has only to think of their fish or vegetable pâtés or terrines.

Spicy country-style terrines

But terrines are not limited to those delicacies cooked in tiny pots (with goose liver pâté the smallest of all). There is another variety of terrine – regardless of whether it is made with goose, duck, hare, venison, pork or liver – which is strongly flavoured and highly seasoned. This is the country-style terrine. Despite their name, these terrines can be found throughout the length and breadth of France whether in Paris or the provinces.

So it comes as no surprise to find that even in the smallest village every other household has its own recipe. And even in the smallest family-run restaurant you will never be disappointed with the 'Terrine du Chef'. Indeed it is often the highlight of the menu, where it often figures under the alternative names of 'pâté de campagne' or 'pâté de la maison'. But this does not affect the quality; they may not all be masterpieces, but they are always good honest pâtés.

Pâté, a high-class sausage?

In France and Belgium pâtés and terrines, galantines and ballotines form a basic part of the national diet, like the German sausage. In no other country in the world is there a trade specially devoted to the pâté to compare with that of the French *charcutier*. The word comes from *chair* (meat) and *cuire* (to cook), that is, 'meat cook', and in France that means pork in particular.

One glance into the window of a French charcuterie is enough to prove that it stocks more varieties of pâté than there are sausages in Germany, and this wide variety is by no means limited to gourmet pâtés. In a way they are sausages in a different form, and one can make this assertion without in any way denigrating the outstanding creations of French and Belgian charcutiers.

It is true that the consumer is often led by the nose by the term 'pâté' which promises so much. But when we come down to it this is a problem that has always been with us and which can be easily resolved. Making your own pies and pâtés with fresh, high quality ingredients is an obvious and very satisfying solution.

Perfect preparation begins with quality

'The juice of the meat and the flavour of fine herbs, wrapped and baked in a thick pastry, with the enclosed filling cooked in its own juices is a widespread refinement in the art of cooking...' A quote from Karl Friedrich von Rumohr. Originally an art historian and writer on art, in 1822 he published his 'Geist der Kochkunst' (Spirit of the art of cooking) under the name of his family cook. This was quite remarkable, for he understood a lot about food and realised that natural ingredients, carefully prepared, improved the flavour of food, improved his very poor state of health and gave him great satisfaction. So he was in fact an early prophet of the recent nouvelle cuisine

The quality and freshness of his raw materials are an absolute must for three-star chef Faugeron, for the continuing reputation of his restaurant depends upon it. To him price is of secondary importance.

movement. An advocate of quality purely and simply.

The need for high quality ingredients, the hallmark of all good food including pâtés and terrines, is thus nothing new. But unfortunately many people forget this – even professional chefs. So, for the pastry, the flour, butter and eggs should be as fresh as possible. Pork fat for terrines should be absolutely fresh, snow-white and firm. This is only obtainable from pigs with a good layer of fat and these are few and far between. And it is obvious that the forcemeat will only be at its best if fish, meat, poultry, game or offal are of top quality. Where vegetables are to be used the best option for the cook is to gather them fresh from his or her own garden. But since this is impossible in most cases, professional chefs try to adopt the standards of the nouvelle cuisine chefs in France: many go off to the markets while the rest of us are still sleeping to get first choice of the freshest foods. Or they order certain ingredients direct from Belgium, France and Italy, with delivery by jet if necessary. For this is the only way they can be certain that meat, fish, vegetables, poultry or game are of best quality. Professional chefs have long had their own sources, and some tradesmen have adapted their businesses to suit their specific needs.

This is all well and good, but what options are there for an ordinary person with a sophisticated palate, who would like to make the occasional pâté but is unsure where to get the best ingredients. Let's be honest about this. Foods offered – even in exclusive food stores and leading delicatessens – are often a disgrace. We are offered limp, obviously old, vegetables. Often we can get only frozen poultry, which is unsuitable for pâtés and terrines. Fresh cream is often hard to come by and herbs show their age through their lack of flavour. Only with butter and eggs can you be reasonably sure of quality.

So, unfortunately the cook has no choice but to get up and go and look for fresh sources. Of course, this takes up a lot of time, but it is time well spent. For you can only make a really good pâté or terrine from top quality ingredients.

The French, Italians and Spanish are much to be envied. Their markets and shops – even in the smallest villages – offer only fresh goods, and in a variety that would make us green with envy.

The person who can buy whatever he or she needs is really fortunate. Using game and game birds, pork and veal, poultry, fish and shellfish, mushrooms and vegetables, you can make the most interesting pâté

The choice available in the market should determine the main ingredient of a pâté or terrine. Even in the market you should check the quality of goods available: not every chicken is slaughtered at the tender age of 6 months.

variations, find new combinations and invent new dishes.

What about decoration? With special cutters, for example, you can make pastry decorations in a variety of geometric, fruit or flower shapes. There are no limits to the imaginative ideas possible. There are limits, however, to the ways in which you can decorate a terrine. Here we are generally restricted to sprigs of herbs, bay leaves and seasonings since the decoration is to be cooked with the terrine.

With pâtés to be eaten cold it is essential to top them up with aspic, for this is the only way of preserving their freshness and moistness. If a terrine is covered with aspic, this is not an essential part of the process, but just one way of enhancing its appearance. The fact that this keeps the terrine moister is merely a pleasant bonus.

Lining a pie or pâté mould with pastry

While it is true that you can make a piecrust with puff pastry and – less often – yeast pastry, the pastry principally used is, and will remain, shortcrust. French pâté chefs, experts in the field, have developed their own methods over years of experience. Many of them maintain that pastry is easier to handle if it is made the evening before, wrapped and left overnight in the refrigerator. One further tip from France: the pastry which covers the base and sides of the tin will need to be slightly thicker if the filling contains a lot of fat. This applies, for example, in the case of strong flavoured, country-style fillings. The thicker pastry absorbs the fat better, which melts during cooking.

For baking you can use almost any type of container – even earthenware casseroles can be lined with pastry – but thinner metal moulds are better. In the tin pastry bakes more evenly, crisper and browner.

Here, once more, there is a lesson to be learnt from the French, for in France – particularly in the homes, where many more pies are baked than here – a lot of time goes into the choosing of the tin mould. There is even one type available which folds flat. Moulds like this make it very easy to remove the pâté or pie from the tin. In general, conical moulds, those that are wider at the rim than the base, are best. These are also quite good for turning out.

With a pastry which contains a lot of fat it is generally unnecessary to grease the mould, but experience has shown that pastry adheres better to the sides of the mould (an essential requisite) if it is lightly greased with butter. With narrow moulds which are more difficult to line, this can make the job much easier.

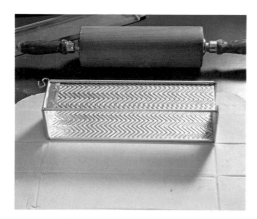

1 **Roll the pastry to a thickness of about 3–4 mm/about ⅛ in.** Press the tin into the pastry to mark the cutting lines. Three pieces, together with the smaller end pieces, are used to line the tin. The fourth, larger piece forms the lid.

2 **Cut off the excess pastry with a pastry wheel** and set aside to use for decoration. Do not cut off any pastry that overlaps at the corners, these will be pressed flat once the pastry is in the mould. This is most important if no fat or gravy is to escape.

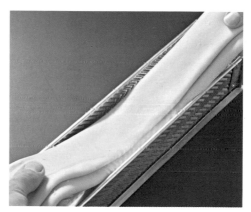

3 **Grease the mould with a little butter.** Sprinkle the pastry lightly with flour and fold together. Transfer carefully to the mould. Unfold to overhang the sides of the mould. Take care not to compress the pastry with your fingers.

4 **Make a small ball from the pastry trimmings** and dip it in flour. Use this ball to press the pastry to the sides of the mould. Using a pastry ball has the advantage of being very gentle on the pastry, its delicacy of touch is difficult to achieve with the fingers.

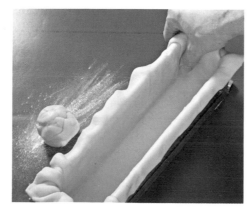

5 **First using the ball of pastry,** then the ball of the thumb, press excess pastry in the corners up towards the rim of the mould. In this way you will get an even overall thickness and the pie will bake and brown evenly.

6 **The pastry should overlap the rim of the tin evenly.** Use scissors to cut a rim of 1–2 cm/½–¾ in. Wrap the remaining pastry for the lid and decoration in foil and leave in the refrigerator until required.

Stock

a fine gravy to complete your pâté

Stock is, so to speak, a flavour concentrate used to enhance the main flavour in a fine pâté or pie. It is made from trimmings, any skin or gristle cut from the meat. The bones are also used and last, but not least, the meat which remains on the bones. Fried with root vegetables, delicately seasoned, and often with wine added, this reduced stock gives the perfect finish to any pâté or terrine. It can be incorporated into the filling or brushed over whole pieces of meat which go into the pâté (in this case venison fillets).

Basic recipe for game stock

5 tablespoons oil
1 kg/2¼ lb game bones
and meat trimmings
vegetables (1 medium-sized onion, 1
carrot, diced)
2 tablespoons tomato paste
2½ litres/4½ pints water
bouquet garni (1 piece celeriac, white of
1 leek, 5 sprigs parsley, 1 bay leaf,
1 sprig thyme)
2 shallots, sliced
1 clove garlic, halved
8 crushed juniper berries
8 white peppercorns
1 teaspoon salt

In a roasting tin, roast the game bones and trimmings for 15 minutes in a very hot oven (240 C, 475 F, gas 9). Add the diced onion and carrot and roast for a further 20 minutes. Add the tomato paste and stir in. Dilute with cold water, stirring in the sediment from the bottom of the tin. Continue roasting until golden brown. Transfer to a large saucepan, add the water, bring to the boil and simmer gently for 2 hours. Remove the scum from time to time. Add the bouquet garni, shallots and herbs for the last 45 minutes. Strain the stock, return to the boil and reduce to the strength required.

1 **Roast the chopped game bones in oil.** Heat the oil in a roasting tin. Add the chopped bones and roast thoroughly all over on the lowest shelf of the oven, stirring from time to time.

2 **Add the vegetables (mirepoix).** Sprinkle the evenly diced vegetables over the bones and brown them. Do not allow them to burn, for this will make the stock bitter. Add the tomato paste and roast until the aroma has developed fully.

3 **Dilute the juices with water.** Add a generous dash of cold water and stir in, incorporating the sediment from the bottom of the tin. When the water has evaporated, repeat the process twice more.

4 **Transfer the roasted bones to a saucepan.** Transfer the mixture of roast bones and vegetables to a large pan and add the cold water. Simmer for a further 2 hours.

5 **Skim the stock.** Fat from the bones, proteins and any impurities rise to the surface. If you are to get a clear stock it must be skimmed repeatedly.

6 **Add the herbs and seasoning.** For the last third of the cooking time add the bouquet garni and herbs. Simmer the stock for a further 45 minutes and carefully remove all fat from the surface. Then strain the stock.

Making a reduced stock for venison fillets. Fry the fillets in oil and remove from the pan. Pour off the oil and melt the butter. Glaze finely chopped shallots in the butter. Dilute with a generous dash of brandy.

Add the highly gelatinous stock. Add the strained stock and herbs. Reduce to a gleaming, thick essence. Strain through a conical sieve over the venison fillets and leave to cool.

Essence for the forcemeat or whole meat

15 g/½ oz butter
25 g/1 oz chopped shallots
3 tablespoons brandy
150 ml/¼ pint jellying game stock
grated rind of ½ orange and ½ lemon
4 crushed juniper berries
ground white pepper

The reduced jellifying stock, further reduced with herbs and alcohol, gives a concentrated essence which, when strained, gives extra flavour to the filling. Alternatively it can be brushed over larger pieces of meat to be included in the pâté.

The venison fillets are thoroughly sealed by frying in oil. Frying makes the meat contract slightly so that it retains its shape in the pâté or terrine.

Filling and sealing the pâté

In the classic pastry covered pâté the filling must be completely wrapped in the pastry so that it is protected and no juices can escape. Joins in the pastry should therefore be brushed with egg yolk and pressed firmly together to seal.

There are no limits to the imaginative ways in which you can decorate a pâté. Possibilities include pinching the edges together with a special tool, marking with a fork or the handle of a spoon, or cutting out or making various decorative pastry shapes which are coated with egg yolk and arranged on the top of the pie.

1 Add the filling. Cover the base of the pastry lined mould with a layer of filling slightly less than 2.5 cm/1 in thick. Press it well into the corners with a spoon so that there are no gaps. The filling should be a fraction deeper around the sides of the mould to form a rim.

2 Add the venison fillets. Cut the tapering ends from the venison fillets so that they will fit closely together in the tin. Place the fillets over the filling and bang the tin several times on a damp cloth.

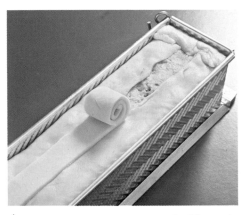

1 Fold the excess pastry over the filling and press down. If it does not meet at the centre, cut a piece of pastry to cover the gap, arrange on the pâté and press the joins together lightly.

2 Seal with the pastry lid. Brush the top of the pâté with a mixture of egg yolk and cream. Cut a thin layer of pastry to the size of the tin, fold into three to make moving it easier and use to cover the pâté.

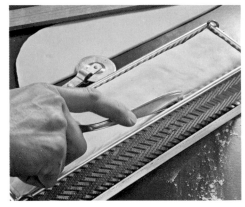

3 Seal the edges. Working out from the centre, press the lid firmly onto the pâté. Press any overlapping edges down inside the tin with the handle of a fork.

4 Decorate the lid. Use a crimper to make a decorative pattern of your own design on the pâté. Alternatively, you could use the prongs of a fork or two teaspoon handles. NB: take care not to cut through the pastry.

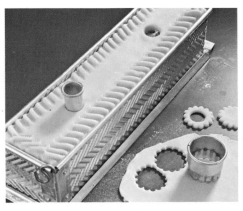

5 Make openings to allow steam to escape during baking. Use a pastry cutter to cut one or two openings in the top of the pâté (the number you need will depend on the size of the pâté), or use a small, sharp knife to make the holes.

6 Add the chimneys. Brush the pâté with a mixture of egg yolk and cream. Place small flower shapes around the openings. Roll pieces of double-thickness foil into tubes and place one in each opening, to prevent any escaping juices marking the top of the pâté.

3 **Sprinkle over the thick, rich stock.** With a tablespoon spread the cool, jellying stock evenly over the venison fillets. This will help the flavour of the stock permeate through the pâté.

4 **Add the second layer of filling.** Cover the fillets with a layer of filling, about 1.5 cm/¾ in deep. As this pâté is to have two layers of venison fillets you will again have to make a rim with the filling.

5 **Add the second layer of venison fillets.** Arrange the fillets as for the first layer, again cover with jellying stock, and top with the remaining filling. Do not overfill the mould. Bang it again on a damp cloth to fill any gaps.

Filling and sealing a terrine

Unlike the pâté, a terrine is baked in the oven standing in a water bath. In a classic terrine the dish is lined with pork fat. For this fresh, rindless fat pork is cut into thin slices. You can place the slices individually between two sheets of waxed paper and beat them until very thin, but be careful not to make any holes or tears. Alternatively, you can line the dish with roasting film or foil: in that case it is important to grease the dish if the terrine is to turn out properly.

1 **Line the dish with slices of fat.** The slices should be very thin, of equal size and without rind. Place them in the dish, overlapping slightly.

2 **The lined dish.** Cut the fat slices for the narrow ends of the dish wide enough to turn the corner and seal it completely. It is important for the filling to be completely covered with fat.

3 **Seal the filled dish.** Fold the excess pork fat into the centre and, working in from the side of the dish, press firmly down. Bang the dish several times on a damp cloth, to fill any air gaps.

4 **Decorate the terrine.** Cut a piece of fat to the correct size to cover the top of the dish. Decorate with the same herbs you have used in the terrine.

Game pâtés and terrines

Were it not for game, pies and their variants, which include terrines and galantines, would be nowhere near as popular as they are. The flesh of game and game birds is a naturally fine product, and needing little embellishment. It is particularly rich in protein, generally low in fat and has a delicious flavour. Nowadays these qualities have come to be even more appreciated when modern rearing and feeding methods rarely produce domestic animals and poultry of suitable quality for pâté making. Nevertheless, not all wild game is of the same quality. The pelt or feathers of fresh-shot game show clearly whether the animal is young and tender or old and tough. And to distinguish one from the other you don't need to know a lot about game or to be a huntsman yourself. With jointed, or even frozen, meat this is no longer possible and it is advisable to buy from a reputable butcher.

The ban on using frozen meat to make pâtés or terrines allows one exception: the consistency of game meat with its low water and fat content means that it freezes better than normal meats. It loses much less liquid during thawing and the quality remains good enough for pâté and terrine making.

The choice of a particular joint is the same as for other types of meat: only the best is good enough for a pâté, and then it must be thoroughly trimmed. This of course gives quite a quantity of offcuts, but they can be used to make excellent stock. It goes without saying that for a country-style pâté you can use cheaper cuts of meat, but it should be prepared with just as much care. The meat must be completely free from skin and gristle.

Venison Pâté

Pâté de chevreuil

150 g/5 oz lean venison
150 g/5 oz lean pork
150 g/5 oz fresh pork fat
pâté salt (page 22)
10 crushed juniper berries
grated rind of 1 orange and 1 lemon
2 venison fillets (total weight about
250 g/9 oz)
2 tablespoons oil
15 g/½ oz butter
25 g/1 oz diced shallot
200 ml/7 fl oz brandy
100 ml/4 fl oz jellifying venison stock
(page 42)
25 g/1 oz coarsely chopped pistachio nuts
50 g/2 oz diced boiled ham
50 g/2 oz diced cured tongue
25 g/1 oz diced truffle
butter for greasing the pâté tin
675 g/1½ lb shortcrust pastry
1 egg for glazing
Madeira aspic to finish
1-litre/1¾-pint pâté mould

Trim all skin and gristle from the venison, pork and pork fat, cut it into fingers and sprinkle with ½ teaspoon salt, 5 crushed juniper berries and half the grated orange and lemon rind. Mince the meat twice through the finest blade of the mincer. Mince the fat once only. Transfer to a bowl,

A classic game pâté made from venison fillet. The flavour is accentuated by a thick game stock. Truffles and pistachios in the filling enhance both the flavour and the appearance.

stand the bowl over ice and work the fat thoroughly into the meat. Finally put the mixture through a sieve. With any forcemeat it is important to chill the meat and fat thoroughly after each stage.

Season the venison fillets with pâté salt, and quickly seal in hot oil. Remove the fillets from the pan and pour off the oil. Melt the butter in the pan and soften the shallots. Stir in the brandy and then add the jellying venison stock. Add the rest of the juniper berries, grated orange and lemon rinds, and reduce to give a thick liquid. Strain over the venison fillets and cool.

Stir the pistachios, ham, tongue and truffle into the forcemeat. Grease the tin with butter and line with pastry. Fill 2–3 cm/about 1 in deep with the forcemeat, slightly deeper around the sides. Place the venison fillets on the filling along the length of the mould and sprinkle with the thick stock. Cover with the remaining filling. Fold the edges of the pastry over the top and cover the pâté with a sheet of pastry. Cut an opening to allow steam to escape, insert a funnel and brush the top with egg.

Bake for 15 minutes at 220 C, 425 F, gas 7, then turn down the oven to 180 C, 350 F, gas 4 for another 25 minutes.

When cool fill any gaps with Madeira aspic, poured in through the steam holes.

Grouse Terrine

Terrine de grouse

450 g/1 lb skinned and boned grouse flesh
350 g/12 oz trimmed pork
1 medium-sized onion
40 g/1½ oz butter
2 teaspoons salt
1 teaspoon mixed seasoning for game
forcemeat
1 teaspoon thyme
1 teaspoon basil
¼ teaspoon ground rosemary
1 bay leaf
8 juniper berries
½ teaspoon dried green peppercorns
1 clove garlic
50 g/2 oz brown breadcrumbs
3 tablespoons cream
1 egg white
100 g/4 oz calf's liver
350 g/12 oz fresh pork fat
25 g/1 oz truffles
350 g/12 oz thinly sliced pork fat
rosemary, thyme, bay leaves and
juniper berries
1·5-litre/2¾-pint casserole dish

Trim the grouse and pork thoroughly, cut into fingers and place in a large bowl. Cut the onion into rings, heat the butter and

soften the onion in it. Leave to cool slightly and then arrange over the meat. Mix the salt with the seasonings and crushed garlic and sprinkle over the meat. Sprinkle the breadcrumbs over the meat. Beat the cream into the egg white and pour over the meat. Cover with foil and leave to chill overnight.

Mince the seasoned meat together with the other ingredients (breadcrumbs, egg white and cream) twice through the finest blade of the mincer. Cut the liver and two-thirds of the pork fat into strips and mince twice. Gradually work the liver and fat mixture into the chilled meat and stir thoroughly until the forcemeat is smooth and shiny. Finely dice the remaining pork fat and truffle and stir into the filling. Line the casserole dish with the slices of pork fat, fill it and cover with pork fat. Decorate with herbs and juniper berries, cover with the lid. Cook in a water bath for 1 hour, in a 180 C, 350 F, gas 4 oven.

A simple terrine with fairly coarse texture, but very spicy and juicy. The same recipe can be used with other game, of your choice.

Checking the cooking time

This is a problem which is by no means restricted to pâtés and terrines, for a correct assessment of cooking times is essential to all types of cooking too. But fine pâtés can prove an expensive mistake if anything goes wrong.

Do not rely on manufacturers' recommendations until you have checked your oven for yourself. It is also inadvisable to rely exclusively on the times and temperatures indicated in this book. They are accurate for the oven we use, but may not be so for yours. So you must check the baking times for each pâté or terrine you make.

This can be done in several ways. For one, you can look down the funnel at the gravy. If it is completely clear, the pâté is cooked. This method will not do, however, if you prefer the meat (for example, breast of chicken) slightly rare.

A more exact method is to test with a skewer. Stick a fairly thin skewer (a trussing needle or similar sized skewer is ideal) into the centre of the terrine or pâté right down to the bottom. Always leave it in the pâté for the same length of time (count from 21 to 30) and then remove it. Draw the needle slowly across your underlip, where the skin is particularly sensitive to temperature. The needle should be hot at the point, warm in the centre and hot towards the top. If it is cold in the centre extend the cooking time.

The third method, testing with a meat thermometer, is the safest method providing the thermometer is working properly. It can be used to check all pâtés, terrines and galantines. Stick the point of the thermometer into the exact centre of the pâté, but not into the funnel, however, for this would give a slightly higher reading. Read off the

thermometer after about 2 minutes. The filling should be at 65–70 C, 150–160 F. Pâtés or terrines which include fillets of meat to be eaten slightly rare should be just over 60 C, 140 F. Do not leave the thermometer in the oven, for this would damage it. For a galantine cooked on the hob, however. you can leave the thermometer in the galantine throughout cooking.

1 **Testing with a skewer is advisable** for all pâtés, terrines and galantines. Stick a fairly thin skewer (a trussing needle is ideal) through the middle of the pâté to the base, and remove it after 10 seconds.

2 **The underlip is especially sensitive** to temperature. You can test the temperature exactly by drawing the needle slowly along the underlip. If the needle is cold in the centre extend the cooking time.

3 **A meat thermometer tells you precisely** when a pâté is cooked. It must be inserted into the exact centre of the filling, to measure the temperature at the centre. But if the sensor of the thermometer is too thick it can leave an unsightly hole.

Highland Pâté

Pâté des montagnes

350 g/12 oz lean venison
250 g/9 oz lean pork
2 teaspoons mixed game seasoning
1 teaspoon basil
½ teaspoon oregano
5 crushed juniper berries
1 clove garlic, crushed
grated rind of 1 orange
1½ teaspoons salt
2 tablespoons oil
2 pork fillets
little salt
25 g/1 oz butter
2 shallots
3 tablespoons gin
150 ml/¼ pint jellifying game stock
1 clove garlic, crushed
5 crushed juniper berries
300 g/11 oz pork fat
1 tablespoon bottled green
peppercorns
100 g/4 oz diced boiled ham
750 g/1½ lb shortcrust pastry
egg yolk and milk or cream for coating
1·5-litre/2¾-pint pâté tin
Madeira or port aspic to finish

Cut the venison meat and pork into fingers. Sprinkle with the seasonings and salt, cover

with foil and leave to stand in the refrigerator.

Heat the oil in a frying pan and quickly fry the thoroughly trimmed and salted fillets (the technical term for this is 'sealing'). Remove from the pan and pour off the oil. Add the butter and glaze the diced shallots. Stir in the gin and add the game stock, garlic and juniper berries. Reduce to a thick liquid and strain through a sieve.

Mince the chilled meat twice through the finest blade of the mincer. Cut the pork fat into similar strips and mince once. Place the meat over ice in a bowl and work in the fat and the thick sauce. Drain the peppercorns thoroughly, coarsely chop and work into the forcemeat with the diced ham.

Cut the chilled, sealed fillets into strips. Line the tin with pastry and add 1 cm ½ in layer of forcemeat. Cover with strips of fillet. Add another layer of forcemeat and press down well. Continue in this way until you have used all the strips of meat and the filling. Cover the pâté with pastry, glaze and bake. When cool fill up the pie with Madeira or port aspic.

Baking time: 55 minutes in all. Begin baking for 10 minutes at 240 C, 475 F, gas 9 and continue at 200 C, 400 F, gas 6.

Complement your venison pâté with a mixture of whipped cream and cranberry sauce, seasoned with a little salt, sugar and ginger.

> ## When stock is included in the list of ingredients,
> you have three options:
>
> **1.** Buy the meat on the bone, and use the bones and any offcuts to make a stock before you begin the pâté.
> **2.** Use tinned stock. There are some good brands available in the shops.
> **3.** The best option of all: make large quantities of stock to use as required. It freezes well.

Wild Boar Pâté

Pâté de marcassin

An easy way of baking a pâté. The stuffing and meat is wrapped in pastry and baked on a baking sheet.

350 g/12 oz boned leg of young wild boar
250 g/9 oz boned loin of pork
300 g/11 oz fresh pork fat
2 teaspoons salt
2 teaspoons mixed game seasoning
½ teaspoon dried green peppercorns
5 crushed juniper berries
½ teaspoon thyme
1 teaspoon oregano
2 cloves garlic
grated rind of ½ lemon
2 wild boar fillets
little salt and pepper
3 tablespoons Armagnac
2 tablespoons oil
20 g/¾ oz butter
40 g/1½ oz shallots, diced
250 ml/8 fl oz game stock
grated rind of ½ lemon
1 good pinch cayenne pepper
5 crushed juniper berries
½ teaspoon thyme
800 g/1¾ lb shortcrust pastry
1 egg yolk and 1 tablespoon cream for
coating
Madeira aspic to finish

Trim the wild boar and pork thoroughly, carefully cutting away all skin and gristle. This should leave about 400 g/14 oz lean meat, which should be cut into strips with the pork fat. Mix the salt with the seasoning, crushed herbs and peeled, crushed garlic. Sprinkle over the meat and fat and grate on the lemon rind. Chill thoroughly.

Trim the boar fillets thoroughly, season with salt and pepper and sprinkle with a little Armagnac. Leave the fillets to marinate for 2 hours and then seal thoroughly in hot oil. Remove from the pan and pour off the oil. Melt the butter in the pan and glaze the shallots. Stir in the remaining Armagnac and add the game stock. Add the seasonings and reduce to a thick liquid.

Mince the meat twice (not the fillets) and the fat once through the finest blade of the mincer. Transfer the meat to a bowl, stand over ice and work a little of the fat at a time into the meat. Finally stir in the cool stock.

Roll out the pastry to 45 × 30 cm/18 × 12 in. Spread half the forcemeat in a strip (about 9 × 35 cm/4 × 14 in) over the lower third of the pastry. Cut both fillets to the same length and place in the centre of the stuffing. Cover with the remaining forcemeat and shape the top into a semicircle.

Press the narrow strip of pastry onto the stuffing and then roll with the stuffing, until the end of the pastry is to the underside. Coat the end with the egg yolk and cream mixture and press down firmly. Cut the remaining pastry into leaf shapes to decorate the top and brush the whole pâté with the egg yolk and cream mixture. Cut a funnel opening and fill with a piece of rolled foil.

Baking time: 45 minutes in all. 10 minutes at 230 C, 450 F, gas 8, then at 200 C, 400 F, gas 6.

When cool fill with Madeira aspic.

Wild Boar Pâté with Venison Fillet

Pâté de marcassin au filet de chevreuil

A fine game pâté based on the above Wild Boar Pâté, with the same quantities of forcemeat and pastry. Replace the boar fillets with 2 venison fillets, use the same seasoning but cover in a pistachio forcemeat. To make this mix 60 g/2½ oz puréed pistachios into 100 g/4 oz wild boar forcemeat. Spread on slices of pork fat and roll around the venison fillets. Stir 40 g/1½ oz chopped pistachios and 25 g/1 oz truffles into the remaining forcemeat.

Serve with ripe sliced persimmon and freshly whipped cream seasoned with grated orange rind and green pepper.

Wild Boar Terrine

Terrine de sanglier

Quite a simple terrine to make, quite coarse in texture, but very moist and tasty.

1 kg/2 lb boned loin of wild boar
1 small onion, chopped
1 clove garlic, crushed
2 teaspoons salt
2 teaspoons pâté seasoning (all-purpose)
1 teaspoon dried green peppercorns
1 teaspoon thyme
1 good pinch ground cloves
1 bay leaf
5 juniper berries
50 g/2 oz crustless white bread
150 ml/¼ pint red wine (strongly-flavoured Rioja)
400 g/14 oz pork fat
1 egg
30 g/1¼ oz truffles, finely chopped
50 g/2 oz shelled pistachios, coarsely chopped
150 g/5 oz pork fat, diced
400 g/14 oz pork fat, thinly sliced
herbs to garnish (bay leaf, thyme)
1.75-litre/3-pint terrine

Thoroughly trim the meat and cut into strips. Place in a bowl with the onion, garlic, salt, seasonings and diced white bread and pour on the wine. Leave to marinate in the refrigerator for 24 hours.

Cut the pork fat into strips and mince with the marinated meat, seasoning and bread (after pouring off the wine) twice through the finest blade of the mincer. Chill thoroughly and beat the egg into the stuffing. Work in the truffles, pistachios and diced pork fat.

Line the terrine with the fat slices and fill with the stuffing. Fold over the excess strips of fat and cover with another slice of fat. Cover the terrine, garnish with herbs and bake standing in water.

Cooking time: about 60 minutes at 160 C, 325 F, gas 3. Delicious served with fresh, sliced figs with curry cream, lightly salted and seasoned with a little lime juice.

Wild Boar Terrine Rioja

Terrine de sanglier 'Rioja'

Replace 300 g/11 oz of the meat with wild boar's liver and omit the pistachios. Marinate the liver for 12 hours in 150 ml/¼ pint Rioja and 40 ml/1½ fl oz Armagnac, and seal in butter. Add the marinade and reduce to a thick liquid. Mince the meat with the liver. Stir the marinade into the stuffing and finally season with rosemary and marjoram.

Partridge Pâté

Pâté de perdrix

4 partridges
5 tablespoons oil
1 carrot, chopped
1 large onion, sliced
1.5 litres/2¾ pints water
bouquet garni (white of 1 leek,
1 piece celeriac, 3 sprigs parsley,
1 bay leaf)
1 teaspoon salt
20 juniper berries
3 small cloves garlic
6 white peppercorns
100 g/4 oz lean pork
225 g/8 oz pork fat
pâté seasoning
ground white pepper
grated rind of ½ orange
15 g/½ oz butter
2 shallots, diced
2 tablespoons brandy
grated rind of ¼ lemon
150 g/5 oz goose liver, marinated in port
50 g/2 oz shelled pistachio nuts
25 g/1 oz truffle, diced
50 g/2 oz salted tongue, diced
butter for greasing
675 g/1½ lb shortcrust pastry
1 egg yolk beaten with 2 tablespoons
cream for glazing
port aspic to finish
1.4-litre/2½-pint pâté mould

Bone the partridges, keeping the breasts to one side. The legs should yield about 250 g/9 oz meat. Roast the bones, skin and trimmings in a meat tin in 3 tablespoons hot oil. After 10 minutes add the coarsely chopped vegetables, and continue roasting, stirring occasionally. Dilute with a little of the water. Transfer to a large saucepan, add

the remaining water, bring to a boil, skim and simmer for 2–3 hours. For the final third of the cooking time add the bouquet garni, salt, 8 of the juniper berries, a clove of garlic and the white peppercorns. Strain through muslin and reduce to 250 ml/8 fl oz.

Cut the meat from the partridge legs, the pork and fat into strips and sprinkle over pâté seasoning, white pepper, half the grated orange rind, a finely chopped clove of garlic and 8 crushed juniper berries. Chill thoroughly. Mince the meat twice through the finest blade of the mincer, the fat once only. Place the meat in a bowl, over ice, and work in the fat. Finally, pass the forcemeat through a sieve.

Rub the partridge breasts with pâté seasoning and ground white pepper, seal in the remaining 2 tablespoons hot oil. Remove from the pan and pour off the oil, melt the butter in the pan and soften the diced shallots. Deglaze with the brandy, add 100 ml/4 fl oz partridge stock (the rest can be reserved for another use), bring to a boil and skim. Strain this essence over the breasts and leave to cool.

Work the lemon rind, the rest of the orange rind and juniper berries, the

remaining clove of garlic, crushed, the diced goose liver, pistachios, truffles and tongue into the forcemeat. Grease the tin with butter, line with pastry and add one third of the forcemeat. Cut the ends from the partridge breasts and place half of them on the forcemeat. Add a second layer of partridge breasts and cover with the remaining forcemeat. Bang the tin several times on a damp cloth. Fold the excess pastry over the filling, cover with a sheet of pastry, decorate with any remaining pastry and brush with the egg yolk and cream mixture. Cut an opening in the top and insert a funnel.

Bake in an oven preheated to 220 C, 425 F, gas 7 for 15 minutes, then reduce the heat to 180 C, 350 F, gas 4 and cook for a further 30 minutes.

Fill the cold pâté with port aspic and serve. If you wish, the pâté can be accompanied with honeydew melon and mint jelly flavoured with Armagnac.

Game Terrine with Truffles

Terrine de gibier aux truffes

1 pheasant, weighing about 800 g/1¾ lb
150 g/5 oz lean venison
150 g/5 oz lean pork
250 g/9 oz pork fat
1 tablespoon pâté seasoning
14 juniper berries, crushed
1 clove garlic, crushed
grated rind of 1½ oranges and ½ lemon
3 tablespoons oil
15 g/½ oz butter
2 shallots, diced
1½ tablespoons brandy
250 ml/8 fl oz jellifying stock
ground white pepper
40 g/1½ oz shelled pistachio nuts,
coarsely chopped
65 g/2½ oz truffles, diced
about 300 g/11 oz pork fat, thinly sliced
250 g/9 oz goose liver, marinated in sherry
100 g/4 oz truffles
sherry aspic to finish
1.25-litre/2¼-pint terrine

Remove the legs and breasts from the dressed pheasant and bone them carefully. The two boned breasts weigh about 200–250 g/7–9 oz, and the legs similarly. Cut the pheasant, venison, pork and fat into strips and add the pâté seasoning, 8 of the juniper berries, garlic, and the grated rind of ½ orange and ½ lemon. Mince the meat twice through the finest blade of the mincer, the fat once only. Over ice, work the fat into the meat and then push through a sieve.

Rub the pheasant breasts with pâté seasoning and seal thoroughly in a frying pan in hot oil. Remove from the pan and pour off the oil. Melt the butter in the pan, glaze the shallots, dilute with brandy and add the jellifying stock. Bring to a boil, skim, add the remaining juniper berries and orange rind, season with ground white pepper and reduce to a thick sauce. Leave to cool.

Work the sauce into the chilled forcemeat and carefully fold in the pistachios and diced truffles. Line the terrine with slices of fat and add one third of the stuffing. With the palm of the hand press out the goose liver until long and flat and wrap around the whole truffles. Place in the tin and cover with stuffing. Add the pheasant breasts as a second layer and cover with the remaining stuffing. Fold over the excess fat and cover with a slice of fat. Bang the terrine several times on a damp cloth and cover.

Cook in a water bath, for 45–50 minutes, in an oven preheated to about 180 C, 350 F, gas 4. Regulate the oven so that the water remains at a gentle simmer.

When cool remove the slice of fat which covers the terrine and glaze the top with sherry aspic.

Add the aspic, but wait until the pâté is quite cool. Meat pies should not be ice-cold; on the contrary, the aspic will bind better to the filling at room temperature. Any split in the pastry can be repaired with butter.

Quail Pâté

Pâté de caille

8–10 oven-ready quails, each weighing
about 100 g/4 oz
5 tablespoons oil
1 carrot, sliced
1 large onion, sliced
1.5 litres/2¾ pints water
bouquet garni (white of 1 leek, 1 piece
celeriac, 3 parsley sprigs, 1 bay leaf)
1 teaspoon salt
20 juniper berries
1 clove garlic
6 white peppercorns
pâté seasoning
15 g/½ oz butter
2 shallots, diced
2 tablespoons brandy
150 g/5 oz lean pork
250 g/9 oz pork fat
grated rind of ½ orange
ground white pepper
50 g/2 oz shelled pistachio nuts
25 g/1 oz truffles, diced
250 g/9 oz goose liver, marinated in dry
sherry
butter for greasing
675 g/1½ lb shortcrust pastry
1 lightly beaten egg for glazing
sherry aspic to finish
1.25-litre/2¼-pint pâté mould or dish

Remove the breasts from the dressed quails. Bone the legs and remove the ligaments. Leave the skin on the legs and breasts as it is particularly flavoursome. The boned, trimmed meat and skin of 8–10 quails gives a quantity of about 250 g/9 oz for the

forcemeat, and the breasts weigh about the same. Roast the bones, ligaments and trimmings in 3 tablespoons of the oil in a meat tin. Add the vegetables, water, bouquet garni, salt, 8 juniper berries, the garlic and white peppercorns to make a stock, strain and reduce to a jellifying stock.

Season the quail breasts with pâté seasoning, seal in the remaining hot oil, remove from the pan and pour off the oil. Melt the butter in the pan and soften the shallots, deglaze with brandy and add 250 ml/8 fl oz stock. Bring to a boil, skim and add 2 teaspoons pâté seasoning and 5 juniper berries, crushed this time. Reduce to a thick liquid and push through a sieve over the breasts. Leave to cool.

Cut the quail meat, trimmed pork and fat into strips, season with pâté seasoning, and add the rest of the juniper berries, crushed, and the orange rind, and ground white pepper. Mince the meat twice through the

finest blade of the mincer, the fat once only. Gradually work the fat into the forcemeat, adding a little quail stock. Push through a sieve. Chill repeatedly after each stage. Work the coarsely chopped pistachios and diced truffles into the forcemeat. Knead the liver thoroughly with the hands and cut into pieces.

Grease the mould or dish with butter, line with shortcrust pastry and add some of the forcemeat. Fill the mould or dish with alternate layers of goose liver, quail breasts and the remaining forcemeat. Fold the excess pastry over the filling, cover with a sheet of pastry, decorate and brush with egg. Cut openings for the steam and insert funnels.

Bake in an oven preheated to 220 C, 425 F, gas 7 for 15 minutes, then reduce the heat to 180 C, 350 F, gas 4 and continue cooking for a further 30 minutes or so.

When cool fill the pie with sherry aspic.

55

Hare Pâté

Pâté de lièvre

1 whole dressed hare
1 saddle of hare
450 g/1 lb pork fat
2 carrots, sliced
1 large onion, coarsely chopped
3 sprigs parsley
250 ml/8 fl oz red wine (Burgundy if possible)
1.5 litres/2¾ pints water
1 teaspoon salt
1 clove garlic
12 juniper berries
10 black peppercorns
1 clove
1 bay leaf
250 g/9 oz lean pork
50 g/2 oz thinly sliced white bread, crusts removed
5 tablespoons cream
1 tablespoon pâté salt
½ teaspoon dried green peppercorns
1 teaspoon thyme
2 tablespoons oil
150 g/5 oz turkey livers
50 g/2 oz walnuts, coarsely chopped
50 g/2 oz pork fat, diced
3 tablespoons brandy
1 kg/2 lb shortcrust pastry
350 g/12 oz pork fat, in thin slices
1 lightly beaten egg for glazing
Madeira aspic to finish
2.5-litre/4¼-pint pâté mould

Cut the dressed hare into joints. Remove the meat from the loin. Cut any other large pieces of meat, particularly from the legs and shoulders, off the bone and trim thoroughly. This should give about 450 g/1 lb lean meat. Remove the fillets from the hare's back. Transfer all the bones and trimmings to a roasting tin. Dice 100 g/4 oz of the pork fat, add it too and roast at 220 C, 425 F, gas 7. After 20 minutes add the vegetables and parsley and roast for a further 30–40 minutes, stirring from time to time. Then transfer the contents of the roasting tin to a large saucepan, add the red wine and water and bring to a boil. Skim the scum from the surface of the liquid until it stops forming. Add the salt, garlic, juniper berries, peppercorns, clove and bay leaf and simmer gently for 30 minutes. Strain the stock and slowly reduce it to about 350 ml/12 fl oz.

Cut the trimmed pork, hare (not the fillets) and the other 350 g/12 oz pork fat into strips. Moisten the thinly sliced bread with the cream, add to the meat and sprinkle with the pâté salt, crushed peppercorns and thyme. Leave to stand for 60 minutes in the

refrigerator and then mince all the ingredients together twice through the finest blade of the mincer. Chill again and push the forcemeat through a sieve.

Heat the oil in a frying pan and quickly seal the turkey livers. Remove from the pan and dice. Work into the forcemeat with the walnuts and diced pork fat. In the same oil quickly seal the four hare fillets, then add the brandy. Remove the fillets from the pan and leave to cool. Add 250 ml/8 fl oz hare stock to the pan, stir well and reduce to about 6 tablespoons.

Line the pâté mould first with pastry, then with the slices of fat. Add half the forcemeat. Wrap the fillets in pork fat and place 2 or 3 alongside each other in the mould. Sprinkle with the reduced stock and cover with the remaining forcemeat. Fold over any excess pork fat and cover with a pastry lid. Decorate and brush with egg. Cut two openings in the lid, insert funnels and bake in an oven preheated to 220 C, 425 F, gas 7 for 15 minutes, then reduce the heat to 190 C, 375 F, gas 5 and bake for a further 1 hour and 10–20 minutes until cooked. If you use a tin of the same volume but narrower than that used for the pâté illustrated, reduce the baking time by up to 20 per cent.

Fill the cooled pâté with Madeira aspic.

Rabbit Terrine

Terrine de lapin

2 rabbits, total weight about 2.5 kg/5½ lb
450 g/1 lb lean loin of pork
2 teaspoons salt
½ teaspoon dried green peppercorns
½ teaspoon ground allspice
1 teaspoon thyme
1 teaspoon fresh chopped lovage
few rosemary leaves
2 bay leaves
500 g/18 oz veal bones
3 tablespoons oil
1 onion, sliced
100 g/4 oz carrots, sliced
100 g/4 oz celeriac, chopped
15 white peppercorns
25 g/1 oz butter
1 rabbit liver
1½ tablespoons brandy
1 clove garlic, crushed
2 shallots, chopped
generous pinch of ground cardamom
1 kg/2 lb pork fat
2 eggs
200 g/7 oz boiled ham, diced
100 g/4 oz mushrooms, coarsely chopped
fresh herbs for decoration
1.8–2-litre/3–3½-pint terrine

Joint and bone the rabbits. When trimmed, the back fillets should give about 250 g/9 oz meat, and the rest of the rabbit should give about 400 g/14 oz after boning and trimming. Keep the fillets to one side to use whole. Cut the remaining rabbit meat into strips with the pork, place in a bowl and season with the salt, green peppercorns, allspice, thyme, lovage, rosemary and 1 bay leaf. Cover the bowl with foil and leave to marinate in the refrigerator.

Chop the rabbit bones and trimmings and veal bones into small pieces, roast in oil, then add the onion, carrot, celeriac, the other bay leaf and 5 white peppercorns. Cover with water to make a stock and then reduce to 250 ml/8 fl oz. Strain.

Heat the butter in a frying pan and quickly fry the rabbit liver and fillets on all sides to seal them. Pour on the brandy, then remove the meat from the pan and leave to

1 Quickly seal the liver and seasoned hare fillets in hot butter. The liver will seal better if cut into cubes. The fillets contract slightly when fried, so will keep their shape when cooked in the terrine.

2 Place the fillets side by side, but first line the terrine with pork fat and cover the base with a 2-cm/¾-in layer of forcemeat. Add the fillets, carefully fill the spaces between them with forcemeat, and press down.

cool. Add the rabbit stock to the juices in the pan and add the crushed garlic, chopped shallots, the remaining 10 peppercorns, crushed, and cardamom. Reduce to about 6 tablespoons, strain through a fine sieve and chill.

Mince the seasoned meat twice through the finest blade of the mincer. Finally mince 350 g/12 oz of the fat and work into the forcemeat a little at a time. Then stir in the eggs and the reduced stock. Chill the forcemeat thoroughly once more, then dice the rabbit liver and work it in, with the diced ham and coarsely chopped mushrooms. Line the terrine with the remaining fat, cut in thin slices, add half the forcemeat, then top with the two fillets. Cover with the remaining forcemeat, seal the top with fat and decorate with fresh herbs. Cover the terrine and bake, in a water bath, for 1 hour–1 hour 10 minutes. Regulate the oven temperature so that the water remains at a gentle simmer.

Rabbit Terrine and Syracuse Tomatoes complement one another admirably. Peeled, diced tomatoes are marinated in olive oil, garlic, spring onion, salt and pepper and served decorated with fresh basil leaves.

Pheasant Terrine with Goose Liver

Terrine de faisan au foie gras

1 hen pheasant
8 tablespoons oil
1 carrot, sliced
1 large onion, sliced
2 litres/3½ pints water
bouquet garni (white of 1 leek, 1 piece celeriac, 3 parsley sprigs, 1 bay leaf)
1 teaspoon salt
2 cloves garlic
22 juniper berries
8 white peppercorns
100 g/4 oz lean pork
250 g/9 oz pork fat
1½ teaspoons pâté salt
grated rind of 1 orange and 1 lemon
15 g/½ oz butter
2 shallots, diced
1½ tablespoons brandy
ground white pepper
65 g/2½ oz shelled pistachio nuts, coarsely chopped
65 g/2½ oz truffles, diced
about 250 g/9 oz pork fat in thin slices
250 g/9 oz goose liver, marinated in port and brandy
port aspic to finish
1-litre/1¾-pint terrine

Remove the legs and breasts from the pheasant and trim them carefully. The two breasts should weight about 250 g/9 oz after trimming, and the two legs about the same. Chop the bones, and roast in a meat tin in 5 tablespoons of the oil, with any trimmings. Add the vegetables, water, bouquet garni, salt, 1 clove of garlic, 8 juniper berries, and the white peppercorns and make a stock. Strain and reduce to about 250 ml/8 fl oz jellifying stock.

Cut the meat from the pheasant legs, the pork and fat into strips and sprinkle with 1 teaspoon of the pâté salt, 8 juniper berries, crushed this time, the second clove of garlic, also crushed, and half the orange and lemon rind. Leave to stand for 60 minutes in the refrigerator, then mince the meat twice and the fat once through the finest blade of the mincer. Place a bowl over ice and work the fat in it into the minced meat, then push through a sieve.

Season the pheasant breasts with the rest of the pâté salt and in a frying pan quickly seal them in the remaining 3 tablespoons hot oil. Remove from the pan and pour off the oil. Melt the butter in the pan and soften the shallots. Add the brandy and the jellifying stock. Bring to a boil and skim. Add the rest of the juniper berries and grated orange and lemon rind, and some

ground white pepper and reduce to a thick liquid, then strain over the breasts and leave to cool.

Carefully work the pistachios and truffles into the thoroughly chilled forcemeat. Line the terrine with the sliced pork fat and add one third of the forcemeat. Add the goose liver, brush with the sauce and cover with forcemeat. Add the pheasant breasts as a second layer and cover with the remaining forcemeat. Fold over the excess fat and cover with another slice of fat. Leave to stand in a cold place.

Cook for about 42 minutes, in a water bath, regulating the oven so that the water remains at a gentle simmer.

When the terrine is cooked and cooled, remove the top slice of fat and cover it instead with a layer of port aspic.

Wild Duck Terrine with Duck Liver

Terrine de canard sauvage au foie de canard

1 whole wild duck
75 g/3 oz lean pork
150 g/5 oz pork fat
grated rind of $\frac{1}{2}$ orange
$\frac{1}{2}$ teaspoon each chopped fresh sage and tarragon
1 teaspoon pâté salt
1 tablespoon oil
15 g/$\frac{1}{2}$ oz butter
25 g/1 oz diced shallots
1$\frac{1}{2}$ tablespoons curaçao
1$\frac{1}{2}$ tablespoons orange juice
100 ml/4 fl oz jellifying game stock
3 juniper berries, crushed
$\frac{1}{2}$ clove garlic, crushed
little fresh sage, tarragon and grated orange rind
100 g/4 oz duck's liver, marinated in Madeira and port
50 g/2 oz boiled ham, diced
25 g/1 oz shelled pistachio nuts, halved
25 g/1 oz truffles, diced
300 g/11 oz pork fat, in thin slices
port aspic to finish
750-ml/1$\frac{1}{4}$-pint terrine

Joint the duck, remove the breasts from the bone and keep to one side. Remove the remaining meat from the bone, remove all skin and ligaments, and weigh off 150 g/5 oz. Cut the duck (except the breasts), pork and fat into strips and sprinkle with the orange rind, herbs and pâté salt. Cover with foil and leave to marinate in the refrigerator.

Mince the meat twice through the finest blade of the mincer, and the fat once. Over ice, work the fat into the minced meat and push through a fine sieve. As with all forcemeat, chill thoroughly after each stage.

Quickly seal the trimmed breasts by frying them in hot oil, remove from the pan and pour off the oil. Melt the butter in the pan and soften the shallots without allowing them to colour. Add the curaçao and orange juice and then the game stock, juniper berries, garlic, herbs and orange rind. Bring to a boil and reduce to a thick essence. Strain the essence over the duck breasts and leave to cool.

Dry the duck's liver on kitchen paper, cut into pieces and work into the forcemeat with the ham, pistachios and truffles.

Line the terrine with slices of pork fat and add about half the forcemeat. Add the breasts, brush with essence and cover with the remaining forcemeat. Fold over the excess fat and cover the top with a slice of fat. Cover the terrine and bake, standing in a water bath, for 45 minutes, regulating the oven so that the water remains at a gentle simmer.

When cool remove the top layer of fat and cover with port aspic.

Country-style Terrine

Terrine de campagne

This real country terrine is surprisingly easy to make, hearty and filling. The smoked pork fat gives the terrine its distinctive spicy flavour.

2 rabbit legs
400 g/18 oz lean pork
200 g/7 oz fresh pork fat
1½ teaspoons salt
½ teaspoon ground black pepper
generous pinch of nutmeg
13 juniper berries
4 bay leaves
1 tablespoon dried herbs (marjoram, thyme, sage and savory)
1½ tablespoons brandy
2 eggs
250 g/9 oz smoked belly pork
300 g/11 oz fresh pork fat in thin slices
butter for greasing
1.2-litre/2-pint terrine

Bone the rabbit legs and remove skin and ligaments. Dice the rabbit, pork and pork fat. Transfer to a bowl, sprinkle with the salt, pepper, nutmeg, 5 of the juniper berries, 1 bay leaf and the herbs, pour on the brandy and mix carefully. Cover with foil and leave overnight to marinate.

Mince the seasoned diced meat and fat a little at a time in a food processor. Chill thoroughly. Work in the eggs and beat the forcemeat vigorously for 5–10 minutes. Remove the rind from the belly pork, cut the pork into small, equal-sized cubes and work into the forcemeat. Check the seasoning – adding more if necessary. Line the terrine with the slices of pork fat, fill with the forcemeat and smooth the top. Garnish with the remaining bay leaves and juniper berries and cover with well-buttered greaseproof paper. Cover the terrine and bake standing in a water bath for 1 hour. Regulate the oven so that the temperature of the water does not rise above 80 C, 176 F. The terrine will shrink slightly during cooking, so fill any gaps around the edges with lard when the terrine is completely cool. The terrine will then keep in the refrigerator for up to two weeks.

This terrine can also be baked in the oven without standing in water. In that case, cook for 1 hour at 220 C, 425 F, gas 7. Cooked like this it will lose more fat, but that is an advantage in that the fat seals the top of the cooled terrine and keeps it moist.

Ham pâté

Pâté de jambon

A delicious loaf-shaped pâté, with a delicate filling of pork and pork loin with truffles and pistachios. Whole or sliced, it has an appetising appearance.

350 g/12 oz lean pork
250 g/9 oz pork fat
1 teaspoon pâté salt
ground white pepper
1 teaspoon each chopped fresh thyme and marjoram
2 cloves garlic, crushed
6 juniper berries, crushed
150 g/5 oz uncooked pork loin, free from bones, fat and gristle, diced
40 g/1½ oz shelled pistachios, halved
25 g/1 oz truffles, diced
butter for greasing
650 g/1½ lb shortcrust pastry
450 g/1 lb piece uncooked pork loin, free from bones, fat and gristle
1 lightly beaten egg for glazing
sherry aspic to finish
1.5-litre/2¾-pint pâté mould

Cut the pork and pork fat into strips, place on a baking sheet and season with pâté salt, pepper, herbs, garlic and juniper berries. Cover with cling film and chill. Mince the meat strips twice through the finest blade of the mincer. Mince the fat once only. Over ice, mix the fat thoroughly into the meat a little at a time and push through a sieve. Don't forget to chill the meat thoroughly after each stage.

Mix the diced pork loin, pistachios and truffles into the forcemeat. Grease the mould and line it with pastry. Add about half the forcemeat to the mould, pressing it to the edges of the pastry. Add the piece of pork loin, cover with the remaining forcemeat and fold over the excess pastry. Cover with a pastry lid. Make one or two openings to allow the steam to escape; decorate the pâté, brush with beaten egg and add foil funnels.

Bake in an oven preheated to 220 C, 425 F, gas 7 for the first 15 minutes, then reduce the heat to 180 C, 350 F, gas 4 and bake for a further 35 minutes, or until cooked.

When cool top up with sherry aspic.

Pâtés and Terrines and Wine

There is no doubt that when we think of pâtés and terrines we cannot help but associate them with French cuisine. But where wine is concerned France, Italy and Germany spring to mind. For all three countries have extensive wine-producing regions with excellent vineyards. Connoisseurs of wine tend, therefore, not to favour one country more than another, but to value highly the best wines produced by all three. There is international agreement about this. It is also agreed that pâtés and terrines and wine belong together. Neither can be fully appreciated without the other. This is true not only of the best wines of Germany, France or Italy, but also of the wines of Spain, Austria or Switzerland.

But there is a great difference between the drinking habits of the Romance countries and Germany. A Frenchman would not dream of eating without a glass of wine. Nor would he dream of drinking wine without eating. In France (and other Romance countries) wine is part of the culture of eating. And according to the French it is for this reason that they produce so many dry wines. For only dry wines go really well with fish and meat, poultry and game. This is slowly coming to be recognised elsewhere too.

In Germany, on the other hand, people like a glass of beer in the early evening. Or they enjoy a bottle of wine in the evening, either at home or in a wine bar. It is the rule to drink without eating. In Germany the habit of drinking wine with meals has been slow to catch on. And lately the trend has changed to producing more dry wines whose labels either bear the word 'trocken' or the yellow seal (which denotes a dry wine). This is fortunate, for only good wines go well with food, so you will do well to serve a good wine with your pâtés and terrines. But which wine goes with which pâté? Here we can only make recommendations; there are no hard-and-fast rules. In general you can rely on your own taste. Connoisseurs of French pâtés and wines say, for example, that it is entirely a matter of taste

whether you serve white or red wine. The main thing is that the wine should be neither too sour nor too heavy. A few examples will provide a few pointers on the greater enjoyment of pâtés and wine but, with the wide range of wines available today, the list cannot claim to be exhaustive. It is hoped that the suggestions below will give you a few ideas to be going on with.

With all types of pâté with game as the main ingredient you can serve full-bodied red wines. This may be a good French Bordeaux or a Languedoc-Roussillon, a wine from the Ahr, from Baden, or a chianti. A sparkling, medium-dry French white wine or one from north or south Austria could just as well be chosen: a Traminer or Gewürztraminer, for example. With a pork or veal pie or pâté serve light, fresh red wines; a Ruländer from the Ortenau region, or a rosé (maybe a Portuguese rosé).

With poultry you can choose between, say, an Italian Orvieto secco, or a Kaiserstühler Ruländer, and there are also the Frankish wines from the Würzburg region or an Austrian wine which bears the good wine seal. Any fish or shellfish pâté needs a dry white wine, for example an excellent, dry Mosel Riesling or one from Alsace. Dry French wines include Entre-deux-Mers, Chablis or a wine from a sandy Portuguese vineyard. For very special occasions you can serve a French champagne or a dry German sparkling wine.

Liver pâtés, whether calf's, goose or other poultry liver, go well with a light, but good-quality red from either France or Germany. Wines produced from the Sauvignon grape, as grown in Baden bei Wien, go excellently with goose liver pâté. The best of the French wines for foie gras is a Sauterne, providing it is not too sweet. The same is also true of Sauvignon wines from Italy.

With Russian pâtés you might like to try a red wine from the Crimea, or a white Crimean sparkling wine.

With heavy English pies rosés or reds are your best bet.

Sweetbread Terrine

Terrine de ris de veau

450 g/1 lb sweetbreads
salt
little white pepper
25 g/1 oz butter
3 tablespoons Armagnac
2 shallots
200 ml/7 fl oz veal stock
½ bay leaf
½ teaspoon basil
¼ teaspoon allspice
1 piece cinnamon
1 clove
300 g/11 oz veal fillet (without fat)
100 g/4 oz lean pork
2 teaspoons pâté seasoning for delicately-
flavoured meat fillings
250 g/9 oz pork fat
1 egg white
100 ml/4 fl oz single cream
100 g/4 oz boiled ham
20 g/¾ oz truffles
400 g/14 oz pork fat, in thin slices
sherry aspic to finish
1.2-litre/2-pint terrine

Stand the sweetbreads under cold running water for 3–4 hours, then blanch for a few moments and carefully remove skin and all veins. Sprinkle the pieces of sweetbread with salt and pepper. Heat the butter in a frying pan, seal the sweetbreads, add the Armagnac and remove from the pan. Lightly glaze the finely chopped shallots in the butter, add the veal stock, herbs and spices (bay leaf, basil, allspice, cinnamon and clove). Reduce the stock to a thick essence, pour over the sweetbreads and leave to cool.

Cut the fillet of veal and pork into strips and sprinkle with salt and the seasoning. Cut the pork fat into similar strips. Chill thoroughly, then mince the meat twice through the finest blade of the mincer and the fat once only. Over ice, work the pork fat into the meat a little at a time. Then push through a fine sieve. Over ice, beat the forcemeat until smooth, gradually work in the egg white and finally beat in the cream a little at a time. Mix the diced ham and sweetbreads into the forcemeat with the essence and diced truffles.

Line the terrine with the slices of pork fat. Add the forcemeat a little at a time and press down firmly to prevent any holes. Smooth the top and cover with fat. Cover the terrine and bake for about 50 minutes in an oven preheated to 180 C, 350 F, gas 4, standing in a water bath. Leave to cool slightly, cover with a board and weight the board with a 1 kg/2 lb weight. When the terrine is completely cool turn it out and scrape off any fat produced by the forcemeat. Remove the top layer of fat and cut a thin layer from the top of the terrine to give a completely flat surface. Place the terrine back in its dish. Pour a thin layer of lukewarm sherry aspic over the top. Leave to set.

This terrine goes particularly well with a fresh endive and orange salad, dressed with vinaigrette and a dash of Bénédictine.

Sweetbread Pie

Tourte de ris de veau

This is a pie which can be served either hot or cold. In a fairly flat pie like this the sweetbreads cook quicker and retain all their moisture. A good variation would be to replace the mushrooms with morels.

1 kg/2 lb veal bones
1.5 litres/2¾ pints water
½ leek
1 stick of celery
1 onion
1 bay leaf
2 cloves
5 white peppercorns
1 teaspoon salt
750 g/1½–1¾ lb sweetbreads
250 ml/8 fl oz white Burgundy
300 g/11 oz lean pork fillet
150 g/5 oz pork fat
15 g/½ oz pâté salt (made with the seasoning for delicately-flavoured meats)
½ egg white
2 teaspoons finely chopped herbs (parsley, rosemary, sage)
800 g/1¾ lb shortcrust pastry
100 g/4 oz mushrooms
1 lightly beaten egg yolk
for glazing
sherry aspic to finish
25-cm/10-in diameter cake tin

Boil the veal bones in the water with the leek, celery, onion, bay leaf, cloves, peppercorns and salt to make a stock, then reduce the volume by half. Soak the sweetbreads, carefully remove the skin and all blood vessels (to leave at least

500 g/18 oz), add to the stock and simmer very gently for about 10 minutes. Transfer the sweetbreads to a narrow container, cover with stock and leave to cool. Strain the remaining stock through a fine sieve, add the wine and reduce to give a thick liquid.

Purée the pork fillet a little at a time in a food processor, and then the pork fat. Season with the pâté salt and beat in the egg white until smooth. Season with the finely chopped herbs.

Roll out the pastry evenly, line the tin, press the pastry to the sides of the tin and cut off any excess. Cover the base and sides of the pie with the forcemeat. Drain the sweetbreads, reserving the thick stock, and arrange over the forcemeat. Fill the spaces between the sweetbreads with mushrooms and pour on the thick stock. Fold any excess pastry over the filling and brush with egg yolk. Cover with a pastry lid and press down firmly around the edges. Cut an opening for the funnel in the centre. Brush the top of the pie with beaten egg yolk. Cut leaves from the leftover pastry and arrange as petals on the pie. Brush the leaves with egg yolk. Make a funnel with foil or greaseproof paper and bake for 45–50 minutes in an oven preheated to 220 C, 425 F, gas 7. If the pie is to be eaten cold, make an aspic with veal stock and sherry and top up the pie.

The most sophisticated Paris creations. You can see and try them at Fauchon's. Among them are a sweetbread terrine with kiwi fruit and a terrine of gourmet vegetables with a variety of meats included. These novel terrines were created by Georges Pralus of Briennon. He describes himself as a 'charcutier and inventor'. He is continually experimenting with new combinations of flavours and new fillings made mainly with new produce: green peppers, exotic fruits and vegetables. Among this wide range of interesting combinations his terrine of rabbit kidney with green peppercorns is notable.

Veal Terrine with Mushrooms

Terrine de veau aux champignons de couche

300 g/11 oz trimmed veal fillet
200 g/7 oz lean pork
575 g/1¼ lb pork fat, in thin slices
salt
½ teaspoon dried green peppercorns
½ teaspoon basil
½ teaspoon sage
½ teaspoon thyme
50 g/2 oz white bread, thinly sliced and crusts removed
1 egg white
6 tablespoons whipped cream
50 g/2 oz butter
2 shallots
200 g/7 oz skinned calf's liver, diced
1½ tablespoons brandy
1½ tablespoons Cointreau
1 clove garlic, crushed
generous pinch of ginger
generous pinch of cardamom
150 ml/¼ pint whipped cream
200 g/7 oz fresh mushrooms

Mushrooms and fresh parsley give quite a dominant flavour, but are particularly good seasonings for veal based terrines.

2 tablespoons chopped parsley
100 g/4 oz boiled ham, diced
1.2-litre/2-pint terrine

Slice the veal fillet and pork. Spread, with 250 g/9 oz of the sliced pork fat, on a baking sheet or place in a large bowl. Sprinkle with 1 teaspoon salt, the peppercorns and herbs and cover with the thinly sliced white bread. Beat the egg white into the 6 tablespoons of whipped cream and pour over the bread. Leave to soak overnight.

Heat half the butter in a frying pan, soften the finely chopped shallots in it and seal the diced calf's liver over a high flame. Add the brandy and Cointreau and simmer for a few moments. Remove the pan from the heat, stir in ½ teaspoon salt, crushed garlic, ginger and cardamom, and cool.

Mince the seasoned meat, fat and bread mixture together with the liver mixture twice through the finest blade of the mincer. Chill thoroughly and then, over ice, beat well, gradually beating in the stiffly whipped cream until the mixture is smooth and shiny.

Wash the mushrooms, cut in half and quickly fry in the rest of the butter, season with salt and parsley. Work this mixture into the forcemeat with the diced ham.

Line the terrine with the remaining slices of fat. Add the filling, cover with more fat, cover the terrine and bake, in a water bath, for 50 minutes in an oven preheated to 180 C, 350 F, gas 4.

Terrine of the House with French Beans

Terrine maison aux haricots verts

200 g/7 oz breast of chicken
450 g/1 lb lean pork loin
2 teaspoons salt
40 g/1½ oz butter
75 g/3 oz finely diced carrot
75 g/3 oz finely diced celeriac
4 shallots, finely chopped
1 clove garlic, crushed
10 white peppercorns
4 allspice berries
½ teaspoon coriander
1 bay leaf
few rosemary leaves
200 ml/7 fl oz Madeira
500 ml/17 fl oz chicken stock
150 g/5 oz calf's liver
350 g/12 oz pork fat
1 egg white
100 g/4 oz French beans
450 g/1 lb pork fat, in thin slices
1.5-litre/2¾-pint terrine

Carefully skin the chicken breast and cut into strips with the pork. Sprinkle with salt. To make the marinade, heat the butter in a frying pan and fry the carrots, celeriac and shallots. Add the coarsely crushed garlic, peppercorns, spices and herbs. Add the Madeira and chicken stock, simmer for 15 minutes, leave to cool and then pour over the chicken and pork. Marinate for at least 12 hours.

Drain the meat thoroughly, strain the marinade through a fine sieve and then simmer gently to reduce to about 150 ml/¼ pint. Cool thoroughly. Carefully skin the liver, cut it into strips and mince with the meat twice through the finest blade of the mincer. Cut the fat into strips and mince once only. Over ice, gradually work the fat into the meat. Stir in the egg white and reduced marinade. Check the seasoning.

Boil the French beans in salted water until half-cooked, plunge into iced water and leave until completely cool. Spread one large or two small slices of fat with a little of the forcemeat, cover with beans and roll up.

When the terrine is sliced the French beans give it an attractive appearance. Their flavour also goes very well with the delicate taste of the calf's liver.

Line the terrine with the remaining slices of fat, half fill with forcemeat. Add the bean rolls, cover with the remaining forcemeat and smooth the top. Cover with fat, cover the terrine and bake standing in a water bath, for 50 minutes in an oven preheated to 180 C, 350 F, gas 4.

Poultry Pâtés and Terrines

Hot or Cold Chicken Pâté

Pâté de poularde chaud ou froid

This pâté is even better hot than cold. It can be served warm with a madeira sauce. If served cold, top up with Madeira aspic.

1 fresh, oven-ready chicken, about
1.5 kg/3 lb
1 teaspoon salt
1 sprig fresh thyme
50 g/2 oz butter, melted
75 g/3 oz shallots, diced
175 g/6 oz fresh mushrooms, sliced
1 teaspoon pâté salt (all-purpose mixture)
1 tablespoon fresh chopped parsley
3–4 fresh basil leaves, chopped
3–4 fresh sage leaves, chopped
3 tablespoons Madeira

Stock
450 g/1 lb veal bones
3 tablespoons oil
1 onion, sliced
1 carrot, sliced
1 small celeriac, sliced
1.5 litres/2¾ pints water
1 clove garlic
8 white peppercorns
½ bay leaf
2 juniper berries
½ teaspoon salt

Forcemeat
250 g/9 oz lean veal (loin)
250 g/9 oz lean pork
250 g/9 oz pork fat
1–2 teaspoons salt
freshly milled white pepper
generous pinch allspice
generous pinch ground ginger
generous pinch mace
generous pinch rosemary
½ teaspoon thyme
½ teaspoon basil
150 ml/¼ pint cream, lightly whipped

Pastry
450 g/1 lb flour
25 g/1 oz fresh yeast
150 ml/¼ pint milk
75 g/3 oz butter
1 egg
1 teaspoon salt
generous pinch of nutmeg

butter for greasing
1 egg yolk, mixed with 1 tablespoon cream
and a generous pinch of sugar
25-cm/10-in diameter tin

Rub the inside of the chicken with salt and place the sprig of thyme inside. Brush with melted butter and roast in a very hot oven, 240 C, 475 F, gas 9, for 12–15 minutes until golden. Leave to cool, then remove the legs. Thinly slice the breast and leg meat and transfer to a bowl. Save the carcass to use for the stock. Lightly glaze the shallots in the cooking juices from the chicken, add the washed, sliced mushrooms, season with pâté salt and simmer for 4–5 minutes. Pour all the contents of the pan over the chicken in the bowl, sprinkle with the chopped herbs and add the Madeira. Cover with foil and leave to stand for 24 hours in the refrigerator.

Cut up the carcass with the skin and any remaining meat and chop the veal bones. Brown lightly in the oil, add the vegetables and soften, then add the remaining stock ingredients. Simmer to make a stock, strain and reduce to 150 ml/¼ pint and, still warm, pour over the chicken and mushrooms, so that the flavour is absorbed by the meat.

Make a forcemeat from the veal, pork, fat and seasonings and, over ice, beat in the lightly whipped cream.

Use the pastry ingredients to make a yeast pastry, following the instructions in the section 'Piecrusts', and when risen, chill in the refrigerator. Roll out two thirds of the pastry into a 33-cm/13-in diameter circle, and line the lightly greased tin. Press firmly to the sides. Add half the forcemeat, covering the sides and base of the tin. Thoroughly mix the seasoned chicken and mushrooms in the bowl and transfer to the tin. The tin should now be three-quarters full. Add the rest of the forcemeat and brush the pastry round the sides of the pâté with egg yolk. Roll out the remaining pastry as thinly as possible and cover the filling. Press the pastry lid firmly to the sides of the pâté with your thumbs. Cut off any excess pastry evenly with a pastry wheel or knife. Work the leftover pastry into a ball, roll out again and cut into small leaf shapes. Brush the top of the pâté with egg yolk and arrange the leaves on the top in a flower pattern, working from the outside to the centre and overlapping the leaves slightly. In the centre cut an opening for the steam, insert a funnel and brush the top of the pâté once more with the egg yolk mixture. Cover the pâté with a cloth and leave to stand for 20–25 minutes at room temperature, then bake for about 50–55 minutes in a hot oven, 220 C, 425 F, gas 7. If the pâté browns too quickly, cover the top with foil.

Chicken Terrine with Liver

Terrine de poulet au foie de volaille

450 g/1 lb chicken breast (about 4 pieces)
2 teaspoons pâté salt (mixture for delicately flavoured meats)
5 white peppercorns, crushed
½ bay leaf
60 g/2½ oz crustless white bread, thinly sliced
25 g/1 oz butter
100 g/4 oz diced shallot
150 ml/¼ pint white wine (Sauterne)
1 egg white
300 ml/½ pint single cream
250 g/9 oz chicken livers (or preferably a mixture of chicken and turkey livers)
3 tablespoons oil
1 tablespoon Calvados
150 ml/¼ pint chicken or veal stock
½ teaspoon chopped basil
1 teaspoon chopped parsley
½ teaspoon salt
freshly milled white pepper
150 ml/¼ pint light red wine
butter for greasing
100 g/4 oz fresh spinach
100 g/4 oz pork fat, cut in thin slices
1 hard-boiled egg, sliced
chicken stock aspic to finish
1-litre/1¾-pint terrine

Cut the chicken breasts into strips and sprinkle with the pâté salt, peppercorns and bay leaf. Arrange the sliced bread over the chicken. Heat the butter in a frying pan and lightly glaze half the diced shallot. Dilute with the Sauterne, reduce to about 3 tablespoons and leave to cool. Whip the egg white into 4 tablespoons of the cream and pour over the bread and meat. Cover with foil and leave to stand in the refrigerator overnight.

Remove any skin or blood vessels from the chicken livers. Heat the oil thoroughly in a frying pan and seal the liver on all sides. Add the Calvados and braise for 2–3 minutes over a low heat. Remove the liver from the pan and add the rest of the shallots. After a few moments add the chicken or veal stock and simmer for a few minutes. Add the herbs and salt and pepper, then the red wine and reduce to a thick liquid. When cool dice the liver, cover with the sauce and leave to stand overnight.

Mince the marinated chicken and bread twice through the finest blade of the mincer, chill and then strain through a fine sieve. Over ice, beat the filling until smooth and gradually work in the remaining cream until the forcemeat shines. Add more seasoning if necessary. Grease the terrine sparingly with butter and add two-thirds of the forcemeat, bringing it up the sides of the dish. Cover with half the lightly boiled, thoroughly drained spinach. Add the diced liver and sauce and cover with the remaining forcemeat. Cover the top with slices of pork fat, cover the bowl and bake standing in a water bath. Regulate the oven so that the water remains at a gentle simmer. When cool remove the slices of fat, cover with the remaining spinach and garnish with egg. Cover with a chicken stock aspic.

Poultry Pâté with Goose Liver

Pâté de volaille au foie gras

1 piece turkey, weighing about
1.25 kg/2½ lb
little pâté salt (for delicate flavours)
1 duck, weighing about 1.75 kg/3¾ lb
200 g/7 oz lean pork
1 teaspoon salt
2 teaspoons thyme
½ teaspoon hyssop
15 white peppercorns
¼ teaspoon allspice
½ bay leaf
2 juniper berries, crushed
1 onion, sliced
1 carrot, sliced
1 piece of celeriac, chopped
1.5 litres/2¾ pints bone stock or water
½ teaspoon basil
2 teaspoons sweet paprika
½ clove garlic
250 ml/8 fl oz red Burgundy
200 g/7 oz goose liver
150 ml/¼ pint vintage port
100 g/4 oz truffles, in pieces
5 tablespoons oil
50 g/2 oz shallots, finely chopped
200 g/7 oz pork fat
butter for greasing
675 g/1½ lb shortcrust pastry
1 egg yolk
port aspic to finish
1.5-litre/2¾-pint pâté mould

Remove the breast from the turkey, trim thoroughly, sprinkle with a little pâté salt and keep to one side to be used whole. For the forcemeat remove the meat from the remaining turkey and the duck, mainly from the breasts and legs. Remove the bones and all skin or gristle. Cut the lean poultry meat (you should be left with about 450 g/1 lb) and pork into strips, sprinkle with salt, 1 teaspoon thyme, the hyssop, 10 crushed peppercorns, the allspice, bay leaf and juniper berries, and leave to stand in the refrigerator for 1–2 hours.

Chop the carcasses of the turkey and duck with the skin and any offcuts and simmer with the onion, carrot, celeriac, stock or water, basil, paprika, garlic, wine and remaining thyme and peppercorns to make a stock, then reduce by half.

Skin the goose liver and remove all blood vessels, knead gently, sprinkle with pâté salt and pour on the port. Cover with foil and place in the refrigerator. When the liver has soaked thoroughly, drain and wrap around the pieces of truffle.

Heat the oil in a frying pan, seal the turkey breast and remove from the pan. In the same oil glaze the shallots and add the jellifying chicken stock. Over a low heat reduce to a thick liquid and strain through a fine sieve over the turkey breast. Leave to cool.

To make the forcemeat mince the seasoned meat twice through the finest blade of the mincer. Cut the fat into strips, mince once and then, over ice, work into the meat in small portions. Push the forcemeat through a sieve and beat firmly for 5–10 minutes until light and airy.

Line the lightly buttered mould with pastry and add half the forcemeat. Add the turkey breast, halved if preferred, the sauce, and the liver and truffles to the pâté. Cover with the remaining forcemeat and smooth the top. Fold any excess pastry over the filling and brush with egg yolk. Add a pastry lid and seal the edges firmly. Decorate with pastry flowers, cut an opening and insert a funnel. Bake for 10 minutes in a hot oven, 220 C, 425 F, gas 7, then reduce the temperature to 200 C, 400 F, gas 6 and cook for a further 40–45 minutes until cooked.

When cool fill with port aspic.

Goose Giblet Terrine

Terrine d'abatis d'oie

giblets of 2 geese (heart, gizzard, neck,
head and wings)
2 goose livers (not force-fed)
800 g/1¾ lb saddle of pork, on the bone
1 carrot, coarsely chopped
1 small onion, coarsely chopped
1 piece celeriac, coarsely chopped
1.5 litres/2¾ pints bone stock or water
10 white peppercorns
1½ teaspoons marjoram
1 teaspoon basil
1 clove garlic
2–3 teaspoons salt
½ teaspoon green dried peppercorns
1 teaspoon mild paprika
1 teaspoon thyme
1 bay leaf
5 allspice berries
50 g/2 oz white bread, sliced and with
crusts removed
150 ml/¼ pint fresh cream
1 egg
2 tablespoons oil
4 shallots, diced
4 tablespoons vintage port
1 tablespoon cranberry sauce
100 g/4 oz lean boiled ham
40 g/1½ oz pistachios, coarsely chopped

300 g/11 oz pork fat in thin slices
1.5-litre/2¾-pint terrine

Remove the flesh of the gizzards from the
tough skin. Remove the arteries from the
hearts and the blood vessels from the livers.
Bone the saddle of pork and trim the meat
thoroughly. Chop the bones. Roast in a
meat tin for 10 minutes with the chopped
necks and heads and the giblet offcuts. Add
the vegetables and after a further 20 minutes
transfer all the ingredients in the meat tin to
a large pan. Add the bone stock and bring to
the boil. Skim and add the white peppercorns, 1 teaspoon marjoram, the basil
and garlic. Simmer gently over a low heat
for 30 minutes, strain and if necessary
remove fat, then reduce to one-eighth the
quantity.

Cut the giblets and pork into strips,
sprinkle with the salt, green peppercorns,
paprika, thyme, bay leaf, allspice and
remaining marjoram and chill. Place the
sliced bread in a large bowl and pour on the
cream and beaten egg.

Heat the oil in a frying pan and
thoroughly seal the liver, remove from the
pan and chill. Glaze the diced shallots in the
same pan, add the port and after 2–3
minutes add the reduced stock and cranberry sauce. Cook the sauce over a very low
heat until syrupy, strain and cool.

Mince the seasoned meat with the bread
(with the cream and egg) twice through the
finest blade of the mincer. Add the sauce
and beat in until evenly incorporated into
the forcemeat. Dice the ham and liver and
stir into the forcemeat with the pistachios.

Line the terrine with the fat slices, add the
forcemeat a little at a time, pressing down
well to make sure there are no gaps. Cover
with pork fat. Decorate with sprigs of herbs,
cover the terrine and bake, standing in a
water bath, in a cool oven, 150 C, 300 F, gas
2, for about 1 hour and 10 minutes.

Polish white cabbage salad. Shred
200 g/7 oz white cabbage and blanch for a
few moments. Cut a fairly sour apple into
thin sticks. Mix with 40 g/1½ oz chopped
pecans or walnuts and dress with a sharp
sauce made from cream, a pinch of
pepper, salt, a little lemon juice and a dash
of Calvados.

A non-fattening, lean terrine containing no fat (in the forcemeat) but very juicy and highly flavoured.
The interest is provided by the highly seasoned giblets. Excellent with a white cabbage salad.

Duck Terrine

Terrine de canard

1 duck, dressed weight 1.75 kg/3¾ lb, with
liver
1.5 litres/2¾ pints water
150 ml/¼ pint red wine
bouquet garni
10 peppercorns
3 tablespoons brandy
2 tablespoons orange juice
2 tablespoons oil
1 small onion, diced
1 clove garlic, crushed
2–3 teaspoons salt
2 teaspoons seasoning mixture for
country-style pâtés
1 teaspoon thyme
1 teaspoon grated orange rind
300 g/11 oz lean pork, cut in strips
300 g/11 oz green pork fat, cut in strips
1 egg
300 g/11 oz pork fat, cut in thin slices
fresh herbs and orange slice to garnish
1.5-litre/2¾-pint terrine

Bone the duck. Remove the breasts and carefully remove skin and ligaments from the remaining meat. Chop the offcuts and bring to the boil with the water, red wine, bouquet garni and peppercorns, then over a low heat slowly reduce to 150 ml/¼ pint, skimming to remove scum and fat from time to time.

Place the breasts and liver in a narrow container, pour on the brandy and orange juice and marinate for 3 hours. Heat the oil, seal the breasts and liver on all sides and remove from the pan. Glaze the onion and garlic and add the marinade and reduced stock. Over a low heat reduce again to about 250 ml/8 fl oz and strain. Add salt, seasoning mixture, thyme and orange rind to the trimmed duck meat (excluding the breasts), the pork and two-thirds of the pork fat, mince through the fine blade of the mincer and work in the egg and cooled sauce to make a smooth forcemeat. Finely dice the sealed liver and the remaining fat and mix into the forcemeat. Line the terrine with the slices of pork fat, add half the forcemeat. Wrap the duck breasts in fat and place one behind the other. Cover with the remaining forcemeat and finally with the excess fat. Garnish with herbs and a slice of orange. Cook for about 1 hour 20 minutes in a cool oven, 150 C, 300 F, gas 2.

Duck Terrine with Truffled Breast of Duck

Terrine de canard au poitrine de canard truffée

200 g/7 oz trimmed duck
100 g/4 oz lean pork
200 g/7 oz pork fat
pâté salt
grated rind of 1 orange
½ teaspoon each chopped fresh sage and mugwort
2 breasts of duck, total weight about 275 g/10 oz
1 tablespoon oil
100 g/4 oz truffles
3 tablespoons port
4 tablespoons jellifying chicken stock
40 g/1½ oz boiled ham
40 g/1½ oz salted tongue
150 g/5 oz foie gras, marinated in brandy and port
20 g/¾ oz shelled pistachios
about 250 g/9 oz pork fat, cut in thin slices
1.25-litre/2¼-pint terrine

Cut the trimmed duck, pork and pork fat into strips, sprinkle with pâté salt, orange rind, sage and mugwort and chill. Mince the meat twice through the finest blade of the mincer, then mince the fat once only. Work the fat into the meat, push through a fine sieve, then beat over ice until the forcemeat is smooth and silky. Chill after each stage.

Season the breasts of duck with pâté salt, seal in hot oil, remove from the pan and cool thoroughly. With a sharp pointed knife, cut a slit along the centre of the breasts. Cut three-quarters of the truffle, preferably one large one, into 2–3-mm/⅛-in slices, dip in port and carefully insert in the slit in the breasts. Pour the chicken stock over the breasts. Finely dice the ham, tongue, the rest of the truffles, and the foie gras, halve the pistachios and stir into the forcemeat with half the stock.

Line the terrine with slices of fat, add about half the forcemeat, bringing it up the sides of the dish slightly. Cut the ends of the breasts straight so that they fit closely together in the terrine, place in it and sprinkle with the remaining chicken stock. Cover with the remaining forcemeat and smooth the top. Bang the terrine several times on a damp cloth to settle the contents. Fold the excess fat over the filling and press down. Top with a whole slice of fat and cover the terrine. Cook for about 45 minutes in a water bath, regulating the oven so that the water remains at a gentle simmer.

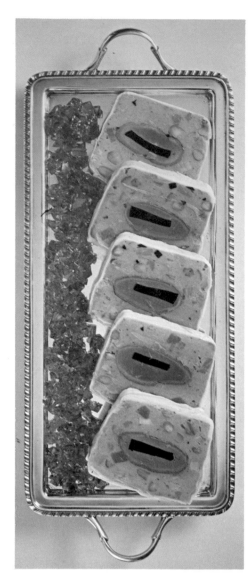

A classic duck terrine, which lends itself to interesting variations. One unusual variation is to replace the truffles inside the breasts with cooked morels soaked in port.

Truffled Turkey Terrine

Terrine de dindon truffée

450 g/1 lb lean breast of turkey
200 g/7 oz lean pork
salt
14 white peppercorns, crushed
generous pinch of ground ginger
generous pinch of cardamom
generous pinch of mace
2 sage leaves
½ bay leaf
65 g/2½ oz crustless white bread, thinly sliced
40 g/1½ oz butter
90 g/3½ oz shallots, diced
4 tablespoons cream sherry
1 egg white
250 g/9 oz turkey liver
2 tablespoons oil
1½ tablespoons Grand Marnier
1 clove garlic
250 ml/8 fl oz jellifying chicken stock
generous pinch of allspice
generous pinch of ground cloves
1 teaspoon grated orange rind
1 teaspoon basil
40 g/1½ oz truffles, diced
150 g/5 oz pork fat, cut in strips
250 ml/8 fl oz single cream
350 g/12 oz pork fat, cut in thin slices
chaudfroid sauce and chicken stock aspic to finish (optional)
1.2–1.5-litre/2–2¾-pint terrine

Cut the turkey and pork into strips, place in a bowl and sprinkle with 1 teaspoon salt, 8 crushed peppercorns, the ginger, cardamom, mace, sage and bay leaf. Arrange the sliced bread over the meat. Heat the butter in a frying pan and glaze half the shallots. Leave to cool slightly and add the sherry and egg white. Pour this mixture over the bread and meat so that it moistens all the bread. Cover with foil and leave to stand in the refrigerator.

Remove any skin and blood vessels from the turkey liver. Heat the oil in a frying pan and seal the liver all over, over a high flame. Add the Grand Marnier. Turn the liver a few times in the pan and then remove. Glaze the rest of the shallots and the crushed garlic in the same pan and add the jellifying chicken stock, allspice, cloves, orange rind, basil, salt and remaining peppercorns. Simmer for about 5 minutes, push through a fine sieve and reduce to a thick liquid. Dice the liver and pour the sauce over the liver, add the truffles, cover with foil and leave to stand in the refrigerator.

Mince the marinated meat with the other ingredients in the bowl twice through the finest blade of the mincer. Then mince the strips of pork fat once only. Over ice stir the fat a little at a time into the meat. Then gradually add the cream and beat until the forcemeat is smooth and silky. Cook a test ball of forcemeat and increase the seasoning if necessary. Stir the diced liver and truffles into the forcemeat with all the sauce. Line the terrine with the slices of fat and add the forcemeat. Cover with a slice of fat, cover the terrine and cook, standing in water, for about 50–55 minutes, regulating the oven so that the water remains at a gentle simmer.

The terrine can be served in the usual way with its covering of fat, or can be covered with a layer of chaudfroid sauce, as illustrated. When cold, turn out the terrine, remove the pork fat and wipe the terrine thoroughly dry with kitchen paper. Line the dish with a layer of chaudfroid sauce made with chicken stock, so that a thin layer adheres to the sides. Return the terrine to the dish and fill any gaps at the side with sauce. Cover the top with a layer of chicken stock aspic.

Pigeon Terrine with Basil

Terrine de pigeon au basilic

4 pigeons
salt
ground white pepper
300 g/11 oz veal bones
½ onion
½ carrot
piece of celeriac
½ teaspoon thyme
½ teaspoon powdered sage
½ teaspoon pink paprika
½ bay leaf
40 g/1½ oz butter
1½ tablespoons brandy
1½ tablespoons Bénédictine
1 shallot, diced
150 ml/¼ pint red Burgundy
20 g/¾ oz dried mushrooms
generous pinch of ground ginger
generous pinch of allspice
generous pinch of mace
200 g/7 oz lean veal (fillet)
100 g/4 oz pork fat
1 tablespoon egg white
1 tablespoon biscuit crumbs
150 g/5 oz single cream
1 tablespoon chopped fresh basil
butter for greasing
50 g/2 oz pork fat, cut in thin slices
600–800-ml/about 1¼-pint terrine

Joint the dressed pigeons, i.e. remove the breasts and meat from the legs, and trim.

Dice the lean meat, you should have about 250 g/9 oz, and place it in a bowl. Sprinkle with salt and pepper, cover with foil and chill.

Make a stock with the carcasses, offcuts, veal bones, vegetables, thyme, sage, paprika and bay leaf, strain and reduce to 150 ml/¼ pint. Heat half the butter in a frying pan and quickly seal the diced meat, stirring continuously. Add the brandy and Bénédictine, stir again and transfer to a bowl. Melt the remaining butter in the pan, glaze the shallot and add the pigeon stock. Add the Burgundy with the dried mushrooms, ginger, allspice and half the mace. Over a very low heat reduce slowly to a thick liquid and strain over the diced pigeon meat. Cover with foil and leave to stand in the refrigerator, preferably overnight.

To make the forcemeat, dice the veal and fat. The small quantities involved are best puréed in a food processor. Over ice first stir in the remaining mace, ½ teaspoon salt and pepper to taste, then the egg white and biscuit crumbs and finally add the cream a little at a time. The forcemeat should be smooth and silky. Stir the diced pigeon meat into the forcemeat with the stock and chopped basil. Grease the terrine with butter and fill with the forcemeat. Cover the top with pork fat, cover the terrine and bake for 35–40 minutes in the oven standing in a water bath. Regulate the oven so that the water remains at a gentle simmer.

Remove the slice of fat from the top of the terrine. It can then be covered with a layer of chicken stock aspic or, as illustrated, with a layer of chaudfroid sauce and decorated with a truffle flower and blanched celery leaves.

Guinea-Fowl Terrine

Terrine de pintadeaux

2 guinea-fowl, weighing 1 kg/2 lb each,
with livers
150 g/5 oz lean pork fillet
3 teaspoons pâté salt (all-purpose
mixture)
50 g/2 oz crustless white bread, thinly
sliced
1 egg
4 tablespoons single cream
2 teaspoons sweet paprika
½ teaspoon allspice
1 bay leaf
450 g/1 lb veal bones
1 onion
1 carrot
1 piece celeriac
1 teaspoon salt
2 sprigs parsley
lovage
8 white peppercorns, crushed
3 tablespoons oil
3 tablespoons Armagnac
50 g/2 oz shallots, diced
1 clove garlic, crushed
250 ml/8 fl oz red Bordeaux
generous pinch of mace
generous pinch of cardamom
grated rind of ½ orange
350 ml/12 fl oz double cream
25 g/1 oz truffles, diced
300 g/11 oz fresh pork fat, cut
in thin slices
Madeira aspic to finish
1.25-litre/2¼-pint terrine

Bone the guinea-fowl, trim the breasts
thoroughly and keep to one side to use
whole. Remove any ligaments from the
other large pieces of meat to give about
300 g/11 oz flesh. Cut the guinea-fowl and
pork fillet into strips and sprinkle with 2
teaspoons pâté salt. Arrange the sliced
bread over the meat. Beat the egg and cream
with the paprika, allspice and ½ bay leaf, and
pour over the bread. Cover with foil and
leave to stand in the refrigerator.

Make a stock from the guinea-fowl
carcasses, skin and offcuts, the veal bones,
vegetables, salt, parsley, lovage, peppercorns, and remaining ½ bay leaf. Strain
and reduce to 500 ml/17 fl oz.

Remove the skin and blood vessels from
the guinea-fowl livers and seal in hot oil
with the lightly salted breasts. Add the
Armagnac and simmer for 1–2 minutes.
Remove the meat from the pan. Add the
shallots and garlic to the juices in the pan,
add 150 ml/¼ pint guinea-fowl stock, simmer for 5 minutes, then add the remaining
stock and the Bordeaux. Add the rest of the

pâté salt, the mace, cardamom and orange
rind and simmer over a low heat to reduce to
a thick liquid. While hot strain over the
breasts and liver and leave to marinate for
at least 2–3 hours.

Cut up the liver and add to the bread and
meat mixture with the sauce. Mince all the
ingredients together twice through the finest
blade of the mincer, chill well and sieve.
Beat the forcemeat vigorously until smooth
and silky. Lightly whip the cream and stir
into the forcemeat a little at a time. Finally
add the diced truffles.

Line the terrine with slices of fat and add
a thin layer of forcemeat. Place the breasts
in the terrine, either one on top of the other
or side by side depending on the shape of the
dish. Cover with forcemeat and press down
well to prevent gaps. Cover with fat, cover
the dish and bake standing in a water bath
for 45–50 minutes. Regulate the oven so
that the water remains at a gentle simmer.

Leave the terrine until completely cold,
then remove the fat from the top and cut
evenly around the sides of the bowl. Wipe
any remaining fat from the top with kitchen
paper and cover the terrine with an even
layer of Madeira aspic.

Guinea-Fowl Terrine with Sweetbreads and Morels

*Terrine de pintade au ris de
veau et morilles*

This is a good example of a terrine with no
fat covering. Instead the dish is liberally
greased with butter. To turn out the terrine,
stand in hot water when cold. If the dish is
lined with roasting film, it will be easier to
turn out.

450 g/1 lb veal bones
1.5 litres/2¾ pints water
bouquet garni (white of 1 leek, small
piece celeriac, ½ small onion, ½ small bay
leaf)
1 teaspoon salt
5 white peppercorns, crushed
300 g/11 oz lean guinea-fowl meat
75 g/3 oz crustless white bread, thinly
sliced
1 egg white, lightly beaten
6 tablespoons single cream
7 g/¼ oz pâté salt
little sage, rosemary, and ground white
pepper
300 ml/½ pint whipped cream
450 g/1 lb sweetbreads
40 g/1½ oz dried morels
1 tablespoon chopped parsley
butter for greasing
1-litre/1¾-pint terrine

Boil the veal bones with the water, bouquet
garni, salt and peppercorns to make a stock
and strain.

Cut the guinea-fowl into strips and place
on a baking sheet. Arrange the sliced bread
over the meat, moisten with the egg white
and cream and sprinkle with the pâté salt,
sage, rosemary and pepper. Cover with foil
and chill. Mince the meat and all the
ingredients in the bowl twice through the
finest blade of the mincer, strain and, over
ice, work in the whipped cream a little at a
time.

Soak the sweetbreads and carefully
remove all skin and blood vessels to give
about 250 g/9 oz flesh. Blanch. Transfer to a
saucepan with half the cooled stock, bring
to the boil, simmer for 10 minutes, then
leave to cool in the stock. Remove the
sweetbreads from the pan and cut into
pieces. Reduce the veal stock to a thick
liquid, dip the sweetbreads in the reduced
stock and chill. Soak the morels, thoroughly
wash away the sand and soak several times
in fresh water until they have completely
swollen up. Boil the morels in the remaining
veal stock for about 25 minutes, then
remove from the pan. Reduce the stock to a
thick liquid and leave the morels to cool in

the stock. Mix the sweetbreads and morels into the forcemeat with the parsley. Grease the terrine with butter, line with heat-resistant film and fill with the forcemeat. Smooth the top and bang the tin several times on a damp cloth. Fold over any excess film, cover the terrine and cook in a water bath for about 40 minutes. Regulate the oven so that the water remains at a gentle simmer.

This terrine is excellent with a grape sauce. Stew skinned grapes in butter, season with lime juice, sugar and a little freshly ground pepper and add a dash of sloe gin.

Fish Pâtés and Terrines

These are the newest and, with a few exceptions, also the lightest of the pâtés and terrines.

Fish or shellfish pâtés or terrines have no long tradition behind them and, with a few exceptions, have in the past been much less popular than those made with pork or game. Their low fat content meant that they did not keep well and, in addition, fish was usually eaten fresh. Fish pâtés and terrines first came into fashion at the turn of the century, made by great French chefs for a gastronomic élite. Nowadays charcutiers offer a wide selection of fish pâtés and terrines, dishes which at one time would never have been included in the stock of a 'pork butcher'.

The reason for the increase in popularity is obviously their slimming aspect, although this is somewhat deceptive, for a good fish pâté includes a lot of calories in the shape of cream and bread or flour panada, which are used as lightening agents. Even so these light, airy creations are less rich than those made with meat. Fish combines excellently with a variety of vegetables and can be served with a wide range of sauces and salads. For these reasons fish pâtés have become popular in the nouvelle cuisine, a branch of cookery which relies heavily upon the freshness and quality of its ingredients.

With fish freshness is of prime importance. With modern methods of transportation this has ceased to be a problem, but you must buy carefully and confine your pâté making to those days when freshly caught fish are available. If you are not sure about the freshness of the fish, it is better to choose a freshwater fish, which fishmongers can keep live in tanks.

Not every fish is equally suitable for use in pâtés and terrines. Of the freshwater fish, pike, with its dense flesh, is especially good, or salmon, and also eel, perch and trout. Whether you choose freshwater or sea fish, the expensive varieties are usually best for a particularly fine dish. Compared with other luxury foodstuffs, truffles for example, even the best fish is not over-expensive. You can make an excellent pâté with inexpensive varieties and combined with vegetables you can use it for a fine, light terrine.

Salmon Pâté

Pâté de saumon

675 g/1½ lb salmon fillet
100 g/4 oz fresh white bread
2 egg whites
475 ml/16 fl oz cream
1 teaspoon butter
50 g/2 oz sliced onion
salt
ground white pepper
generous pinch each of nutmeg and English mustard powder
25 g/1 oz diced truffle
butter for greasing
675 g/1½ lb shortcrust pastry
1 egg yolk and 2 tablespoons cream for coating
white wine aspic to finish
1.75-litre/3-pint terrine

Remove any bones from 350 g/12 oz of the salmon and cut it into strips. Remove the crust from the bread, slice thinly and pour over the egg whites and 100 ml/4 fl oz of the cream. Melt the butter, glaze the onion without allowing it to colour and then leave to cool. Place the salmon, bread and onion on a baking sheet and sprinkle with 1 teaspoon salt, pepper to taste, nutmeg and mustard. Mince twice through the finest blade of the mincer. As with any forcemeat, chill well after each stage. Push through a sieve and gradually work in the rest of the cream.

Remove any bones from the rest of the salmon fillet and season with salt and pepper. Work the truffles into the forcemeat. Grease the dish with butter and line with pastry. Place half the forcemeat in, lay the salmon fillet along the centre and cover with the remaining forcemeat. Fold over any excess pastry and cover the top with a sheet of pastry. Decorate the pâté, make an opening in the lid and insert a funnel. Brush the top of the pâté with the egg yolk and cream mixture.

Bake for 40 minutes in all, 15 minutes in a very hot oven, 240 C, 475 F, gas 9, then lower the temperature to 220 C, 425 F, gas 7 and cook for a further 25 minutes. When cool top up the pie with white wine aspic.

Chef's Fish Terrine

Terrine de poisson du chef

1 teaspoon butter
1 sliced shallot
175 g/6 oz white fish fillet, e.g. sole or turbot
salt
ground white pepper
generous pinch each of nutmeg and English mustard powder
1 egg white, lightly beaten
25 g/1 oz flour panada
175 ml/6 fl oz whipped cream
100 g/4 oz flat mushrooms, cleaned and diced
225 g/8 oz salmon trout fillet, diced
200 g/7 oz turbot fillet, diced
100 g/4 oz lobster claw meat, diced
25 g/1 oz green beans, diced
40 g/1½ oz carrots, diced
16–20 leaves fresh lemon balm
butter for greasing
1-litre/1¾-pint terrine

Melt the butter, glaze the shallot in it without allowing it to colour and leave to cool. Cut the fish fillet into strips and sprinkle with ½ teaspoon salt, pepper to taste, the nutmeg, mustard and shallot. Mince the fish twice through the finest blade of the mincer. Over ice beat in the egg white a little at a time. Sieve the flour panada a little at a time into the forcemeat and work in. Push the forcemeat through a sieve and beat until smooth and silky. Work in the whipped cream a spoonful at a time. Chill after each stage.

Blanch the mushrooms, drain and leave to cool. Season the salmon trout and turbot with salt and pepper and fold, with the lobster, diced vegetables and lemon balm, into the forcemeat. Grease the dish with butter, line with heat-resistant film and fill with the forcemeat. Bang the dish several times on a damp cloth and seal.

Cook for about 45 minutes in a water bath. Regulate the oven so that the water remains at a gentle simmer.

Eel Terrine

Terrine d'anguille

1 teaspoon butter
1 shallot, sliced
65 g/2½ oz fresh white bread
½ egg white, lightly beaten
2 tablespoons single cream
150 g/5 oz pike fillet
salt, ground white pepper, nutmeg and
English mustard powder
150 ml/¼ pint whipped cream
4 tablespoons chopped dill
500 g/18 oz fresh eel, boned and skinned
200 g/7 oz smoked eel fillet
butter for greasing
chopped dill and white wine aspic to
finish
1-litre/1¾-pint terrine

Melt the butter, glaze the shallot in it and
leave to cool. Remove the crust from the
bread, slice thinly and moisten with the egg
white and single cream. Remove any bones
from the pike fillet, cut into strips and place
on a baking sheet with the moistened bread
and shallot. Sprinkle with salt, pepper,
nutmeg and mustard. Mince twice through
the finest blade of the mincer. Push through
a sieve and beat until smooth and silky.
Gradually beat in the whipped cream and
finally add half the dill.

Fillet the skinned fresh eel and carefully
flatten with the back of a kitchen cleaver, i.e.
beat flat without damaging the fish. Cut into
equal pieces to fit the size of the dish, and
sprinkle with salt, pepper, nutmeg, mustard
and the remaining dill. Cut the smoked eel
into strips the same length as the dish.
Grease the dish and line it with heat-
resistant film. Place the fresh eel in the dish,
skin side outermost, leaving no gaps. Cover
with about one-third of the forcemeat,
bringing it up the sides of the dish. Fill the
dish with layers of smoked eel and
forcemeat, finishing with a thin layer of
forcemeat. Bang the dish several times on a
damp cloth, fold the excess film over the top
and seal the dish.

Cook for about 40 minutes in a water
bath, regulating the oven so that the water
remains at a gentle simmer.

When cool turn out the terrine, sprinkle
with chopped dill, coat with several layers of
white wine aspic and sprinkle again with
a little more chopped dill.

Line the dish with eel fillets. Cut the fillets to the
same length and sprinkle with dill. Line the dish
with film and lay the fillets side by side to leave
no gaps. Then fill the dish with the pike
forcemeat and smoked eel fillets.

Fish Pâté in Brioche Pastry

Poisson en brioche

1 teaspoon butter
1 shallot, sliced
200 g/7 oz fish fillet, e.g. sole
salt
ground white pepper
generous pinch each of nutmeg and
English mustard powder
1 egg white, lightly beaten
40 g/1½ oz flour panada
200 ml/7 fl oz whipped cream
1 teaspoon each chopped dill and tarragon
500 g/18 oz flour
25 g/1 oz fresh yeast
1½ tablespoons milk
1 egg
65 g/2½ oz melted butter
350 g/12 oz salmon fillet
1 lightly beaten egg for coating

Melt the butter and glaze the shallot in it
without allowing it to colour. Leave to cool.
Cut the sole into strips and sprinkle with ½
teaspoon salt, pepper to taste, the nutmeg,
mustard and shallot. Mince the fish twice
through the finest blade of the mincer. Over
ice beat the egg white a very little at a time
into the fish. Sieve the panada into the fish a
little at a time and beat in thoroughly. Push
the forcemeat through a fine sieve and beat
until smooth and silky. Beat in the cream a
spoonful at a time. Finally add the herbs.

Sift the flour into a bowl and make a well
in the centre. Stir the yeast into the
lukewarm milk, pour into the well and mix
with a little of the flour. Leave to rise for 15
minutes at room temperature. Stir the egg, ½
teaspoon salt and a pinch of nutmeg into the
melted butter and work into the yeast
mixture and remaining flour in the bowl.
Beat until you have a light dough and leave
to rise for another 15 minutes. Cover with a
damp cloth and leave to stand in the
refrigerator for a further 15 minutes, so that
the pastry will be chilled before coming into
contact with the heat-sensitive filling. Roll
out the pastry to 4 mm/¼ in thick and use a
cutter to cut 2 fish shapes, or cut around a
cardboard pattern.

Cover one piece of pastry with half the
forcemeat, leaving 2 cm/¾ in free around the
edge. Place the salmon fillet in the centre of
the forcemeat, cover with the remaining
forcemeat and smooth the top to seal the
salmon fillet completely. Brush the edges of
the pastry with egg. Lay the second sheet of
pastry carefully over the filling and press the
edges firmly together, making sure to leave
no air gaps between pastry and filling. Cut

the remaining pastry to make a mouth and fins, brush with egg and press onto the fish. Leave to rise at room temperature for 15 minutes, then decorate as required. Cut out the eye, insert a funnel and brush the pastry all over with egg.

Bake in a hot oven, first at 220 C, 425 F, gas 7 for 10 minutes, then at 200 C, 400 F, gas 6 for a further 35–40 minutes or until cooked.

Use scissors to cut scales. This is a simple way of decorating the fish. Leave to rise at room temperature for 15 minutes and then cut with a small pair of scissors to make scales. But be careful not to hold the scissors too straight to avoid cutting right through the pastry. Finally brush with egg following the direction of the scales, so that only the tips of the scales brown during baking.

Rainbow and Salmon Trout Terrine

Terrine de truites arc-en-ciel et truites saumonées

½ tablespoon butter
40 g/1½ oz sliced shallots
90 g/3½ oz fresh white bread
1 egg white, lightly beaten
4 tablespoons single cream
250 g/9 oz salmon trout fillets, skinned and boned (from about 500 g/18 oz salmon trout)
a little salt, ground white pepper and nutmeg
250 ml/8 fl oz whipped cream
2 tablespoons chopped dill
4 trout, each weighing about 300 g/11 oz
butter for greasing
200 g/7 oz smoked trout fillet
1-litre/1¾-pint terrine

Melt the butter, glaze the shallots in it and leave to cool. Remove the crust from the white bread, slice thinly and moisten with the egg white and cream. Cut the salmon trout into strips and arrange on a baking sheet with the moistened bread and shallots. Season with salt, pepper and nutmeg. Mince twice through the finest blade of the mincer. Push through a sieve and beat until smooth. Gradually work in the whipped cream and fold in half the dill.

Before you use the trout they should be left to stand in the refrigerator for at least 12 hours because fillets of fresh-caught trout contract too much when cooked. Fillet the trout and season the fillets. Grease the terrine with butter, line with heat-resistant film and then with the fillets, placing them skin side outermost and leaving no gaps between. Sprinkle with the remaining dill. Cut the smoked trout into pieces, fold into the forcemeat and fill the dish. Bang it several times on a damp cloth. Fold the excess film over the filling and seal the terrine.

Cook for about 40 minutes in a water bath, regulating the oven so that the water remains at a gentle simmer.

Sole Terrine with Lobster Filling

Terrine de sole au homard

15 g/½ oz butter
40 g/1½ oz shallots, diced
150 g/5 oz unpeeled prawns
100 g/4 oz fresh lobster meat
65 g/2½ oz crustless fresh white bread, sliced thinly
1 egg white
4 tablespoons single cream
a little salt, ground white pepper and nutmeg
25 g/1 oz fresh lobster roe
300 ml/½ pint whipped cream
25 g/1 oz diced truffles
50 g/2 oz diced mushrooms
450 g/1 lb sole fillets, skinned
150 g/5 oz cooked lobster meat
butter for greasing
celery leaves, cooked carrot slices and truffle pieces to garnish
fish stock aspic to finish
1-litre/1¾-pint terrine

Heat the butter, glaze the shallots in it and leave to cool. Shell the prawns, cut along the back, remove the gut and place on a baking sheet with the lobster. Cover with the shallots and white bread. Beat the egg white with the cream, season with salt, pepper and nutmeg and pour over the bread. Chill, then mince with the prawns and lobster twice through the finest blade of the mincer. Sieve the lobster roe into the forcemeat and mix in, then sieve the forcemeat. Beat thoroughly and add the whipped cream a little at a time. Fold in the truffles and mushrooms. Chill thoroughly after each stage.

Flatten the sole fillets and season with a little salt. Grease a terrine with butter and line with heat-resistant film. Line the tin with the sole fillets, placing the skin side outermost and leaving no gaps between them. Add some of the lobster forcemeat, bringing it up the sides of the tin. Then add the cooked lobster meat. Cover with the remaining forcemeat and bang the tin several times on a damp cloth. Fold over the excess sole fillets and cover with the film. Seal the tin and cook standing in a water bath for about 40 minutes, regulating the oven so that the water remains at a gentle simmer.

Garnish with blanched celery leaves and flowers made from boiled carrot and truffle. Cover with a fish stock aspic.

Sole Terrine with Goose Liver

Terrine de sole au foie gras

This is an unusual combination which gives a very good flavour. The recipe is a variation of the preceding Sole Terrine with Lobster Filling recipe, with the lobster and prawns in the stuffing replaced by fresh salmon trout, skinned and boned. The cooked lobster is replaced by 150 g/5 oz fresh goose liver, with all skin and nerves removed, kneaded with a little pâté salt and shaped into a roll, the same length as the tin. The roll of liver is placed in the middle of the terrine embedded in the stuffing. When completely cool cover the terrine with fish stock aspic to seal in the flavour.

The cooking time is about 40 minutes in a water bath.

This terrine goes well with a celery salad. Cut the celery into very thin sticks and braise in highly seasoned veal bone stock; the celery should still have a 'bite'. When cool flavour with a little brandy and dress with vinaigrette sauce.

Salmon Trout Terrine with Oyster Paste

Terrine de truites saumonées au parfait d'huîtres

Salmon trout forcemeat
150 g/5 oz salmon trout fillet
25 g/1 oz crustless fresh white bread
1 small egg white
3 tablespoons single cream
25 g/1 oz sliced onion, softened in butter
½ teaspoon salt
ground white pepper and English mustard powder
about 150 ml/¼ pint whipped cream
Oyster forcemeat
40 g/1½ oz oyster flesh
40 g/1½ oz turbot fillet
15 g/½ oz crustless fresh white bread
1 small egg white
2 tablespoons single cream
salt, ground white pepper and cayenne pepper
about 100 ml/4 fl oz whipped cream

butter for greasing
1 teaspoon chopped dill
25 g/1 oz carrot, in julienne strips
25 g/1 oz green Kenya beans
500-ml/17-fl oz terrine

Prepare the two forcemeats separately.
Grease the terrine with butter and line with heat-resistant film. Transfer about three-quarters of the salmon trout forcemeat to a piping bag fitted with a plain nozzle. Pipe into the terrine and smooth up along the sides with a palette knife. Sprinkle with the dill and then fill with layers of oyster forcemeat and boiled carrot fingers and beans, boiled but still firm. Cover with the remaining salmon trout forcemeat. Seal the terrine and bake standing in a water bath for about 25–30 minutes, regulating the oven so that the water remains at a gentle simmer.

Salmon Terrine

Terrine de saumon

Salmon forcemeat
225 g/8 oz salmon fillet
50 g/2 oz crustless fresh white bread
1 egg white
5 tablespoons single cream
25 g/1 oz onion, sliced
½ teaspoon butter
1 teaspoon salt
freshly ground white pepper
little cayenne pepper
about 250 ml/8 fl oz whipped cream

575 g/1¼ lb salmon fillet
little salt and freshly ground white pepper
20 g/¾ oz finely diced truffle
1-litre/1¾-pint terrine

Prepare the salmon forcemeat and chill it.

Spread about half the forcemeat onto a piece of roasting film, covering an area about the same size as the terrine. Cut 375 g/13 oz salmon fillet to exactly the same size and lay it over the forcemeat, skin side uppermost, and season it. Keep a little forcemeat to one side and stir the truffle into the remainder and spread over the salmon. Season the remaining salmon fillet and place along the centre of the forcemeat. Place in the terrine with the film, bang several times and cover with the remaining forcemeat. Fold over the excess film, bang again, seal and cook in a water bath for about 42 minutes, regulating the oven so that the water remains at a gentle simmer.
Garnish the salmon terrine with whirls of cream and caviar and serve on top of finely diced fish stock aspic.

Turbot Terrine with Fresh Basil

Terrine de turbot au basilic frais

Turbot forcemeat
250 g/9 oz turbot fillet
100 g/4 oz fresh white bread
1 egg white
6 tablespoons cream
1 teaspoon butter
2 sliced shallots
1 teaspoon salt
ground white pepper
a pinch each of nutmeg and English mustard powder
250 ml/8 fl oz whipped cream
Turbot and spinach filling
75 g/3 oz spinach
about 10 fresh basil leaves
350 g/12 turbot fillet
salt and ground white pepper
20 g/¾ oz diced truffle
butter for greasing
white chaudfroid sauce to finish
1-litre/1¾-pint terrine

Remove any bones still in the turbot fillet and cut into strips. Remove the crust from the white bread, thinly slice and moisten with the egg white and cream. Melt the butter and glaze the shallots in it without allowing them to colour. Leave to cool. Place the turbot, bread and shallots on a baking sheet and season with salt, pepper, nutmeg and mustard. Mince twice through the finest blade of the mincer. Push the forcemeat through a fine sieve and beat until it becomes silky. Over ice beat in the cream a spoonful at a time.
Quickly blanch the spinach and basil separately, place immediately in iced water and leave until completely cool. Drain the

spinach and place on roasting film. Drain and finely chop the basil leaves. Season the turbot fillet to be used whole with salt and pepper, lay over the spinach and, using the film to help you, wrap the spinach around the fish. Stir the diced truffle and basil into the forcemeat. Grease the terrine with butter and line with roasting film. Add half the forcemeat and in the centre place the turbot fillet wrapped in spinach. Cover with the remaining forcemeat. Bang the tin several times on a damp cloth and seal.

Cook in a water bath for about 35–40 minutes, regulating the oven so that the water remains at a gentle simmer.

When cool turn the terrine out and cover with a white chaudfroid sauce made with fish stock. Decorate to your choice, for example with carrot hearts and pieces of truffle.

Salmon Mould

Tourte de saumon

Pike forcemeat
300 g/11 oz pike fillet
½ teaspoon butter
25 g/1 oz sliced shallots
1 teaspoon salt
freshly milled white pepper
little nutmeg and English mustard powder
1 large egg white
60 g/2½ oz flour panada
350 ml/12 fl oz whipped cream
Salmon forcemeat
150 g/5 oz salmon fillet
½ teaspoon butter
15 g/½ oz sliced onion
½ teaspoon salt
freshly ground white pepper
little nutmeg and English mustard powder
1 medium egg white
25 g/1 oz flour panada
175 ml/6 fl oz whipped cream
Salmon rolls
350 g/12 oz salmon fillet
salt and freshly ground white pepper

butter for greasing
fish stock aspic to finish
1-litre/1¾-pint dome-shaped mould

Prepare the two forcemeats separately.

For the salmon rolls, cut 200 g/7 oz salmon fillet lengthways into sheets 4–5 mm/¼ in thick. Place, touching each other, on heat-resistant film, sprinkle with salt and pepper and spread thinly with about 175 g/6 oz pike forcemeat. Use the film to help you roll the salmon, tie securely in place and poach for about 10 minutes in the oven in well-seasoned fish stock. Leave to cool in the stock and chill.

Grease the mould with butter and line with heat-resistant film. Cut the salmon roll into thin slices and line the mould. Add about half the remaining pike forcemeat, cover with the remaining salmon fillet and cover with the rest of the pike forcemeat. Then cover with salmon forcemeat. Bang the mould several times on a damp cloth, seal and cook in a water bath for about 60–65 minutes, regulating the oven so that the water remains at a gentle simmer.

Turn out the salmon mould, cover with a thin layer of light fish stock aspic and garnish with whirls of cream and pieces of truffle.

Lobster Terrine with Vegetables

Terrine de langouste aux légumes

250 g/9 oz lobster meat
salt
ground white pepper
generous pinch cayenne pepper
1 egg white, lightly beaten
50 g/2 oz flour panada
100 ml/4 fl oz single cream
200 ml/7 fl oz whipped cream
1 lobster tail, weighing about
350–400 g/12–14 oz
lemon juice
50 g/2 oz each celery and carrots, boiled and then diced
50 g/2 oz peas
butter for greasing
white chaudfroid sauce and fish stock aspic to finish
celery leaves and chives to garnish
900-ml/1½-pint terrine

Cut up the lobster and sprinkle with salt, pepper and cayenne pepper. Mince twice through the finest blade of the mincer. Over ice beat in the egg white a little at a time. Then sieve the flour panada a little at a time into the forcemeat and mix in. Push the forcemeat through a sieve and work in first the single cream, then the whipped cream a spoonful at a time.

Place the lobster tail on a small wooden board and tie it so that it lies straight. Boil

An effective decoration – made from very simple ingredients. Arrange blanched celery leaves and chives over a coating of chaudfroid sauce and cover the whole with fish aspic.

for 5 minutes in water with a little salt, pepper and few drops lemon juice and then leave to stand in the water for 15 minutes. Transfer to the wooden board and leave to cool, then remove the shell. Fold the boiled, diced celery and carrot and the peas into the forcemeat. Grease the terrine with butter and line with roasting film. Add half the forcemeat, top with the lobster tail and cover with the remaining forcemeat. Seal the terrine.

Cook for about 40 minutes in a water bath, regulating the oven so that the water remains at a gentle simmer.

When cool cover the terrine with a white chaudfroid sauce made with fish stock and cream and garnish with celery leaves and chives. Cover with fish stock aspic.

Individual Salmon and Rainbow Trout Terrines

Petites terrines de saumon et truites arc-en-ciel

200 g/7 oz salmon fillet, skinned
a little salt, freshly ground white pepper, cayenne pepper and English mustard powder
1 large egg white, lightly beaten
40 g/1½ oz flour panada, sifted
200 ml/7 fl oz whipped cream
1 tablespoon chopped dill
400 g/14 oz trout fillet, skinned
butter for greasing
white chaudfroid sauce to finish
4 cups or small moulds, each 200 ml/7 fl oz capacity

Cut the salmon fillet into strips, season with salt, pepper, cayenne and mustard and chill. Mince twice through the finest blade of the mincer, and, over ice, gradually work in the lightly whisked egg white and flour panada.

A good gift suggestion. Cook the individual terrines in cups and then garnish decoratively. Add a saucer and side plate to make a most attractive gift.

Push the forcemeat through a sieve and beat in the whipped cream a little at a time. Finally stir in the dill. Chill once more.

Sprinkle the trout fillet with salt, and cut to fit the moulds. Grease the moulds well and line with the trout fillets, placing them skin side outermost and leaving no gaps between them. Fill any small gaps with little pieces of fillet. Add the forcemeat and smooth the top. Cook standing in a water bath for 15–18 minutes, regulating the oven so that the water remains at a gentle simmer.

When cool cover the terrines with a white chaudfroid sauce made with fish stock and garnish decoratively, for example with pieces of truffle and slices of carrot.

Snail Pâté

Pâté d'escargots

1 teaspoon butter
40 g/1½ oz sliced shallots
40 g/1½ oz fresh white bread
½ egg white, lightly beaten
1 tablespoon single cream
100 g/4 oz lean veal
a little salt and ground white pepper
100 ml/4 fl oz whipped cream
200 g/7 oz canned snails
1 tablespoon each Pernod and brandy
6 tablespoons jellifying veal stock
2 small cloves garlic, crushed
1 teaspoon each chopped fresh thyme and marjoram
butter for greasing
300 g/11 oz shortcrust pastry
1 egg and 2 tablespoons cream
750 ml/1¼-pint pâté mould

Melt the butter, glaze the shallots in it and leave to cool. Remove the crust from the bread, cut into thin slices and moisten with the egg white and cream. Cut the veal into strips and place on a baking sheet with the moistened bread and half the glazed shallots, and season. Mince twice through the finest blade of the mincer. Push the forcemeat through a fine sieve and beat until smooth and silky. Gradually beat in the whipped cream, chilling well after each stage.

Strain the snails through a sieve and cut each in half, keeping the liquid to one side. Add the Pernod and brandy to the rest of the glazed shallots, dilute with the veal stock and snail liquid. Add salt and pepper, the garlic and half the herbs. Reduce to a thick liquid, strain through a sieve, add the snails and leave to cool. Work into the forcemeat with the remaining thyme and marjoram. Grease the mould and line it with pastry. Fill with the snail forcemeat. Fold over the excess pastry and top with a sheet of pastry. Cut an opening for the steam, decorate the pâté, brush with the egg and cream mixture and insert a funnel.

Bake for about 30 minutes in all, first in a very hot oven, 240 C, 475 F, gas 9, then lower the temperature to moderate, 180 C, 350 F, gas 4 and cook for a further 15 minutes or so, until cooked.

Deliciously wrapped in brioche pastry, and decorated with cut-outs the exact shape of the 'leaves' of a globe artichoke, this must be one of the most beautiful and satisfying of vegetable-based pâtés. It would make an elegant centrepiece to a fine but informal buffet table.

Artichoke Pâté

Pâté d'artichauts

150 g/5 oz pork fat
200 g/7 oz veal, trimmed
200 g/7 oz pork, trimmed
2 tablespoons oil
65 g/2½ oz diced onion
275 ml/9 fl oz fresh cream
2 egg whites
salt
1 teaspoon pâté seasoning (for delicate meats)
1 teaspoon basil
12 bottled or canned artichoke hearts
freshly ground white pepper
a little ground ginger
250 ml/8 fl oz dry white wine
1½ tablespoons good brandy
50 g/2 oz shelled pistachios, coarsely chopped
150 g/5 oz boiled ox tongue, diced
butter for greasing
yeast dough made with 500 g/18 oz flour
1 egg yolk for coating
Madeira or sherry aspic to finish
1.2-litre/2-pint mould or dish

Finely dice and freeze the pork fat. Dice the veal and pork. Heat the oil in a frying pan, glaze the onion and spread over the meat. Beat 4 tablespoons of the cream with the egg whites, 1 teaspoon salt, the pâté seasoning and basil and pour over the meat. Cover with foil and leave to stand for a few hours in the refrigerator.

Thoroughly drain the artichoke hearts (you can of course use fresh artichokes if preferred), place in a narrow container, sprinkle with salt, pepper and ginger and add the wine and brandy. Marinate for 2–3 hours.

Purée the marinated meat with its other ingredients in a food processor. Use the frozen fat to cool the meat, adding a few cubes to each portion you purée. Beat the forcemeat with a wooden spoon until smooth and silky. Then gradually beat in the remaining cream and increase the seasoning if necessary. Finally fold in the coarsely chopped pistachios and diced ox tongue.

Grease the tin with butter (an oval soufflé tin is best). Roll out about two-thirds of the pastry to about 3 mm/⅛ in thick and line the tin. Leave 2 cm/¾ in extra pastry around the edges. Add two-thirds of the forcemeat. Drain the artichokes very well and press them base down into the forcemeat. Cover with the remaining forcemeat. Brush the inside of the pastry rim with egg yolk, roll out the remaining pastry to make a lid, place over the filling and press the edges firmly together. Cut off any excess pastry and reroll the offcuts. Cut into leaves which look like artichoke leaves, brush the top of the pâté with egg yolk and arrange the leaves on top to overlap. Cut an opening in the centre for the steam, insert a funnel and brush the top with egg. Bake in a hot oven, 220 C, 425 F, gas 7 for 55–60 minutes.

When cold top up the pâté with Madeira or sherry aspic.

Vegetable Terrine with Goose Liver

Terrine de légumes au foie gras

400 g/14 oz trimmed chicken breast
25 g/1 oz butter
65 g/2½ oz shallots, diced
50 g/2 oz celeriac, diced
65 g/2½ oz crustless white bread
2 egg whites
400 ml/14 fl oz cream
salt and freshly ground white pepper
grated rind of ½ lemon
generous pinch of allspice
200 g/7 oz fresh artichoke hearts (about 6–10 artichokes)
150 g/5 oz carrots
150 g/5 oz green beans
300 g/11 oz fresh goose liver
150 ml/¼ pint port
65 g/2½ oz truffles
300 g/11 oz pork fat, cut in thin slices
1.5-litre/2¾-pint terrine

Dice the chicken breast and place it in a bowl. Heat the butter and glaze the diced shallots and celeriac. Spread over the chicken. Cut the bread into small pieces and add to the bowl. Beat the egg whites with 4 tablespoons of the cream, 1 teaspoon salt, pepper to taste, the lemon rind and allspice and pour over the bread. Cover with foil and leave to stand overnight.

Wash the artichoke hearts thoroughly, trim the carrots and beans, then blanch one after the other in salted water and transfer to iced water.

Season the goose liver (after removing all blood vessels), cover with the port and leave to marinate, preferably overnight. Then knead a few times in the marinade. On a large piece of foil place the pieces of liver side by side in a row. Cut the truffle into slices (saving offcuts to go in the forcemeat) and place between the pieces of liver. Shape the liver into a compact roll. Chill thoroughly.

Purée the seasoned chicken with the bread, egg white and cream in a food processor. Over ice, beat the forcemeat until light and fluffy and gradually beat in the

A **vegetable terrine** made up of a delicious blend of flavours, but which you can easily vary; for example, replace the vegetables (artichoke hearts, carrots and beans) with various kinds of mushroom: 200 g/7 oz open mushrooms, 150 g/5 oz chanterelles and 150 g/5 oz wild mushrooms. The mushrooms are cut into pieces, braised in butter and sprinkled generously with chopped parsley and a little basil. Cool thoroughly before folding into the forcemeat. This mushroom terrine can be served with a cold chive sauce and a green salad.

remaining cream. Dice the artichoke hearts and truffle offcuts and fold into the forcemeat. Line the terrine with the slices of pork fat and add about one-third of the forcemeat. Intersperse the beans and carrot (cut into fingers). Place the goose liver roll along the centre of the terrine and fill it with the remaining beans, carrots and forcemeat. Cover with fat, seal and cook, standing in a water bath, for 50–55 minutes, regulating the oven so that the water remains at a gentle simmer.

Broccoli Terrine

Terrine de brocoli

Broccoli filling
400 g/14 oz broccoli, cleaned
2 egg whites
1 teaspoon salt
freshly ground white pepper, nutmeg and ground ginger
100 ml/4 fl oz double cream
Celeriac filling
400 g/14 oz celeriac, cleaned
2 egg whites
1 teaspoon salt
freshly milled white pepper
generous pinch of garlic salt
100 ml/4 fl oz double cream

butter for greasing
250 ml/8 fl oz light chaudfroid sauce
150 g/6 oz broccoli florets
light aspic to finish

Simmer the broccoli in salted water for 10–12 minutes. Leave to cool and drain thoroughly. Purée in a food processor. Beat the egg whites a little at a time into the broccoli. Add salt, pepper, nutmeg and ginger and then, over ice, beat in the lightly whipped cream a little at a time.

Quarter the celeriac and cook in salted water until soft. Prepare a celeriac filling as for the broccoli.

Grease the terrine with butter and fill the dish with 2 alternate layers of broccoli and celeriac filling. Seal the terrine and cook for about 45 minutes in a water bath, regulating the oven so that the water remains at a gentle simmer.

When cool cover the top of the terrine with a layer of chaudfroid sauce. Top with steamed broccoli florets and cover with a light aspic.

Mushroom Terrine à la Maison

Terrine de champignons à la maison

25 g/1 oz butter
100 g/4 oz shallots
200 g/7 oz lean veal fillet, diced
50 g/2 oz crustless white bread

1 egg white
250 ml/8 fl oz cream
salt
ground white pepper
generous pinch each of ground ginger,
allspice and mace
800 g/1¾ lb mixed mushrooms (flat, field,
button, chanterelles), cleaned
3 tablespoons oil

½ clove garlic, finely chopped
200 ml/7 fl oz jellifying chicken stock
1 teaspoon dried basil
½ teaspoon dried thyme
½ teaspoon dried sage
½ teaspoon crushed caraway seeds
100 g/4 oz truffles
butter for greasing
1–1.25-litre/1¾–2¼-pint terrine

Heat 15 g/½ oz of the butter, glaze half the sliced shallots in it and spread them over the veal. Cut the bread into small pieces and add to the veal. Beat the egg white into 3 tablespoons of the cream, add ½ teaspoon salt, pepper to taste and the spices and pour over the bread. Cover with foil and leave to stand, preferably overnight.

Cut the larger mushrooms into fairly large pieces and leave small ones whole. Heat the oil in a frying pan and add all the mushrooms at one go. Braise the mushrooms for a few minutes, continually shaking the pan, and transfer to a sieve. Keep the mushroom juice to one side. Melt the remaining butter in the pan, glaze the shallots and garlic, then add the mushroom juice and chicken stock. Add the herbs, caraway and salt and, over a moderate heat, reduce slowly to a thick liquid. Strain over the mushrooms through a conical sieve and stir in well. Cover and leave to stand overnight.

Purée the veal, bread, egg white and cream mixture a little at a time in a food processor. Chill thoroughly, then beat until light and fluffy. Gradually beat in the rest of the cream until the forcemeat is smooth and silky. Fold the marinated mushroom mixture and chopped truffles into the forcemeat. Grease the terrine with butter, fill with the forcemeat. Shake the terrine to make sure there are no air gaps in the stuffing. Seal the terrine and cook standing in a water bath, for 45–50 minutes, regulating the oven so that the water remains at a gentle simmer.

A vegetable terrine, very light in consistency, which when cooked is just firm enough to cut. It can also be served hot (without the chaudfroid sauce of course) with chervil or chive sauce.

The strongly flavoured chaudfroid sauce with which the terrine is covered provides a contrast in flavour with the delicately flavoured stuffing. The decoration is made with cut-outs of hard-boiled egg and braised carrot. The stems are thin sprigs of chives.

Individual Mushroom Terrines

*Petites terrines de champignons
de couche*

A veal forcemeat, as given in the recipe for Mushroom Terrine à la Maison goes particularly well with the flavour of mushrooms. Or you can use the same quantity of a fine chicken forcemeat.

25 g/1 oz butter
50 g/2 oz finely diced shallots
350 g/12 oz cleaned mushrooms, diced
about ½ teaspoon salt
freshly ground white pepper
generous pinch of mace
generous pinch of ground ginger
2 tablespoons chopped fresh herbs
(parsley, basil, rosemary, hyssop)
500 g/18 oz veal or chicken forcemeat
butter for greasing
chaudfroid sauce to finish
6–8 150-ml/¼-pint moulds

Heat the butter in a frying pan, glaze the shallots in it and add the mushrooms. Sauté the mushrooms for 3–4 minutes, shaking the pan continuously. Sprinkle with salt, pepper, spices and herbs, stir in and leave to cool. Mix into the forcemeat. Grease the moulds lightly with butter, fill with forcemeat and smooth the tops. Cook, standing in a water bath, for 18–20 minutes, regulating the oven so that the water remains at a gentle simmer.

Tip the cold terrines out onto a cooling tray and cover with white or green chaudfroid sauce.

Chanterelle Terrine

Terrine de chanterelles

1 tablespoon butter
2 sliced shallots
50 g/2 oz fresh white bread
½ egg white, lightly beaten
2 tablespoons single cream
150 g/5 oz lean veal
little salt and ground white pepper
150 ml/¼ pint whipped cream
675 g/1½ lb fresh, whole, small chanterelles
3 tablespoons oil
40 g/1½ oz diced shallots
150 ml/¼ pint jellifying veal stock
1 teaspoon chopped caraway seeds
2 tablespoons chopped parsley
butter for greasing
port aspic to finish
1-litre/1¾-pint terrine

Melt 2 teaspoons of the butter, glaze the sliced shallots in it and leave to cool. Remove the crusts from the bread, thinly slice and moisten with the egg white and single cream. Cut the veal into strips and place on a baking sheet with the moistened bread and shallots. Season. Mince twice through the finest blade of the mincer. Push the forcemeat through a fine sieve and beat until smooth and silky. Gradually add the whipped cream and beat in thoroughly. Chill thoroughly after each stage.

Braise the chanterelles in the oil and drain through a sieve. Glaze the diced shallots in the remaining butter and add the veal stock. Add the caraway and reduce to a thick liquid. Push through a sieve, add the drained chanterelles and simmer for a few moments. Leave to cool and then stir into the forcemeat with the parsley. Grease the terrine with butter, add the forcemeat and bang several times on a damp cloth. Seal and cook, standing in a water bath, for about 35 minutes, regulating the oven so that the water remains at a gentle simmer.

When cool cover the terrine with an aspic made with port and finely chopped parsley.

Mushroom Terrine

Terrine de cèpes

1 tablespoon butter
40 g/1½ oz sliced shallots
40 g/1½ oz fresh white bread
½ egg white
1 tablespoon single cream
100 g/4 oz lean veal
little salt and ground white pepper
100 ml/4 fl oz whipped cream
500 g/18 oz fresh flat mushrooms, sliced
2 tablespoons oil
40 g/1½ oz diced shallots
150 ml/¼ pint jellifying veal stock
1 teaspoon crushed caraway seeds
1 clove garlic, crushed
1 tablespoon finely chopped chives
butter for greasing
Madeira aspic to finish
750-ml/1¼-pint terrine

Melt 1 teaspoon of the butter, glaze the sliced shallots and leave to cool. Remove the crusts from the bread, thinly slice and moisten with the lightly whisked egg white and cream. Cut the veal into strips and place on a baking sheet with the moistened bread and shallots. Season. Cover with foil and chill. Mince twice through the finest blade of the mincer. Push through a sieve and beat until smooth and silky. Gradually beat in the whipped cream.

Braise the mushrooms in the oil and drain through a sieve. Glaze the diced shallots in the remaining butter, add the jellifying veal stock, caraway and garlic and reduce to a thick liquid. Push through a sieve. Add the mushrooms and simmer for a few minutes. Leave to cool then fold into the forcemeat with the chives. Grease the terrine with butter, fill with the mushroom forcemeat, bang the dish several times on a damp cloth and seal.

Cook for about 30 minutes in a water bath, regulating the oven so that the water remains at a gentle simmer.

When cold cover with Madeira aspic.

Aspic Jellies and Sauces

Many galantines, terrines or other types of cold pies and pâtés would be unthinkable without aspic jellies or chaudfroid sauces. These may be the crystal-clear cubes of aspic, served on the plate with a slice of pâté, or a fine ivory-coloured coating of chaudfroid sauce on a duck galantine. Both increase one's enjoyment of the dish tremendously. They improve the taste by bringing out the flavour of the pâté and visually they set off a real culinary masterpiece. They also have a very practical effect. Aspic jellies and sauce coverings help the pâté to keep, preserving its freshness for longer.

Whether your aim is decoration or freshness, you should pay a lot of attention to your aspics and sauces. They can complement a pâté or terrine admirably and their flavour will bring out the flavour of the pâté, even though they may be rather time-consuming to make. The bones or carcass of the meat used for the pâté are boiled to make a stock, thus you will use a game stock with a venison pie or chicken stock for a poultry galantine. This stock forms the basis of an aspic or chaudfroid sauce. There should be no foreign taste to disturb the unity of the pâté when you top up a pâté with aspic or cover a galantine.

Crystal-clear perfection

How long aspic jellies have been used in pâté-making cannot be ascertained with any certainty. But aspic as a separate dish was not unknown to the Romans. Their aspic must have been rather cloudy for the method of clarifying aspic with egg white was not discovered until La Varenne came along. At least it was he who published the method for the first time in his book *Le Cuisinier françois*. An auspicious time for the art of cookery, at least for cold cookery. Of course a cloudy aspic of unclarified stock tastes just as good, but just imagine an aspic pâté with its brightly coloured vegetables without its clear, shining coating. Not to mention the various aspic jellies which are served in cubes with pâté and melt tenderly on the tongue.

In the old days considerable time was spent making a form of gelatine from gristle and bones, particularly calf's feet which had to be boiled for hours on end. One highly flavoured type of aspic, known in Bavaria as *Knöcherlsulz*, is still made in this way. But now this long process can be eliminated for good quality gelatine is available in powder or leaf form and has a completely neutral taste. It is a natural product, consisting of soluble proteins, animal proteins, treated in a certain way. But other modern aids, in the shape of instant stock, create more problems. High quality instant gelatines or aspic powders are very practical and can be used quite well with a simple, strongly-flavoured country-style terrine. But if you are making a gourmet game terrine with truffles, with its expensive ingredients and time-consuming preparation, you cannot risk spoiling the excellence of the finished result by using anything other than a home-made aspic, preferably made with the original stock.

Chaudfroid – first warm, then cold

Louis Alexandre Berthier, Marshall of France, was eating a chicken fricassée, but was called away from the table for a considerable length of time. He returned to find the fricassée cold and congealed. Louis was angry, but continued his meal – and discovered how good the food tasted cold. From that time on this dish, which the Marshall named *Chaudfroid* was never missing from his banquet table. In English the term means something like 'First hot, then cold'.

The term has come to be used in cooking for any dish which is prepared hot but intended to be eaten cold. With terrines and galantines we have the chaudfroid sauces, covering sauces. They are not transparent like aspics and completely mask the beautiful terrine or galantine, so a variety of colours have been introduced for these coatings. A chaudfroid sauce made from a light stock and white sauce, or as made more frequently today from light stock and reduced cream, is white in colour. This gives a particularly beautiful cream-coloured sauce. It can, however, be made shades of green, pink or red by adding spinach, lobster roe or tomato paste. To make a brown chaudfroid sauce, for *demiglaces*, jellifying brown stock is used. This concentrated stock also guarantees a concentrated flavour. So a good chaudfroid sauce should not be considered merely as a decorative element which helps preserve freshness, to be left on the side of the plate like a sausage skin. Its flavour should not compete with that of the terrine, but its flavour and seasoning should complement that of the terrine. They should be related in taste. If you make a stock specially for the sauce this is no problem; a fish stock for a fish terrine, a poultry stock for a duck terrine, for example. But as with aspic jellies, these sauces can also be flavoured with wine or spirits to give highly satisfactory results.

Chaudfroid sauces and aspics are often used together to decorate a terrine or galantine, as, for example, with a terrine covered in white chaudfroid sauce: this forms an excellent base for a decoration of herbs, truffles or vegetables. The decoration is then covered with a layer of crystal-clear aspic. This prevents it being disturbed when the terrine is sliced.

Aspic jelly, a shimmering complement to pâtés and terrines

The basis is always a meat or fish stock, preferably made with the carcass or bones from the meat used in the pâté. Veal bones can be added to the stock for they contain a lot of natural gelatine and have a relatively neutral taste. This stock is then clarified before gelatine is added to make an aspic.

It is always clarified with egg white. Egg white is used in the following recipe and in the alternative method on the next page. Beef is also used in this recipe as a clarifying agent which gives a good flavour without detracting from the natural flavour of the stock.

Aspic jelly, clarified with egg white

This is a basic recipe which provides for a wide range of variations. You can alter the seasoning to suit the recipe. Or the wine. Use Madeira and port, for example, for meat or poultry stock, a sparkling, dry Riesling, Chablis or Champagne for a fine fish stock. But only good quality ingredients should be used. This is particularly true of the gelatine. Only good quality aspic powder or, better still, gelatine leaves, will be neutral in flavour.

100 ml/4 fl oz egg white,
beaten until soft peaks form
1 small onion, finely diced
50 g/2 oz leeks, finely diced
50 g/2 oz celeriac, finely diced
few stems of parsley
1 teaspoon salt
8 white peppercorns
1 piece bay leaf
1 litre/1¾ pints light stock (meat, poultry
or fish, depending on the type of pâté)
100 ml/4 fl oz white wine or 3 tablespoons
wine vinegar
40 g/1½ oz aspic powder or leaf gelatine

1 **Tip the finely diced vegetables** and seasonings into the egg white. The egg white should have been whipped until soft peaks formed. Work the ingredients in with your hand or a wooden spoon.

2 **Tip the egg white and vegetable mixture into the stock.** The stock should be cold at this stage. Place over the highest possible heat and whisk continuously with a hand whisk.

3 **Beat firmly with the whisk,** scraping round the base of the pan to prevent the egg white solidifying. It is easier if you use a spatula for this. Bring to the boil and reduce the heat.

4 **The egg white separates** and floats on the surface. Add the white wine or vinegar. Simmer the stock very gently for 40–50 minutes without allowing it to boil. This gives the stock time to absorb all the flavour from the vegetables and seasonings.

5 **The stock is clarified.** You can see from looking at the pan that the egg white has absorbed even the tiniest impurities, leaving the stock completely clear. Line a conical sieve with filter paper and strain the hot stock. An alternative method is shown on the next page. A sheet of muslin is attached to the legs of an upturned kitchen stool.

6 **Add the gelatine to the clarified stock.** If the stock has become too cool during filtering, reheat to allow the gelatine (powder or leaves), previously soaked in cold water, to be completely dissolved.

7 **A crystal-clear aspic of exactly the right consistency,** firm enough to cut but still tender. 40 g/1½ oz aspic powder or gelatine to 1 litre/1¾ pints stock is about the average requirement. This quantity will keep the aspic firm at normal room temperature.

Aspic jelly clarified with egg white and beef

A method of preparation which gives a particularly fine result, a real 'gourmet' aspic. The addition of beef to the vegetables, together with egg white, guarantees superb quality. Shin of beef is particularly good as it contains a lot of gelatine. But it must be absolutely free from fat. It is minced through the largest blade of the mincer (known as the 'pea blade') or finely chopped. It is important to beat the meat vigorously into the egg white and vegetables. Use a strong wooden spoon, or better still, work it in thoroughly by hand.

150 g/5 oz clarifying meat (fat-free shin of beef)
25 g/1 oz carrots
25 g/1 oz leeks
25 g/1 oz celeriac
25 g/1 oz onion
1 or 2 small tomatoes
1 clove garlic
10 white peppercorns
1 teaspoon salt
1 small piece bay leaf
3 large egg whites
1 litre/1¾ pints light stock
(game, poultry or meat)
100 ml/4 fl oz white wine
40 g/1½ oz aspic powder or leaf gelatine

The stock must be completely free from fat. If you allow the stock to become cold the fat will solidify and is easy to remove. Remove any tiny particles from the surface with a piece of filter paper.

1 **Prepare the ingredients.** Mince the beef through the largest blade of the mincer. Dice the vegetables and peel the tomatoes. Crush the garlic and lightly crush the peppercorns.

2 **Mix the meat and vegetables together** and add the salt, bay leaf and egg white. Work the ingredients thoroughly together with a wooden spoon or, better still, by hand, so that all the ingredients bind as well as possible.

3 **Add the stock.** Place the pan on the hob and add the stock, from which you have carefully removed all fat. Turn up the heat to the highest setting and boil for a few minutes.

4 **Stir the stock.** A spatula is best because its flat shape makes for extra contact with the base of the pan and prevents the egg white sticking before it separates. Then simmer gently for 40 minutes without allowing to boil.

5 **The egg white has separated** and has taken even the smallest impurities out of the stock. Add the white wine and stir in very gently.

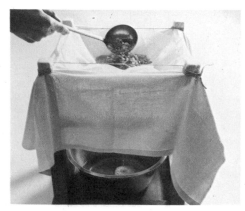

6 **Filter the stock through a sheet of muslin.** Attach the muslin to the feet of a stool. Line with filter paper, place a bowl under the cloth and pour all the contents of the pan into the cloth. Warm the stock and dissolve the softened gelatine in the stock.

Coating with warm aspic, which the experts call 'glazing'. A thin layer of suitably flavoured aspic jelly makes slices of pie or pâté look as if they have been prepared individually, giving an appetising shine and bringing out the colour. Brush on the aspic gently with a wide brush. To glaze delicate decorations sprinkle on the aspic with the brush.

Flavouring with wine

By far the most popular are the Southern wines, Madeira and port. But sherry, tokai and full-bodied white wines, such as a Muscatel, give a good flavour.

200 ml/7 fl oz Madeira to 1 litre/1¾ pints stock is about the average requirement, but you should always adjust the amount of wine to suit the type of pâté you are making. It is advisable to test by adding to a small amount first, for many wines can make the stock cloudy.

Aspic temperature
Regardless of whether you are topping up a pâté or covering a galantine, the correct temperature of the aspic jelly is always important. It should be used just before it reaches setting point, while still slightly fluid, but allowing it to set as quickly as possible once used. There is a very simple and reliable method of checking the temperature.

Pour a little liquid aspic into a bowl and keep the remaining warm aspic to hand. Place the bowl in iced water and stir gently with a small slotted spoon or pastry brush. Vigorous stirring would cause bubbles which would not look very good when poured over a terrine. Before setting you can see clearly that the aspic becomes slightly thick. Remove from the water at once and use. This ideal temperature period is quite short. If the aspic in the bowl begins to set, add a little of the warm aspic and if necessary cool again until you have the right consistency.

Chaudfroid, a coating sauce for cold dishes

Unlike a transparent aspic, this aspic-based sauce is an opaque covering for terrines and galantines. It encloses the pâté, protecting it from the air and keeping it fresh, as well as setting off its flavour. Last but by no means least it is an effective form of decoration, whose colour can be easily varied.

Light chaudfroid sauce was once, and still is today to a lesser extent, made with a velouté, i.e. a white *roux*-based sauce. This can taste very good but tends to be rather sticky. A more modern method is to bind with gelatine, which, when used with reduced cream, is light and airy. A good compromise is to use an aspic sauce with a little starch for binding and some gelatine.

This combines the advantages of aspic with the smoothness of a flour-based sauce.

The basic recipe for the light sauce allows an almost limitless colour variation. Spinach, tomato paste, saffron or lobster roe can be used for colouring, but the flavour of the colouring agent must harmonise with the flavour of the dish. As with aspic jelly, you should use a suitably flavoured stock.

For the brown chaudfroid no cream is used. Here the fat-free, brown, jellifying chicken, game or veal essence provides the colour. The sauce is thus semi-transparent, but particularly strong in flavour. It is generally used with strongly flavoured terrines or to contrast with a particularly delicately flavoured pâté. Thus a brown chaudfroid sauce can give the final touch to a delicately flavoured veal terrine.

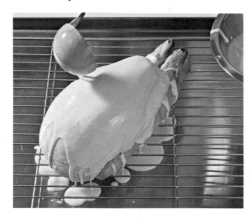

Stir the chaudfroid sauce until cold. Place half the sauce in a bowl in iced water and stir very gently with a ladle to avoid bubbles. If it becomes too firm it can be diluted with a little of the warm sauce – but only as long as it has no lumps. In that case the sauce must be dissolved again.

The exact temperature is important. The sauce should begin to set (begin to thicken), then it is ready to use. With galantines in particular make sure that the sauce is completely fat-free, otherwise the sauce will separate. Wipe the skin of the galantine dry with kitchen paper.

Natural Chaudfroid

1.5 litres/2¾ pints fat-free light veal, poultry or fish stock
600 ml/1 pint single cream
40 g/1½ oz cornflour
1 tablespoon dry white wine
20 g/¾ oz gelatine
salt and freshly ground white pepper

These ingredients give 1 litre/1¾ pints chaudfroid sauce

Reduce the stock over a moderate heat to about 600 ml/1 pint. Reduce the cream by half (300 ml/½ pint) and pass through a fine sieve into the stock. Dissolve the cornflour in the white wine and use to bind the sauce. Bring to the boil once, remove from the heat and stir in the softened gelatine until dissolved. Put the sauce once more through a fine sieve or, better still, through muslin and season. The seasoning will depend on the type of galantine or terrine to be covered.

The basic flavour of the chaudfroid can be varied by using a reduced mushroom, asparagus or other suitable stock.

Chaudfroid sauce and aspic jelly combined for a duck terrine. The dish is lined with hot chaudfroid. The terrine is returned to the dish after removing the fat layer and covered with chaudfroid. This coating is decorated and covered with a light aspic jelly.

 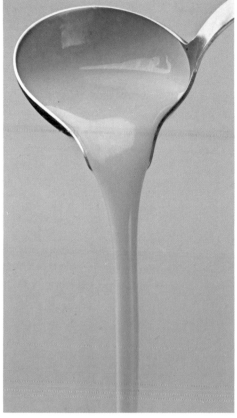 

### Red Chaudfroid	### Green Chaudfroid	### Brown Chaudfroid

1.5 litres/2¾ pints fat-free light veal, poultry or fish stock
25 g/1 oz cornflour
1 tablespoon water
½ teaspoon sweet paprika
1 tablespoon light stock
150 g/5 oz tomato paste
600 ml/1 pint single cream
20 g/¾ oz gelatine
salt, sugar, white pepper and cayenne pepper

These ingredients make 1 litre/1¾ pints sauce

Reduce the stock over a moderate heat to about 750 ml/1¼ pints. Dissolve the cornflour in the water and use to bind the stock. Stir the paprika into the 1 tablespoon light stock and stir thoroughly into the sauce with the tomato paste. Boil through once. Reduce the cream to 300 ml/½ pint and pass into the stock through a hair sieve. Bring back to the boil, remove from the heat and stir in the softened gelatine until dissolved. Sieve again and season.

300 g/11 oz fresh spinach
1.5 litres/2¾ pints fat-free light veal, poultry or fish stock
600 ml/1 pint single cream
40 g/1½ oz cornflour
1 tablespoon water
20 g/¾ oz gelatine
salt and white pepper

These ingredients make 1 litre/1¾ pints sauce

Mince the spinach leaves, squeeze in a cloth and catch the juice in a bowl. Heat the juice slowly in a saucepan, stirring continuously. Any bits of leaf which rise to the surface should be removed with a small fine sieve. Then strain through a hair sieve. Reduce the stock over a moderate heat to about 750 ml/1¼ pints. Reduce the cream by half and strain into the stock. Dissolve the cornflour in the water and bind the sauce. Bring to the boil once, remove from the heat and stir in the softened gelatine until dissolved. Stir in the spinach juice, sieve the sauce again and season.

1.5 litres/2¾ pints fat-free, highly jellifying veal, game or poultry stock
15 g/½ oz cornflour
3 tablespoons sherry or Madeira
20 g/¾ oz gelatine
salt and white pepper

These ingredients make 1 litre/1¾ pints sauce

Reduce the stock over a moderate heat to 1 litre/1¾ pints, skimming continuously and pass through a hair sieve. Dissolve the cornflour in the sherry or Madeira and bind the stock. Bring to the boil once, remove from the heat and stir in the softened gelatine until dissolved. Sieve again and season.

The brown chaudfroid contains no cream and remains semi-transparent.

Liver Pâtés and Terrines

Liver pâtés are a culinary delicacy, but goose liver pâté or goose liver terrine, blasphemously called pâté, is the jewel of these delicacies. As the following chapter deals with liver pâtés in general, with special attention obviously given to goose liver pâtés, we must first look at the history of liver pâté in general. First of all we discover that at all periods of history man has been in the habit of fattening animals which were intended for eating purposes. This was equally true of poultry, pigs or other domestic animals. This was not so much intended to produce better meat, as to produce bigger, tenderer, juicier liver. A favourite animal, and possibly the first domestic animal, was the goose, which was domesticated in ancient times. 'The birds of Arabia, anointed with myrrh, flying over Egypt like clouds'. Migratory birds in fact. Geese were cooked on glowing embers, and it was not long before they were beginning to be fattened. Sculptured reliefs like the one in the illustration offer a striking example of this. Geese were portrayed on frescoes, and also on grave paintings, usually in scenes where they were being force-fed.

Our illustration shows a reproduction from the grave paintings of a high Egyptian official called Ti, who is remembered as Pharoah's only friend. It is from a period 2,500 years before Christ and clearly shows that force-feeding of geese was by no means a French invention and could certainly not have been discovered by the French several centuries later.

The ancient Romans later perfected the art of feeding pigs on huge quantities of figs to increase the size of the livers which were eaten roasted, but also used to make pâtés. When man finally discovered that cranes, pheasants, storks and peacocks were also quite good to eat, they were also force-fed. They were kept in so-called *ornithos*. They were fed principally on noodles, barley bread and masticated wheat bread, but geese were specially fed on figs. As early as Cato's time (234–149 BC) his *De agri cultura* contains advice on force-feeding geese. The drive for increased sensual satisfaction has been present in every age.

Then, in the second half of the eighteenth century, pâté de foie gras was discovered in a most spectacular way. It is thought to have been discovered in 1762 (but many historians give other dates) by Jean-Pierre Clause, cook to the governor of Alsace, Marshall de Contades. Anyone who knows anything of the customs of the time will not be surprised that the cook dedicated the dish to his master, calling it initially Pâté à la Contades. It is an established fact that this was a pâté encased in pastry, without truffles. Thus it was rather similar to goose liver pâté cooked in brioche or shortcrust pastry, which is one of the noblest dishes known to us. For this pâté, whose popularity naturally spread at lightning speed, tradition demanded that you use the livers of geese fattened in Alsace. One of the most select delights of the art of cooking had been born.

One may regret it or not, but for the normal consumer, or to put it better, for the gourmet with a small budget, a goose liver will not be beyond his means, but is nevertheless a considerable investment.

But liver pâtés don't necessarily have to be goose liver pâtés: you can make excellent pâtés with the liver of other birds. A fattened duck's liver is second in taste only to goose liver, but due to increased demand they have become almost as expensive. But turkey or chicken liver, mixed with a good quantity of pork or poultry, makes excellent forcemeat. And livers of this kind, in direct contrast with fattened livers, are not exactly offal products but are extremely inexpensive. They can never replace the fattened liver for they have not received the same special treatment and their naturally much stronger flavour makes then unsuitable for pure liver forcemeat, but as a flavouring ingredient in a forcemeat, well-seasoned and maybe marinated, they produce their full aroma.

Amidst the prestige attributed to foie gras, the best of the pâtés, those made with pig's or calf's liver have gone almost unnoticed. These are the most popular types of pâté and they include wonderful, melting forcemeats, delicately seasoned and marinated, with truffles or other fine ingredients. A calf's liver pâté made with high quality, fresh ingredients can impress even the most spoiled gourmet. Even Danish liver pâté, strongly flavoured and solid, is not to be overlooked, to say nothing of the Belgians who know a lot about liver pâtés.

Goose liver, home-made or bought?

This is a question you never need ask, not in this book at least. Inevitably, bought products can never have the same flavour as something freshly made, and this is especially true of a gourmet dish such as goose liver. Anyone who has made a terrine with a good liver and has tasted the uncooked liver after it has marinated for 24 hours, must have asked themselves why on earth it has to be cooked, for they taste excellent even uncooked. But a goose liver terrine is merely poached very gently in the oven and remains a delicacy of the first rank. But the problem is that the consumer seldom has the chance to compare. For the average man goose liver means bought goose liver, either semi or fully preserved in earthenware dishes or tins which line the shelves of our delicatessens. Unlike France, goose liver terrines are seldom sold here in the piece for slicing. So a good tip, if you want goose liver, is to make sure you buy it fresh or, better still, make it yourself.

It is certainly not difficult to make goose liver pâté. The method of preparation presents no problems at all. But where in this country can you find a market stall, as you can in France, which simply sells goose livers, as ours sell vegetables? And even if you could find somewhere to buy it, who

Even for French housewives goose livers, like these in Périgueux market, are not cheap. So you must check very carefully for quality and look for a liver of the right colour and the required consistency.

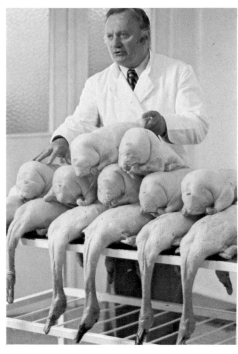

Best quality geese are a must for Monsieur Grimand, but they are not difficult to come by with the quantities available in Gascony. He makes huge quantities of goose liver terrines. One of his best products is his pâté de foie gras *en brioche*.

Bought or freshly made goose liver pâté? For beginners it is not easy to tell the difference, for both home-made and bought blocks of liver pâté can be the same shape. It is only when you taste it that you can tell the difference. One sure way to success for the gourmet: buy a fresh goose liver and make your own pâté.

would be capable of judging its quality? This needs a lot of experience which here only top chefs possess (and they also know how to get hold of fresh goose liver). There are several different opinions concerning goose liver. There are experts who will not buy extremely large, light-coloured liver – the less fat the liver contains the lighter it is in colour. They prefer a yellow to amber colour. But you can't go on colour alone for you never know what the goose may have been fed on. And the colour of the food affects the colour of the liver. Other signs which experienced pâté chefs look for are: the liver should give slightly under thumb pressure and the depression remain visible. The two sides should also separate easily, they should be firm and should not spring back together like rubber. Fattened geese weigh 6–8 kilos/13–18 lb with livers weighing 700–1000 g/$1\frac{1}{2}$–$2\frac{1}{4}$ lb.

In Gascony and Périgord it is mainly grey Gascony geese which are used for goose liver. In Alsace they use white geese, and also in Poland and Hungary. It is only in Gascony that goose liver pâté makers are self-sufficient and use their own products. Périgord and Alsace import a lot of liver from the Eastern bloc and Israel. It is interesting to note that long ago Marx Rumpolt was using liver from Bohemia. In his cookery book of 1587 he writes, 'I had a goose liver, fattened by Bohemian Jews, which weighed just over three pounds. This can also be made into a purée.'

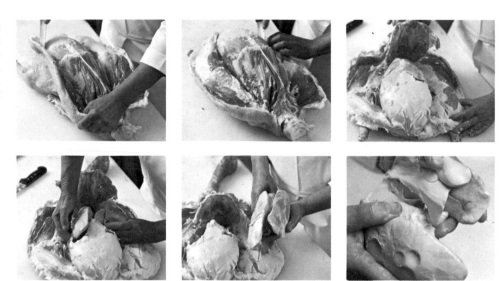

To remove a goose liver requires great care in cutting open the goose. Cut from the neck along the breast and cut the breast meat off the rib cage. Lift off the carcass to leave the liver exposed, embedded in fat. Lift out carefully. It separates very easily from the fat and can then be tested for quality. Thumb pressure should leave a lasting depression and the two sections of the liver should be firm and pull apart easily without springing back together like rubber.

Confit, when the goose is merely a by-product

Confit, a speciality of south-west France, is often served in this area where geese are reared for their livers. Confit is a traditional dish found throughout France. It can also be made with turkey or duck, but is best when made with goose as this is particularly rich in fat which is an essential part of *Confit d'oie*. So as to use all the goose, as well as the liver, goose liver manufacturers also make confit.

Joints of goose simmer in a generous amount of goose fat over a low heat until cooked and juicy.

Confit d'oie

Joint the goose. Add 25 g/1 oz salt per 1 kg/2 lb meat. Cover and leave to stand for 24 hours in a cold room or in the refrigerator. Rub the pieces of goose. Warm a generous quantity of goose fat to lukewarm, but not completely melted. Add the pieces of goose so that they are covered by fat. Simmer over a low heat. Add 1 unpeeled clove garlic and 5 cloves and 5 peppercorns for each 1 kg/2 lb goose fat. Cook for up to 3 hours, stirring frequently. Prick the meat with a trussing needle. If it is soft and gives off clear juice, lift out of the fat with a slotted spoon. Remove bones if preferred. Line an earthenware pot with fat, fill with the joints of goose and cover with goose fat. Leave to stand in a cool place for 2 days. Top up with hot goose fat. Leave to set. Then add a layer of lard. Cover with greaseproof paper and press down. Seal with greaseproof paper. Serve cold or rewarmed.

Home-made confit. French housewives always store it in earthenware pots. Shops sell it in glass bottles.

Goose liver terrine

Terrine de foie gras

It is interesting to note that foie gras, as it is called in the French-speaking countries, means fattened goose liver. (Fattened duck's liver is called foie gras de canard.) And it has been traditional to fatten geese for at least 150 years in France. Even before farmers in Gascony and Périgord began doing it, fattening of geese was an organised industry in Strasburg. Later they began fattening ducks too to produce fattened duck's liver. At one time this was on

A foie gras specialist par excellence! M. Jean Legrand is a master chef in the classic mould. For him, the quality of the goose liver he meticulously chooses to make his masterpiece is of paramount importance. Crucial too is the temperature of the water bath in which he cooks the terrine – it must not exceed 80 C, 176 F.

account of their lower price. But today they cost almost as much as goose livers, although experts claim they are of inferior quality. And they are certainly right in that goose liver has the better flavour.

One is quite justified in describing pâté de foie gras as the most luxurious of all pâtés, providing that the ingredients are of top quality. This is what basically guarantees the ideal ratio of protein to fat in the liver, a ratio which can only be achieved by force-feeding, no matter how unpleasant this may be for the goose. It is surprising how easy it is to make such an expensive, luxury pâté. The series of photographs below illustrate the traditional method. Here the terrine is cooked in the oven standing in a water bath. But many of these methods have now disappeared. Not only in industry, but famous chefs too cook goose liver pâté by the quick method, wrapped in foil. Or they are cooked in steamers which work like pressure cookers. There is disagreement about the resulting flavour, but we believe that traditional methods give better results.

No matter how much one likes exact recipes, no precise quantities can be given for terrine de foie gras, the reason being that quantities depend on the weight of the goose liver and it is not possible to buy these by the gramme or ounce. A liver of about 800 g/1¾ lb – a medium-sized liver – is just right for a terrine holding 1 litre/1¾ pints. In the following recipe there are no seasonings or alcohol – except for the pepper, salt, port and dash of brandy used in the marinade. You are free to decide what additional seasoning you prefer. For every 500 g/18 oz liver you can add ½ teaspoon of the seasoning mixture for delicately flavoured meat (page 22). Or add a little allspice. You can also add extra flavour to the marinade

with Armagnac. But the alcohol content should not be too high or it can give the liver a strong flavour.

> 1 fattened goose liver,
> weighing about 800 g/1¾ lb
> 1 teaspoon salt
> freshly ground white pepper
> 250 ml/8 fl oz vintage port
> dash of brandy
> port aspic to finish
> 1-litre/1¾-pint terrine

This terrine can also include truffles. For this about 100 g/4 oz boiled black truffles are placed in a row in the centre of the terrine, so that they come in the centre of each slice when it is cut.

Cooking time is 35–40 minutes in a water bath, with water at 80 C, 176 F. As with any terrine, you will have to check the water temperature for – despite the claims made by manufacturers – oven temperatures often vary.

Alternatively you can use duck liver for this recipe and for any recipe which uses goose liver.

1 **Break up the goose liver.** Break each section into several pieces and where necessary carefully remove any skin or blood vessels. Work carefully, avoiding damaging the liver more than necessary.

2 **Knead the carefully trimmed liver until soft.** Opinions on whether or not you should knead the liver differ considerably. Many people only knead the firm ends where the liver comes to a point. But our chef kneads the whole liver until soft.

3 **Season the liver with salt and pepper.** If you want to add additional seasonings you are free to do so. But a good goose liver has so much natural flavour that salt and freshly ground pepper are sufficient.

4 **Marinate the liver.** Transfer the liver to a bowl and add the port. A dash of brandy will add extra flavour. Old Armagnac is used for this in Gascony.

5 **Knead in the marinade.** Work the liver gently with your fingers to prevent breaking it up more than necessary. Cover with foil and leave in a cool place to marinate for 24 hours.

6 **Fill the terrine.** Arrange the pieces in the dish one at a time. Press down lightly to ensure that there are as few air gaps as possible between them. This will give a homogenous terrine when cooked.

7 **Flatten the top,** i.e. even out the surface with your hands to get rid of any gaps. You can gently press down the liver again with your hands.

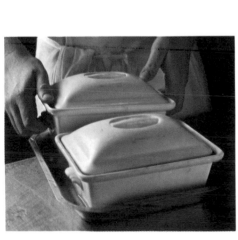

8 **Cover with the lid** and place in a water bath in the preheated oven. The water temperature should be exactly 80 C, 176 F (about 140 C, 275 F, gas 1, oven temperature). Check with a thermometer where possible.

9 **Leave the cooked liver terrine to stand for at least a day** before turning out. If any fat has come out of the terrine during cooking it can be removed when you turn it out. Then return the pâté de foie gras to the dish and cover with a thin layer of port aspic. This is primarily a protective layer which prevents the terrine drying out, but it also adds to the flavour, providing of course the flavour of the aspic goes with the flavour of the terrine.

Goose Liver in Brioche Pastry

Foie gras en brioche

Illustrated on page 100

1 goose liver, weighing about
800 g/1¾ lb
7 g/¼ oz pâté salt (made with the mixture
for delicately flavoured meats)
½ teaspoon ground white pepper
250 ml/8 fl oz vintage port
1½ tablespoons Armagnac
port aspic to finish
2–2.5-litre/3½–4½-pint tin or mould

Brioche pastry
450 g/1 lb flour
25 g/1 oz fresh yeast
scant 150 ml/¼ pint milk
150 g/5 oz butter
2 eggs
1 teaspoon salt
½ teaspoon sugar
egg yolk for glazing

Carefully remove all skin and arteries from the goose liver. Season the liver and any pieces which have come away when cleaning the liver with the pâté salt and pepper. Place in a bowl and add the port and Armagnac.

Cover with foil and leave to marinate in the refrigerator for 24 hours. The liver is shaped to give it a good solid shape in the brioche. The best way to do this is to use a loaf tin slightly smaller (to allow for the thickness of the pastry) than the tin you use to cook the brioche. Remove the liver from the marinade and place in a sieve. Boil the marinade, reduce to about 2–3 tablespoons and leave to cool. Press half the liver into the tin, add the reduced marinade and then the remaining liver. Turn out of the tin when ready to place in the brioche.

Sieve the flour into a bowl. Stir the yeast into the lukewarm milk until it dissolves. Melt the butter, leave to cool and stir in the eggs, salt and sugar. Add the dissolved yeast and butter mixture to the flour and work in to give a smooth, dry dough. If it is too firm add a little more milk. Leave the dough to rise for 30 minutes at room temperature. Roll out to a sheet about 60 × 40 cm/24 × 16 in. Place in the loaf tin so that it overlaps the tin evenly all round. Add the pre-shaped goose liver, brush the pastry edges with egg yolk, fold the dough over the filling and press firmly down to enclose the filling completely. Cut a cross into the top with a sharp knife. Make two openings and insert two funnels. With yeast dough you should not use foil or greaseproof paper, for yeast

dough expands during baking and could easily squash funnels of this type: two small round metal cutters are ideal. Leave the pâté to rise for a further 20–30 minutes at room temperature (on no account should it be allowed to become warmer than room temperature). It should almost double in volume. Then brush the top with egg yolk and bake for 45–55 minutes in an oven preheated to 200 C, 400 F, gas 6. When completely cool (leave to cool overnight if possible) top up the brioche with port aspic.

Chicken Liver Terrine

Terrine de foies de volaille

This recipe is suitable not only for chicken liver, but also for turkey liver or unfattened duck or goose liver. The terrine is equally good in a pasta shell. It can include various pieces of meat, e.g. chicken breasts sealed in oil, or can be varied by adding diced truffles, pistachios, mushrooms or calf's liver marinated in Armagnac.

250 g/8 oz chicken livers
150 g/5 oz pig's liver
350 g/12 oz piece lean pork
350 g/12 oz piece pork fat
grated rind of ½ orange
2 teaspoons sweet paprika
½ teaspoon bottled green peppercorns,
crushed
generous pinch of ginger and allspice
1 teaspoon basil
½ teaspoon thyme
½ teaspoon rosemary
1 bay leaf
1½ tablespoons Armagnac
40 g/1½ oz crustless fresh white bread
50 g/2 oz shallots, diced
1 clove garlic, crushed
4 tablespoons single cream
1 egg white
2 teaspoons salt
400 g/14 oz pork fat, cut in thin slices
1.2-litre/2-pint terrine

Remove any skin and blood vessels from the livers. This should leave about 300 g/11 oz liver. Cut the liver, pork and pork fat (without any rind) into strips. Arrange in layers in a shallow dish, sprinkle on the orange rind, paprika, peppercorns, ginger, allspice, herbs and Armagnac. Thinly slice the white bread and arrange over the meat. Sprinkle the shallots and garlic over the bread. Beat the egg white and cream together and pour over the ingredients in the bowl. Cover with foil and leave to stand in the refrigerator for at least 3–4 hours, but preferably overnight.

Chicken liver forcemeat, a blending of simple ingredients flavoured with Armagnac. If you do have them to hand, other, more exotic poultry livers can be used equally successfully instead. In that case you might also consider letting your imagination have freer rein with the other ingredients – truffles, pistachios, wild mushrooms for example.

Mince all these ingredients (liver, meat, fat, seasonings, bread and liquid) twice through the finest blade of the mincer, or purée a little at a time in a food processor. Over ice, beat with a wooden spoon until smooth and silky and work in the salt. Line the terrine with slices of fat, fill with the forcemeat and cover with more fat. Decorate the top with herbs. Cover the terrine and bake in the oven standing in a water bath, regulating the oven so that the water remains at a gentle simmer.

The terrine will have a more unusual flavour if baked without the water bath. With this method it will lose more of its fat but this has the advantage of acting as a seal when cool, keeping the terrine very moist. In this case, bake for 45–50 minutes in a moderately hot oven, 200 C, 400 F, gas 6.

Individual Liver Pâtés in Brioche Pastry

Petits pâtés de foie en brioche

No one can explain why it should be so, but liver pâtés are particularly delicious baked in brioche dough. It is not only goose liver which goes well with this slightly sour dough, any kind of liver goes with it equally well.

You can make these individual pâtés using the pastry for Goose Liver in Brioche Pastry (recipe opposite) and the filling for the Chicken Liver Terrine. You will need 8–12 small brioche tins, round or oval. Line the tins with pastry rolled to 3–4 mm/¼ in thick and fill with the forcemeat. Brush the edges of the pastry with egg yolk, add a pastry lid of the same thickness, and press the edges carefully together to seal. Cut off any excess pastry. Cut small openings in the top for the steam to escape. Decorate the pâtés and brush with egg yolk. Insert the funnels and leave the pâtés to rise at room temperature. Bake in a hot oven, 220 C, 425 F, gas 7 for 20–25 minutes. After baking leave the brioches until completely cool and top up with port aspic.

Truffled Liver Pâté

Pâté de foie truffé

350 g/12 oz calf's liver
2 tablespoons oil
2 teaspoons sweet paprika
100 g/4 oz pig's liver
300 g/11 oz piece lean pork
50 g/2 oz shallots, sliced
20 g/¾ oz butter
100 ml/4 fl oz vintage port
1½ tablespoons Armagnac
25 g/1 oz crustless fresh white bread
1 egg white
1½ teaspoons salt
½ clove garlic, crushed
½ teaspoon dried green peppercorns
½ teaspoon basil
1 teaspoon pâté seasoning (for delicately
flavoured meat)
250 g/9 oz pork fat
100 g/4 oz boiled ham
1 kg/2 lb shortcrust pastry
40 g/1½ oz black truffles
1 egg for coating
1.5–1.8-litre/2¾–3-pint pâté mould

Dice the trimmed calf's liver. Heat the oil in a frying pan and quickly seal the liver, shaking the pan continuously. Sprinkle with the paprika and keep one third to one side to use whole. Cut the carefully trimmed pig's liver and pork into strips and transfer to a bowl with two-thirds of the fried liver. Glaze the shallots in the hot butter, add the port and Armagnac and slowly reduce to about half the quantity. Cut the bread into very thin slices and arrange over the meat and liver mixture. Add the egg white and sprinkle with the salt, garlic, peppercorns, basil and pâté seasoning. Finally pour on the cooled shallot and port mixture and leave to stand.

Cut the pork fat into strips and mince with the seasoned meat and liver mixture twice through the finest blade of the mincer. Over ice, beat the forcemeat until smooth and light. Fold the diced fried liver and diced ham into the forcemeat. Line the mould with pastry and add half the forcemeat. Place the pieces of truffle in a row along the centre and cover with the remaining forcemeat. Cover with a pastry lid and decorate with overlapping pastry leaves. Cut an opening in the centre, insert a funnel and glaze the top with egg.

Bake for about 55 minutes; first for 15 minutes at 220 C, 425 F, gas 7, then at 190 C, 375 F, gas 5 until cooked.

Calf's Liver Terrine

Terrine de foie de veau

This is a particularly fine and moist liver terrine. The ingredients and method of preparation are the same as the recipe for Truffled Liver Pâté, with the pig's liver replaced by pork. The truffles are not used whole, but chopped and folded into the forcemeat. The diced ham is omitted. Line a 1.5-litre/2¾-pint terrine with 350 g/12 oz sliced pork fat or grease the terrine with butter. Cook standing in a water bath, for 50–55 minutes, regulating the oven so that the water remains at a gentle simmer.

This terrine goes very well with a fine orange sauce. To make this reduce freshly squeezed, strained orange juice with sugar and fine strips of orange rind. When it has reduced to a thick liquid leave to cool and season with a little cayenne pepper, Cointreau and vintage brandy.

Black Truffles and Goose Liver

'When you say truffle you are referring to something great', according to Jean-Anthelme de Brillat-Savarin, writer and authority on the pleasures of the table (1755–1826). In his book *La Physiologie du Goût* (*The Philosopher in the Kitchen*) he described the truffle as 'the black diamond' of cooking and did not overlook a warning on its erotic effect on both sexes. This effect was confirmed by George Sand (1804–1876) when she wrote 'the truffle is the black magic apple of love'. This famous campaigner for women's right to free love ought to have known what she was talking about. But we know nothing about the amount of truffles she actually ate. Many famous writers have mentioned truffles, among them Alexandre Dumas (1824–

1895). The creator of the 'Lady of the Camelias' called the truffle 'the holy of holies'. Truffle is a word which centuries of gourmets have been unable to utter without heaping praises upon it. There is no doubt that the mere mention of the word sets gourmets reeling. Gourmets of centuries gone by and of the first decades of the present century were able to eat their fill of truffles, for then they were inexpensive and widely available. Things have changed a great deal in the last few years. Today you need a full purse or a cheque book when you go to buy truffles. For in the shops 1 kg/2 lb can cost up to £300. It has always been expensive to have a refined palate! This is equally true of the incomparably tender and flavoursome fattened goose liver. This now costs between £35 and £45 per kg/2 lb. Both these are exclusive ingredients for exquisite dishes, but the most exquisite of all are the black Périgord truffles. This is their botanical name rather than a description of their place of origin, referring to winter truffles. They can just as easily come from Provence or Spain. Truffles have become an essential feature of haute cuisine, and so has the foie gras from which the most delicious terrines are made. Doubt it or not, it is nevertheless a fact that only force-fed geese produce large livers. The animals

are reared for the first 5–6 months on free-range methods, like Bresse chickens, so that natural feeding can give flavour to the meat and liver. Then they are force-fed for 21 days. For this a maximum of 20 geese are kept in a small, dark enclosure. Four times a day each goose is force-fed 500 g/18 oz maize, usually with an electric feeder. A spindle in the feeder chops the feed and delivers it to the feed-pipe. If the goose were left to its own devices it would eat 500 g/18 oz of feed per day at most. To make the maize more digestible and easier to dispense it is poached with a little salt and fat. Farmers from Gascony, Alsace and Périgord, who specialise in rearing geese, maintain that the geese – which are usually quick to become angry – undergo this torture as quietly as mice. But then geese can't talk.

Whether one agrees or disagrees with these methods, foie gras is indeed a delicacy and when prepared properly and combined with truffles has a flavour impossible to equal. Of course the one can be eaten without the other, for example, natural goose liver terrine, which consists entirely of marinated, seasoned liver and has a pure liver flavour. Or truffles, poached for 5 minutes in port, Madeira or champagne, and eaten with nothing more than bread, salt and butter. But a foie gras pâté with truffles is for many gourmets a dish which must have been invented in heaven. Usually a dish of this kind takes pride of place in top restaurants, being the high point of the menu, coming at the start of the meal and setting the tone for what is to follow. For a terrine is always an hors d'oeuvre: whether plain or truffled they caress the palate in an indescribable way, and have brought sighs of pleasure to the lips of many. The skill of a professional chef in the restaurant kitchen is required to produce this enjoyment. It takes an expert in his field who has his own recipes at his fingertips, and years of experience in handling basic

problems. They are symbiotic, found mainly with oak trees. A network of fungus threads, the mycel, spreads 10–30 cm/4–12 in below the ground. Where there are truffles no grass will grow. Farmers in Perigord say 'the earth burns'. In fact the presence of truffles beneath an oak destroys any other vegetation. This is a reliable sign that truffles can be found here, but one still cannot predict with any accuracy where they grow. Man's sense of smell is not keen enough for him to be able to detect them, so pigs and dogs are used to smell out the truffles. There is also a small fly which lays its eggs where truffles are to be found, and this can often point the way.

In Périgord Madame rears grey geese with 'golden livers'. Continually increasing demand sends the price of this delicacy ever higher.

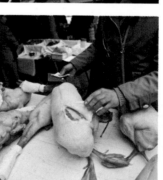

'Diamond trading' in the street. Every Wednesday – from November to March – ordinary people can buy truffles in Perigueux market. Although truffles are not exactly cheap even here, not to mention the price of goose liver, it is quite common for people to make their own foie gras. And no one buys the liver in the goose like a pig in a poke. The seller will willingly cut a window at the right point on the bird.

ingredients to make a perfect terrine. Their handling of the expensive ingredients must be faultless.

Like all foods truffles also have their own history. Long ago Marcus Gavius Apicius, the much-quoted author of the oldest existing Roman cookery book, appreciated the value of truffles. Natural, undamaged and, above all, dry truffles were layered in jars with sawdust, sealed with gypsum and then stored in a cool place. In the first volume of his four-volume work he also describes a sauce to accompany truffles. We are not surprised to read that it is made with honey, oil, pepper, lovage and coriander. But the fact that it also contained fish brine, a favourite sauce of the time, might make us shudder slightly. To bring out the full flavour of the truffle he recommended braising in a mixture of oil, wine, honey, mint, rue and pepper.

In the course of the centuries other truffle recipes were developed; today, perhaps surprisingly, more so than ever before. Despite their high price great chefs in France, and gradually in other countries too, are beginning to use this supreme delicacy more generously. Its price seems to present no problem. But, from the botanical viewpoint, truffles still present

Pigs are still the best truffle hunters. They have only one disadvantage: they like eating truffles too. The truffle farmer has to act quickly and divert the pig with a little sweet corn if he is to harvest his valuable fungus untouched by the pig. Dogs are less self-centred. They enjoy hunting for their masters and gladly give up their prey, but they have to be given the scent of the special truffle smell. There is also a type of fly which is a reliable guide to the whereabouts of the black diamonds. When the sun is low in the sky the truffle hunter walks slowly over the bare ground: anywhere he sees the fly taking to the air, he can be sure to find truffles.

Danish Liver Terrine

Leverpostej

This simple country-style terrine is a kind of culinary common property shared by all Danes. There is scarcely anybody who does not like it, scarcely a housewife who doesn't know how to make it. It is usually made with pig's liver but for special occasions this is mixed with calf's liver.

In Denmark Leverpostej is usually found as part of a cold buffet, providing all the ingredients for guests to make up their own *Smørrebrøds*. But in this country Danish liver pâté can be served as an hors d'oeuvre for a simple menu or as a supper dish.

Delicious: cranberries to go with it and bring out the flavour. A creamy béchamel sauce is used as the panada (technical term for the lightening agent).

575 g/1¼ lb pig's liver
350 g/12 oz pork fat
1 onion
2 eggs
2 anchovy fillets
salt
½ teaspoon dried green peppercorns
½ teaspoon allspice
¼ teaspoon ground cloves
¼ teaspoon ground ginger
25 g/1 oz butter
2 tablespoons flour
200 ml/7 fl oz fresh cream
150 ml/¼ pint meat stock
400 g/14 oz pork fat, cut in thin slices

1 **Trim the liver thoroughly,** i.e. remove blood vessels and skin. The sharper the knife the less liver you will lose. Coarsely dice the liver and pork fat. Peel and chop the onion.

2 **Liver and bacon** are minced twice through the mincer. Mince the onion with the last of the meat. Cover the bowl and leave in a cool place (but not in the refrigerator) until ready to continue with the mixture. Meanwhile prepare the other ingredients and make and cool the béchamel sauce.

3 **Beat the eggs, puréed anchovy fillets, ½–1** teaspoon salt, the peppercorns and spices in a basin until thoroughly mixed. Heat the butter for the béchamel sauce and cook the flour in the butter. Beat in the cream and stock. Boil through for a minute, and add 1 teaspoon salt.

4 **Leave the béchamel sauce (panada) to cool.** Then beat in the egg mixture until smooth. Finally add the liver, fat and onion mixture. Beat carefully and thoroughly until smooth and elastic.

5 **Line the base and sides of a 1.5-litre/2¾-pint mould** with slices of fat, so that they overlap the sides generously. Add the terrine mixture in an even layer, using a pastry scraper. Smooth the top of the terrine.

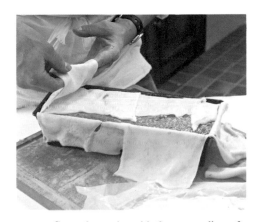

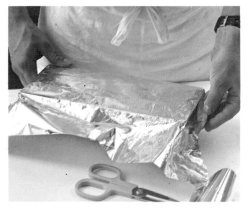

Although not authentically Danish the following variation on liver pâté is very tasty. The ingredients for the above recipe remain unchanged. In addition 250 g/9 oz calf's liver is carefully skinned and cut into small cubes, about 5 mm/¼ in square. Marinate the liver in a bowl with 1 tablespoon orange juice and 4 tablespoons vintage port. Season with a little freshly ground pepper and allspice. Marinate for 2–3 hours, add salt and then fold into the prepared liver mixture.

6 **Cover the terrine with the excess slices of fat.** Fold over a long side first, then a short side, then other long side and finally the remaining short side. The terrine should be completely covered by fat, to prevent it drying out during cooking.

7 **Cover the mould with foil,** securing the edges firmly. Bake in a water bath in an oven preheated to 180 C, 350 F, gas 4 for 90 minutes on the middle shelf. Remove from the oven. Remove the foil and leave to cool, then cover again and store in a cool place.

Galantines

GAME AND POULTRY LUXURIES

This is the most 'galant' of the pâtés, for without doubt the term galantine is of French origin from the word *'galant'*, meaning elegant or gentlemanly. It is an accepted fact that galantines were already being eaten in the days of the knights. It is also a fact that pâtés in pastry, made to resemble the animal in question as nearly as possible, formed the high point at banquets throughout the civilised world. With pheasant pâtés, for example, the bird was recreated with great exactitude: feathers were cut out of thin sheets of pastry, shaped and attached to the body one at a time. For magnificent swan pies a wire framework had to be made to hold these enormous confections together. These were real works of art, using a lot of pastry and little filling, certain to win the approval of the guests. Another favourite method was to stick the plucked feathers back into the cooked pastry to give the natural effect expected by the guests. This method does not sound particularly appetising, but it did allow the recreated bird to appear in all its glory to form a magnificent centrepiece for the grandest banquets.

But whenever too much emphasis is placed upon the appearance of the food, whether in pâté making or in cooking in general, it usually follows that the flavour suffers. Architectural cooking has only one aim – appearance – and those who cared more about flavour had to seek another means of expression. And they found it by sticking to the fundamental principles of pâté making, as presented by Habs and Kasner in their *Appetit-lexika* published in 1894. 'The more beautiful the drapery of the clothes, the more beautiful must be what they contain.' In other words, the pâté should be appetising in appearance, and the filling of the highest quality. This is an aim which can be achieved with carefully prepared galantines. In French dictionaries they were prosaically described as 'meat aspics', which was technically incorrect and in no way typical of the usually flowery language of French cuisine. Galantines are more, much more than this. At their finest they are a quite exceptional culinary delicacy.

On the one hand there are the classic examples, where the filling is served in the boned meat or just in its skin: in the case of chickens, for example, or pheasant, duck or separate joints such as shoulder of lamb, breast of veal or even pig's trotters – the Italian speciality known as *Zampone*. Boning can be a time-consuming job, for you have to keep the shape of the animal or the joint. This can be achieved, for example, by leaving the feet and wings intact. Making the stuffing and filling the animal is then the easiest part of the process. Prepared in this way the animal can retain its original shape even after cooking.

But modern tastes have had an effect on the techniques used by professional chefs. For some time now this kind of time-consuming galantine has been replaced by a more modern variation, by a rolled pâté. These usually come undecorated like a simple sausage. Neither is rolled pâté a particularly inspiring description of them, but luckily their appearance is in direct contrast to their wonderful flavour. Pâté rolls can be made with boned poultry, fish fillets or even seaweed (see our recipe for Galantine of Scallops). In every case galantines are poached in a suitable stock, but can be baked in the oven or smoked at a later stage. Nouvelle cuisine – for example – has become famous primarily through such creations as fish galantine.

Whether we are speaking of a true galantine or a pâté roll, their fillings are always excellent. For festive occasions master chefs will, even today, make a chicken or pheasant galantine, for example, in its original shape or even stuff a wild boar's head in the traditional way. This is entirely for the sake of appearance.

Any garnish used should take into account that one is dealing with a real luxury pâté. Thus any ingredients from simple carrots and leeks on the one hand to expensive truffles on the other can be used here. And classic French cuisine has created true works of art without sacrificing anything of the flavour.

There are also the ballotines, little sisters to the galantines. These take the form of stuffed chicken joints, for example legs or breasts, whose shape should remain recognisable after stuffing. They can be made in exactly the same way as galantines.

Duck pâté roll, the galantine rationalised. Free from elaborate decoration and reduced to its essential elements, its appearance bears little relationship to the classic galantine of cooking history. The basic criterion of cooking a stuffing in boned meat has, however, been followed and, correctly prepared, the galantine is one of the most luxurious members of the pâté family.

Boning poultry or duck for a galantine

As with many other pâtés and terrines, a galantine is a delicious filling in an edible case. In this instance the case is not made of pastry but from the flesh and skin of the animal in question – in this case a duck. And there is one other important difference: galantines are not baked, but poached in stock, that is, cooked in liquid. The original galantine took the form of a stuffed animal, retaining its original shape as closely as possible and boned only in so far as this would facilitate carving. Typical examples of this method are stuffed chicken with feet and wings, or Italian *Zampone*, stuffed pig's trotters. The main drawback with galantines of this kind is that when carving a chicken, for example, the first few slices take all the breast, leaving only the filling.

The galantine rationalised The fact that cooks are not only artists but can also think scientifically is demonstrated by the invention of the rolled galantine. Here the meat, poultry, breast of lamb or game is completely boned, covered with the stuffing, possibly topped with other ingredients, before being rolled. This galantine, which has now become a pâté roll, is cooked in foil or wrapped in a cloth. Meat and filling is thus distributed more or less evenly in every slice.

1 **Trim the bird.** Place the plucked, dressed, washed and singed duck breast side up on a board. Using a sharp knife or poultry scissors chop off both wings at the elbow joint.

For a galantine only the best is good enough

Domestic poultry, at least the smaller varieties such as duck, chicken, guinea-fowl and pigeon, are, together with game birds, the perfect basis for a galantine. But even with these you should look for the best possible quality. Best quality poultry will be more tender and, in addition, boned poultry provides the perfect casing for a galantine.

It should go without saying that fresh meat must be used, never frozen. But the poultry industry has created a situation where for the consumer, chicken and deep-freezing seem made for one another.

This is not true in France where 80 per cent of poultry is bought fresh. In other countries, however, buying fresh birds may cause some problems, for they are not available in every shop and

they may often be expensive, sometimes much more expensive. Recently the increasing demand for quality has caused more fresh birds to become available in the shops, and naturally reared chickens or ducks are available on the market at moderate prices. Large stores with good food departments may offer them at very good prices as loss leaders. But there is a kind of quality guarantee with poultry, for which you will have to dig rather deeper into your pocket. Even here quality has its price. With ducks the best are the fleshy migratory ducks from the Loire Valley (known as Barbary ducks in France), which contain almost no fat and at 1.5 to 2 kg/$3\frac{1}{4}$–$4\frac{1}{2}$ lb are the ideal weight for galantines. With fresh chickens or hens France also offers quality controlled poultry in the form of Breton chickens (gourmets swear by them) or Bresse chickens. There certain rules of poultry raising have become legal requirements such as, for example, the ruling of 10 square metres of ground per bird. Only those farmers who adhere strictly to the regulations are entitled to label their chickens 'Poulet de Bresse', and the consumer can, through the labelling, trace the chicken back to the original farmer. This is made possible by a ring bearing the production number which is attached to the leg of every chicken.

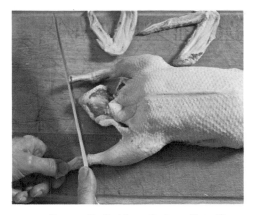

2 **Remove the feet from the legs.** Cut off both lower legs at the knee joint. It is necessary to remove the tips of the wings and legs at this stage to facilitate further boning.

3 **Cut the duck open.** Turn the duck over onto the breast. Working from the neck (previously removed) to the tail (parson's nose) cut the skin along both sides of the back bone.

4 **Loosen the wings at the shoulder.** Locate the joint with your fingers and cut through the fulcrum with a sharp knife, holding the wing bone in your left hand and turning it slightly in the joint.

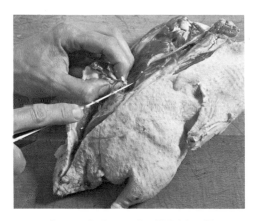

5 **Loosen the legs at the thigh joint.** Treat the legs as you did the wings. Again locate the joint with your fingers and loosen the legs from the thigh joint.

6 **Loosen the carcass.** Hold the duck firmly in the left hand. With a sharp knife cut along the rib cage to remove the meat. Cut with the blade of the knife towards the carcass, not the meat.

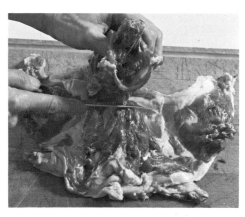

7 **Remove the breast bone.** Here special care is needed for the breastbone joins directly onto the skin. The skin must not be damaged during this stage so hold the breast bone up well away from the skin while you cut.

8 **Cut around the wing bone.** Cut through the ligaments around the knuckle of the bone. Scrape the meat off the bone with a small knife. Pull the bone through holding the meat firmly in place.

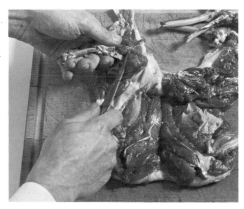

9 **Remove the ligaments.** Deal with the leg bones in the same way as the wings. Remove the wing and leg ligaments, using pliers where necessary.

10 **Even out the duck meat.** Cut off the parson's nose. Cut off the strips of skin at the base of the breasts which have no meat on them, so that all the skin is now covered with meat.

1 **Stuff the duck.** Spread evenly with about half the forcemeat. Cut the ends of the sealed breasts to straighten them, place along the centre of the forcemeat, brush with the cooled essence and cover with the remaining forcemeat.

2 **Seal the duck.** First fold the tail end over the forcemeat and then fold over the neck end. Press down to seal all the joins, so no filling can escape. Shape to an even, thick roll.

3 **Wrap the galantine.** For this use either heat-resistant film, e.g. roasting film, or a tea-towel. Place the galantine on the film and wrap firmly but not too tightly.

Duck Galantine

Galantine de canard

2 ducks, each weighing 1.5–2 kg/3¼–4¼ lb
3 bouquets garni
100 g/4 oz lean pork
250 g/9 oz pork fat
pâté salt
grated rind of 1 orange
3 fresh sage leaves, chopped
40 g/1½ oz diced boiled ham
40 g/1½ oz chopped pistachios
20 g/¾ oz truffles, diced
2 tablespoons oil
chaudfroid sauce to finish

Carefully bone the ducks. Set one duck aside to be used whole. Boil half the bones with one bouquet garni to make a stock in which the galantine will be cooked.

Finely chop the remaining bones and simmer with vegetables, second bouquet garni and seasoning to make a stock. Strain through a sieve, add further seasoning and reduce to a thick essence.

Set the duck breasts aside to be used whole. Remove all skin and ligaments from the remaining duck meat (there should be about 225 g/8 oz) and cut into strips with the pork and fat. Sprinkle with pâté salt, the orange rind and sage. Chill. Mince the meat twice through the finest blade of the mincer, the fat once only. Chill again. Work the fat into the meat a little at a time, finally add 2 tablespoons of the duck essence and then strain through a fine sieve. Fold in the ham, pistachios and truffles.

Season the duck breasts with pâté salt, seal in hot oil, remove from the pan, drain and pour on the remaining duck essence.

Trim the reserved boned duck and spread with about half the forcemeat, top with the breasts, brush with about 2 tablespoons essence and cover with the remaining forcemeat. Roll the duck from the tail to the neck, wrap in roasting film and tie into place with twine. Poach gently in sufficient duck stock to cover, with the third bouquet garni, for 40 minutes per kg/2 lb weight. Do not exceed the cooking time. Test with a needle to check when cooked. Leave the galantine to cool in the stock. Weight with a board and a 1–2 kg/2–4 lb weight and leave in a cool place for 24 hours. Then remove from the stock, remove the film, thoroughly wash off all fat under warm running water and wipe dry. The galantine is now ready for covering with a light chaudfroid sauce.

Duck galantine, alternative method

(Illustrated on page 114)

Prepare the forcemeat as in the recipe alongside, changing only the additional ingredients. Fold 100 g/4 oz marinated foie gras of goose or duck, strained through a sieve, 65 g/2½ oz shelled and quartered almonds, 65 g/2½ oz boiled, diced smoked tongue and 40 g/1½ oz diced truffles into the forcemeat. Omit the duck breasts. Spread the forcemeat along the centre of the duck from neck to tail and fold the two sides over the forcemeat, carefully sealing the joins. In this way the stuffed galantine follows the natural shape of the duck. It is also wrapped in roasting film or a tea-towel and bound with twine.

4 **Bind the galantine.** Seal both ends of the film with thread and knot firmly into place. The galantine should not be wrapped too tightly for it expands during cooking and could cause the film to split.

5 **Tie up the galantine.** Tie with twine at about 3-cm/1-in intervals. Take the twine through the cross pieces and secure each with a running knot. Finally, knot firmly.

6 **The galantine made by method 1.** A cross-section of the galantine rolled from tail to neck, showing that by this method the rolled breast and leg meat is evenly distributed.

Poaching the galantine. Make a stock with duck bones, bouquet garni and seasoning, strain and simmer the galantine in the stock with a bouquet garni. Make sure that the water temperature remains at a constant 80°C/176°F from the time you put the galantine into the stock until it is cooked. Check the temperature repeatedly with a thermometer. The cooking time for a galantine depends on its weight. It needs 40 minutes per kg/2 lb. Leave the galantine to cool in the stock, weight with a board and a 1–2-kg/2–4-lb weight and leave to stand for 24 hours in a cool place. Then remove from the stock, take off the wrapping, carefully wash off any fat under warm running water, wipe dry and cover with a light aspic or chaudfroid sauce.

Wild Duck Galantine

Galantine de canard sauvage

1 wild duck
pâté salt
a little mugwort, sage and basil
150 g/5 oz fattened duck's liver
a little salt and white pepper
100 ml/4 fl oz vintage port
150 g/5 oz wild duck breast meat,
trimmed (or breast of domestic duck)
100 g/4 oz lean pork loin
2–3 crushed juniper berries
grated rind of $\frac{1}{2}$ orange
$\frac{1}{2}$ clove garlic
150 g/5 oz pork fat
65 g/2$\frac{1}{2}$ oz diced smoked tongue
65 g/2$\frac{1}{2}$ oz diced boiled ham
25 g/1 oz chopped pistachios
20 g/$\frac{3}{4}$ oz truffles, diced

Bone the wild duck as shown in the photographs on pages 116–117. Trim to shape, so that the meat is evenly distributed over the whole skin. Sprinkle with 1 teaspoon pâté salt and finely rubbed dried herbs. Boil the carcass, ligaments and trimmed skin to make a stock. Strain.

Remove the skin from the fattened duck's liver together with any blood vessels. Add salt and pepper and marinate in the port.

Dice the duck breast meat and pork loin. Sprinkle with 1 teaspoon pâté salt, the juniper berries, orange rind, garlic and a little of the dried herbs and chill. Dice the pork fat and deep-freeze. In a food processor purée small amounts of seasoned meat and frozen fat. Chill thoroughly once more. Push the marinated duck's liver through a fine sieve and work into the forcemeat. Chill again and then sieve.

Fold the tongue, ham, pistachios and truffles into the forcemeat. Lay the boned duck out on a board and spread with the forcemeat. Roll up, bind in roasting film or a tea-towel and leave to stand in a cool place.

Poach the galantine in the stock for 45–50 minutes.

A particularly fine variation of this recipe is Wild Duck Terrine with Truffled Liver. For this the duck is boned in the same way as the Chicken Galantine on page 124. The stuffing is made up, omitting the duck liver and diced truffles. 250 g/9 oz fattened duck liver is marinated in port and a dash of brandy. 75 g/3 oz truffles in large pieces are wrapped in the liver and embedded in the centre of the stuffing. Sew up the duck and return as closely as possible to its original shape and poach in stock.

Galantine of River Trout

Galantine de truites de torrent

15 g/½ oz butter
20 g/¾ oz onion, sliced
100 g/4 oz salmon trout fillet, skinned
25 g/1 oz crustless fresh white bread,
thinly sliced
½ small egg white
1–2 tablespoons single cream
a little salt, ground white pepper, nutmeg
and English mustard powder
100 ml/4 fl oz whipped cream
1 heaped teaspoon chopped dill
7 river trout fillets, skinned,
weighing about 75 g/3 oz each

Melt the butter, glaze the sliced onion
without allowing it to colour and leave to
cool. Cut the trout fillet into strips and
arrange on a flat dish, cover with the onion
and thinly sliced white bread. Moisten with
the egg white and cream, sprinkle with the
seasoning, cover with film and chill. Mince
all these ingredients twice through the finest
blade of the mincer, strain through a sieve,
beat well and, over ice, gradually beat in the
whipped cream. Finally stir in the dill.

Flatten the trout fillets with the back of a
kitchen cleaver, season with salt, cut to
shape where necessary and place touching
side by side, skin side uppermost, on a large

piece of roasting film. Fill any gaps between
the fillets with small pieces of fish. Transfer
the forcemeat to a piping bag and pipe onto
the fillets to cover completely. Use the foil to
help roll the galantine and tie into position.
Poach in fish stock or salted water for about
30 minutes, with water at a gentle simmer.

Scallop Galantine

Galantine de coquilles Saint-Jacques

1.5 kg/3 lb fish trimmings (head, bones,
skin etc.)
2 litres/3½ pints water
juice of ½ lemon
250 ml/8 fl oz white wine
bouquet garni (white of 2 leeks, 1 small
parsley root, 1 small sprig thyme, ½ small
bay leaf)
½ small onion
½ small clove garlic
3 white peppercorns, crushed
1 clove
salt
1 teaspoon butter
25 g/1 oz sliced shallots
200 g/7 oz scallops, without roe
50 g/2 oz crustless fresh white bread,
thinly sliced
1 egg white
3 tablespoons single cream

ground white pepper and
nutmeg
175 ml/6 fl oz whipped cream
250 g/9 oz seaweed

Wash the fish trimmings, place in the cold
water and bring to the boil with the lemon
juice and wine. Skim thoroughly, add the
bouquet garni, onion, garlic, peppercorns,
clove and 1 teaspoon salt and simmer for 30
minutes. Strain the stock through muslin.

Heat the butter, glaze the sliced shallots
and leave to cool. Wipe the scallops dry, cut
into strips, arrange on a flat dish and cover
with the shallots and thinly sliced white
bread. Moisten with egg white and cream
and sprinkle with a little salt, pepper and
nutmeg. Chill. Mince the scallops, shallots
and bread twice through the finest blade of
the mincer, stir well and push through a
sieve. Over ice, beat the forcemeat until
smooth and silky. Then beat in the whipped
cream a little at a time. Chill repeatedly after
each stage.

Wash the seaweed, blanch for about 10
minutes and transfer immediately to lightly
salted iced water and leave until completely
cool. Drain the seaweed thoroughly and
spread over a large sheet of roasting film to
cover an area 18 × 20 cm/7 × 8 in. Transfer
the chilled forcemeat to a piping bag and
pipe over the seaweed without moving the
seaweed from position. Using the film to
help you, roll the galantine lengthways,
bind and poach in the fish stock for about 30
minutes with the liquid at a gentle simmer.

Classic Galantines

When too much attention is paid to the appearance of the food (at least in pâté making) it follows logically that the flavour of the dish suffers as a consequence. The galantine was the way out of the dilemma for those who were concerned about flavour. It was made with the best meat and finest fillings and the shape of the animal was preserved into the bargain. More recently this type of galantine has been largely replaced by the rationalised pâté roll, but the traditional galantine has not disappeared completely. For festive occasions a hen or boar's head is still stuffed in the old way, although this method of preparation is used mainly for poultry. Skilful boning which retains the bones which give the bird its shape (feet and wings), stuffing and trussing creates a new bird which retains the shape of the original.

The extra ingredients included should be ideally suited to the luxury of the pâté. So, various ingredients such as carrots and leeks on the one hand, and delicious truffles on the other, give ample opportunity to let your imagination take flight; the essential thing is that they should look good.

Chicken Galantine

Galantine de poulet

1 chicken weighing, without neck and giblets, about 1–1.25 kg/2–2½ lb, weight without carcass: about 575–750 g/1¼–1½ lb (the weight of the stuffing should be about the same as the bones)
pâté salt
carcass, neck and giblets (without liver), made up to 450 g/1 lb with chicken bones if necessary
2.5 litres/5 pints water
2 teaspoons salt
75 g/3 oz leeks (white only)
75 g/3 oz celeriac
½ bay leaf
5 white peppercorns, crushed
½ onion
150 g/5 oz fattened goose liver
250 ml/8 fl oz milk
1 tablespoon port
1 tablespoon Armagnac

Season the boned chicken with 1 teaspoon pâté salt and chill. Chop and wash the chicken bones. Finely chop the carcass, neck and giblets. Add to a pan of cold water with the chicken bones and bring to the boil. Pour off the water. Bring the bones back to the boil in the measured water, add the salt and skim. Simmer for 1 hour, repeatedly

Boning a chicken for a galantine made in its original shape

In contrast to the rolled galantine, this chicken galantine is only partially boned. It is essential to use a fresh chicken with the skin completely undamaged. Use a chicken which still has its feet, for these are cut off short of the joint to prevent the skin receding. With the carcass, the bones in the body cavity are removed completely, but the leg and wing bones are left in the chicken to help preserve its original shape. Further preparation is as for the rolled galantine.

1 **Cut off the neck and feet.** Push back the skin and chop off the neck as close to the base as possible. Chop off the feet short of the joint to prevent the skin receding during cooking.

2 **Cut through the skin along the backbone.** Starting from the tail – which should be left intact – make a sharp cut along the backbone to the neck. Remove the glands and any fat.

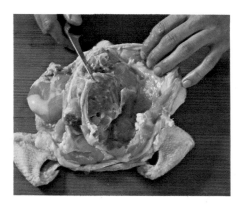

3 **Remove the carcass.** Working to left and right along the backbone separate the meat from the carcass and fold open. Hold the rib cage with the left hand and carefully separate the breast bone from the skin.

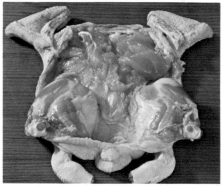

4 **The boned chicken.** Carefully lift out the carcass, taking care not to damage the skin. Leg and wing bones remain in the chicken. Lay out flat on a board and sprinkle with pâté salt.

5 **Fill the chicken with forcemeat.** The quantity should roughly correspond to the volume of the carcass. Arrange the forcemeat from neck to tail along the centre of the chicken. Do not overfill.

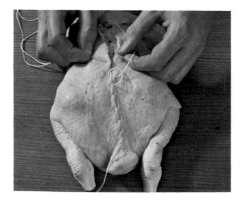

6 **Sew up the chicken.** Pull the skin together from each side. With a darning needle sew up from tail to neck. Tie off the ends of the thread and sew up the tail.

7 **Truss with twine.** Take the thread under the chicken and cross under the thighs. Wrap the twine inwards over the thighs and tie firmly to bring the legs close together.

8 **Tie the base of the chicken.** Bring the ends of the twine forward under the wings, take them back round the legs and knot to secure legs and wings firmly to the body.

skimming of the foam as it forms. Tie together the leeks, celeriac and bay leaf to make a bouquet garni, add to the stock with the crushed peppercorns and onion and simmer gently for a further 30 minutes. Again, skim off any fat and scum and strain through muslin.

Carefully remove the skin and blood vessels from the goose liver and place in the milk. This 'washes out' any remaining blood. After 1 hour remove the liver and wipe dry on kitchen paper. Mix the port and Armagnac. Season the liver with pâté salt, place in a small bowl and cover with the port and Armagnac mixture. Marinate for several hours.

Forcemeat and filling

100 g/4 oz trimmed chicken meat
100 g/4 oz lean pork
150 g/5 oz pork fat
pâté salt
freshly ground white pepper
1 teaspoon chopped rosemary
1 teaspoon chopped sage (2 leaves)
100 g/4 oz boiled ham
25 g/1 oz truffles

Cut the trimmed chicken, pork and fat into strips, sprinkle with pâté salt, pepper and the finely chopped herbs and chill. Mince the meat through the finest blade of the mincer, chill again and repeat. Finally mince the fat and chill both meat and fat. Then mix the fat into the meat, increase the seasoning if necessary and chill in the refrigerator. With a metal scraper to help you push the forcemeat through a sieve and chill again. Dice the ham and truffles.

Break the marinated liver into small pieces and mix with the ham and truffles carefully into the forcemeat. Spread the forcemeat over the boned chicken and sew together. With your hands re-form the chicken to its original shape as closely as possible and truss with twine to help keep its shape. Wrap in roasting film which should fully enclose the galantine without being too tight. Tie up both ends. Heat the chicken stock to 80°C/176°F and cook, allowing 40 minutes per kg/2 lb weight. You will have to calculate the time taking account of the weight. During cooking keep the liquid temperature at exactly 80°C/176°F. Leave the chicken galantine to cool in the stock and then weight with a 1 kg/2 lb weight. Place in the refrigerator for 24 hours before removing the wrapping.

If the galantine is to be covered with aspic or chaudfroid sauce, you will have to wash off any fat under warm running water before drying with kitchen paper.

Chicken galantine with a light chaudfroid sauce. The sauce should suit the flavour of the galantine. In this instance chicken stock is used in the sauce. The forcemeat is made from the recipe alongside, but without the added goose liver.

Stuffed Goose Neck

Cou d'oie farci

giblets of 2 geese (neck and head, crop,
heart and unfattened liver)
1 teaspoon salt
a little ground white pepper, mace,
allspice, sweet paprika and marjoram
½ clove garlic, crushed
40 g/1½ oz butter
150 g/5 oz lean pork
2 tablespoons white breadcrumbs
1 tablespoon oil
2 tablespoons diced onion
2 tablespoons vintage port
6 tablespoons veal stock
a little fresh thyme, hyssop and lovage
75 g/3 oz frozen diced pork fat
50 g/2 oz boiled ham
50 g/2 oz shelled pistachios
1 litre/2 pints chicken stock

Cut round the skin on both necks below the
head and pull off the skin. Remove the
tough skin from the meaty part of the crops.
Remove the blood vessels from the hearts
and livers. Transfer the giblets to a bowl and
sprinkle with salt, pepper, mace, allspice,
paprika, marjoram and garlic. Heat the
butter in a frying pan and quickly seal the

giblets, continuously shaking the pan, and
then chill. Dice the pork and add to the
giblets. Sprinkle with the breadcrumbs.

Heat the oil in a frying pan and glaze the
diced onion. Add the port and veal stock,
then the herbs, and reduce to a thick liquid.
Strain over the giblets and pork. Leave to
marinate.

Purée the thoroughly chilled mixture of
giblets, pork and reduced stock with the
frozen diced fat in a food processor. Fold
the diced ham and coarsely chopped
pistachios into the forcemeat.

Sew the neck skins together along one
side and fill with the forcemeat, making sure
you leave no air gaps. Sew up the stuffed
neck, cook for about 20 minutes, in the
chicken stock, maintaining the liquid at a
gentle simmer, and leave to cool in the
stock.

Stuffed Pig's Trotters

Zampone

2 pig's trotters, each weighing about
800–1000 g/1¾–2 lb
550 g/19 oz lean pork loin
350 g/12 oz pork fat
about 15 g/½ oz pâté salt
freshly ground white pepper
fresh thyme and marjoram
12 juniper berries, crushed
3 cloves garlic, crushed
200 g/7 oz diced smoked tongue
450 g/1 lb uncooked pork fillet, diced
75 g/3 oz shelled pistachios
beef stock for cooking

Scald the trotters and scrape off any bristles
with a sharp knife, taking care not to
damage the skin. Remove the inside of the
trotters as far as the toes, so that the skins
are completely free from meat. Soak for 24
hours.

Cut the pork and fat into strips, sprinkle
with pâté salt, pepper, herbs, juniper berries
and garlic and chill. Mince the pork twice
through the finest blade of the mincer.
Mince the fat once only, work into the meat
and push the forcemeat through a sieve.
Finally fold in the tongue, pork fillet and
pistachios. Dry the trotters and stuff with
the forcemeat, leaving no air gaps, but not
overfilling. Sew up the ends with strong
thread. (It will be easier to sew the thick skin
if you make the holes in advance.) Prick the
stuffed trotters several times with a thin
trussing needle, to allow air to escape during
cooking. Wrap with strips of linen about
5 cm/2 in wide and secure with thread. This
will help the trotters keep their shape during
cooking and prevent the skin splitting.
Cook in beef stock for about 3½ hours,
maintaining the temperature of the liquid at
a gentle simmer, and leave to cool in the
stock.

Even better smoked. Both neck of goose and
Zampone are suitable for smoking. You can get
your butcher to smoke them or, better still,
smoke them yourself. Smoking gives both a
particularly spicy flavour and will help them to
keep longer.

Stuffed Breast of Veal

Punta di vitello ripieno

1 kg/2 lb boned, trimmed breast of veal
salt and white pepper
400 g/14 oz lean veal
300 g/11 oz lean pork loin
200 g/7 oz pork fat
2 teaspoons pâté seasoning (all-purpose mixture)
1 teaspoon thyme
1 teaspoon basil
1 bay leaf
20 g/¾ oz butter
1 small onion, cut into rings
1 clove garlic, crushed
1½ tablespoons Grappa (Italian brandy)
2 slices bread, without crust
1 egg
3 tablespoons single cream
100 g/4 oz diced boiled ham
100 g/4 oz braised mushrooms
1 tablespoon chopped parsley
25 g/1 oz chopped truffles
veal stock for cooking

Cut a slit in the breast of veal and rub the inside with salt and pepper. Leave to stand in the refrigerator. Cut the veal, pork and pork fat into strips, transfer to a bowl and sprinkle with 1 teaspoon salt, the pâté seasoning and herbs. Heat the butter in a frying pan, glaze the onion and crushed garlic and add the Grappa. Allow to cool slightly and pour over the meat. Crumble the bread over the meat. Beat the egg into the cream and pour over the bread. Cover the bowl with film and leave to stand in the refrigerator for 3–4 hours.

Mince the meat and all the other ingredients in the bowl twice through the finest blade of the mincer. Over ice, beat the forcemeat until smooth and silky and then fold in the ham, mushrooms, parsley and truffles. Stuff the breast of veal and sew up with a cotton thread. Cook in highly seasoned veal stock for 1 hour or so, maintaining the liquid at a gentle simmer, and allow to cool in the stock.

Stuffed Wild Boar's Head

Hure de sanglier farcie

The original idea of stuffing a wild boar's head was probably suggested by its elongated shape which seems made for stuffing. But probably many hunters also wanted to impress their guests with its frightening, yet beautiful, appearance. It is a classic French preparation and included more for historical than culinary interest.

1 small young boar's head, weighing about 4–4.5 kg/9–10 lb
pâté salt
ground white pepper
chopped fresh marjoram
chopped fresh thyme
2 tablespoons chopped parsley
100 g/4 oz diced onion, glazed in butter
3 cloves garlic, crushed
450 g/1 lb lean wild boar meat
225 g/8 oz lean pork loin
450 g/1 lb fat (use wild boar fat if possible)
juniper berries
grated lemon rind
25 g/1 oz diced onion
15 g/½ oz butter
200 g/7 oz diced wild boar fillet
2 tablespoons oil
3 tablespoons brandy
100 ml/4 fl oz wild boar essence
200 g/7 oz uncooked pork fillet, diced
75 g/3 oz shelled pistachios
40 g/1½ oz truffles, diced
200 g/7 oz foie gras, seasoned with pâté salt and marinated in port and brandy
The boiled and pickled tongue of the wild boar can also be diced and included

The truffled trophy

To describe this procedure in great detail might be said to be akin to 'taking coals to Newcastle', for anyone who is willing to have a go at this recipe must either be a very expert or a very brave cook. Nevertheless it is quite an experience to make this, the king of the galantines. And, without doubt, young boar's meat served in the

boar's head with truffles makes a really attractive dish. Beginners are advised to use a young boar, for they are smaller and easier to handle.

The head should be cut from the body with as much of the neck as possible. Bristles are removed by scalding the head. It is best to begin with the water at 45°C/113°F and to increase the temperature slowly to about 60°C/140°F maximum. Shave off the bristles with a sharp knife (or razor blade), taking care not to damage the rind. Then soak the boar's head for at least 12 hours.

Rub the head with pickling salt, place in an earthenware jar, cover with pickling brine, cover and leave to stand in the refrigerator for about 24 hours. Rinse several times before proceeding.

The inside of the boar's head is removed from the lower jaw side. Cut the skin between the bones of the lower jaw and cut the skin free of the cranial bone at each side. Cut out the ear muscles but leave the ears in place on the head. This leaves only the skin with the flesh attached to it. In the meantime make the stuffing to go in the head and prepare the other ingredients to be included in the stuffing.

After soaking, dry the head thoroughly. Place on a board. Carefully sew up the eye, ear and snout opening to prevent the stuffing escaping. Turn the head upside down and season the inside with salt and pepper. Mix together 1 tablespoon each

marjoram and thyme, the parsley, glazed onion and one crushed garlic clove and spread evenly over the inside of the head.

Cut the wild boar meat, pork and fat into strips, season with pâté salt, pepper, marjoram, thyme, crushed juniper berries, lemon rind, and another crushed garlic clove, and chill. Soften the onion in the butter and cool. Mince the seasoned meat and onion twice through the finest blade of the mincer, the fat once only. Over ice, beat the fat into the meat mixture. Chill well.

Seal the diced wild boar fillet in oil, then remove from the pan. Deglaze the pan with brandy, then add the wild boar essence (made from reduced boar stock), 8 crushed juniper berries, marjoram, thyme, lemon rind, and the remaining garlic. Boil until well reduced, then strain over the diced sealed boar fillet. Cool.

Mix the diced boar fillet, pork fillet, pistachios, truffles and broken up foie gras into the forcemeat. Stuff the head so that when it is sewn together along the lower jaw it regains its original shape. Seal the remaining opening at the neck with a piece of soaked bacon rind and sew to the skin of the boar's head. Wrap the head firmly in roasting film or a cloth.

Use the wild boar bones and vegetables to make a light stock. Strain and season well. Cook the boar's head in the stock at a maximum temperature of 80°C/176°F – at higher temperatures the skin will split. Test with a needle to ascertain when it is cooked through. Make sure that the head is completely covered with stock throughout the cooking time, adding more liquid as the stock evaporates. Leave the head to cool in the stock.

During cooking the head will contract slightly, regaining (almost) its original shape. Of course when you carve the head the slices will be of different sizes, which can be annoying when you want to carve equal portions. This can be overcome by cutting away some of the rind on the underside before stuffing. In this case you should bind up the head with a strip of linen, applied like a bandage. But do not bind too tightly so that the stuffing can expand slightly during cooking. (Secure the bandage with a cotton thread.)

Cooking time: about 3–3½ hours.

It is traditional to glaze the boar's head with a brown chaudfroid sauce or brown aspic. This goes well with the flavour and enhances the frightening appearance of the head. This recipe can also be adapted to make a rolled pâté. Serve with rose-hip sauce and apples, mushrooms or glazed chestnuts, braised in white wine.

The Outsiders among Pâtés

Timbales, parfaits, mousses – all are dishes to set the pulse of the serious gourmet racing. If we disregard for the moment Antoine Carême's large timbales, these are the smallest of the great pâté family. But are they really pâtés? This is a difficult question to answer for while these outsiders all have some feature in common with the pâté or terrine, be it the shape, the forcemeat or the filling, some of them differ widely from the accepted form of the terrine or pâté. So should they be included within the scope of this book? As with other types of pâtés, when correctly prepared they are the finest of delicacies and their refined method of preparation is proof that they are closely related to pâtés. Yet, compared with large pies or galantines, many of these recipes are relatively easy to make.

Mousse, a delicate foam

In French the word simply means 'foam'. In German the mousse is defined as a foam loaf, not a particularly apt description, for these, the lightest of all pâtés, do not even have their shape in common with a loaf. They are pâtés made with aspic. The basic ingredient is always a fine purée of vegetables, poultry, ham, game, poultry liver, fish or shellfish, and this is combined with gelatine and whipped cream. This purée can be easily made in a blender or food processor. The mousse can be made in moulds of a variety of shapes, but is usually served turned out of the mould. It is not essential to cover them with a layer of aspic even though this has one definite advantage: the tender, creamy mousse tastes particularly fresh under its aspic (which should naturally harmonise with the flavour of the mousse) and it is well protected against absorbing flavours from other foods, in the refrigerator for example. It should be unnecessary to add that, with mousses, fresh, high-quality ingredients are as essential as they are with pâtés.

Parfait (the French word means complete, perfect) is the term used to describe the finest forcemeat made either with aspic, that is, bound with gelatine, or with egg white and poached standing in water. The term very accurately describes this very fine and tender dish and is almost synonymous with the term mousse. There is not really much difference between a poached parfait and a terrine cooked without its coating of pork fat. Their light consistency and the opportunity they offer for variation makes them a favourite of the new, light style of cuisine. Experiments have been carried out and new creations invented from

Poultry liver mousse, a very tender delicacy made from turkey liver and foie gras. It is excellent served with papaya stewed in sugar, vintage Tokay and a dash of pepper.

ingredients which were once thought unsuitable for pâté making. Think of the light, airy hors d'oeuvres made from puréed vegetables. Fish and shellfish too are an ideal basis for these light forcemeats and offer a wide range of possible combinations with vegetables.

Timbales are moulds with a filling of some kind and the master chef and pâtissier, Antoine Carême, whom we have already mentioned, invented some extremely complicated timbales. Cooked or uncooked ingredients arranged in layers in a charlotte mould, poached and then turned out were real works of art and a favourite highlight of menus in nineteenth-century France. Some of these creations are still popular today, like the Timbale à la milanaise.

The first timbales must have been pâtés in the shape of a kettle drum (the French word *timbale* means 'kettle drum') which were baked blind, that is, without the filling. In the course of time these changed in shape to become conical. These were filled with forcemeat and baked, or filled with stewed meat. Eventually the best-loved and finest timbales came to omit the pastry altogether. Fine forcemeats, usually bound with egg or egg white, were poured into small, individual moulds greased with butter. Any type of meat or fish suitable for pâté making is also suitable for a timbale. But you can also make wonderfully tender timbales with puréed vegetables and, served with a suitable sauce, these make an excellent hors d'oeuvre. And they have one definite advantage: they are quick to make. More exquisite still are the filled timbales. The outside is a tender forcemeat, filled with a fine stew and sealed with forcemeat. They are poached in a water bath. You will often find timbales on many menus, unfortunately, which prove to be stews served in small individual dishes. Here any relationship with pâtés ends.

Assorted tartlets

No one can say precisely where they came from or how long they have been made. They have more in common with pâtés than many others of the same family. They are small tartlets, baked blind, in shortcrust or sometimes puff or yeast pastry. Beyond this they become less easy to define. The rest relies upon the cook's imagination. Even the shape of the tartlet can be varied, but they should always bear some resemblance to a small flan. They can be plain or fluted, round, oval or square in shape. The size should always be adequate for one serving. They can be filled with stew while still warm, covered with forcemeat and baked, or covered with sauce and browned under the grill. Or, if preferred, they can be filled with cold ingredients and served cold.

Poultry Liver Mousse

Mousse de foies de volaille

Illustrated on page 130

300 g/11 oz turkey liver
100 g/4 oz pork fat
100 ml/4 fl oz vintage port
1½ tablespoons Armagnac
1 teaspoon salt
½ bay leaf
1 small sprig thyme and lemon balm
freshly ground white pepper
25 g/1 oz butter
300 g/11 oz fattened goose liver
3 leaves gelatine
3 tablespoons chicken stock
100 ml/4 fl oz cream
250 ml/8 fl oz light chicken aspic
900-ml/1½-pint mould or 6
150-ml/¼-pint individual moulds

Remove all skin and blood vessels from the liver. Coarsely dice the fat and place in a bowl with the liver. Add the port, Armagnac, salt, herbs and pepper. Cover and marinate overnight in the refrigerator.

Drain off the marinade and quickly fry the liver and fat in the hot butter, shaking the pan continuously. Remove from the pan and leave to cool. Add the drained marinade to the cooking juices, reduce to a thick liquid and leave to cool.

Purée the chilled liver and fat in a food processor with the reduced marinade. Push the prepared goose liver through a fine sieve. Over ice, beat into the turkey liver forcemeat. Dissolve the softened gelatine in the warmed chicken stock and stir it into the forcemeat. Add the cream and extra seasoning if necessary. Transfer to a mould, or moulds, coated with chicken aspic. Leave

to cool in the refrigerator and cover the top with chicken aspic. Leave until completely set. To turn out the mousse stand in hot water for a few moments and slide the delicate mousse very gently onto a flat dish.

Broccoli Flan

Tourte de brocoli

sherry aspic for coating
250 g/9 oz venison fillet, fried and well seasoned, then thinly sliced
2 slices carrot
2 slivers of truffle
350 g/12 oz broccoli, cleaned
½ teaspoon salt
freshly ground white pepper
generous pinch of nutmeg,
thyme and basil
6 leaves gelatine
6 tablespoons brown game stock
250 ml/8 fl oz lightly whipped cream
500 g/18 oz puff pastry
1 egg yolk for coating

Coat two deep soup plates with sherry aspic and leave to set. Arrange the thinly sliced venison fillet in a circle over the aspic. Place a slice of boiled carrot and a piece of truffle in the centre of each circle.

Cook the broccoli in salted water until soft, drain and leave to cool. Purée in a blender and, if necessary, push through a fine sieve. Add the seasonings. Dissolve the softened gelatine in the hot game stock and stir into the broccoli purée, which should be at room temperature. Then gradually beat in the lightly whipped cream and transfer to the soup plates coated with aspic and venison. Smooth the tops and leave the

mousse in the refrigerator to set.

Roll out the puff pastry to about 4 mm/¼ in thick and cut a 4 cm/1½ in wide ring of pastry the same size as the plate to go around the mousse. It can be either plain or fluted. Roll out the remaining pastry once more very thinly. Cut two rounds the same size as the rings and transfer to a baking sheet. Brush with egg yolk, top with the rings of pastry and brush these too with egg yolk. Leave to stand for 15 minutes and then bake in a hot oven, 220 C, 425 F, gas 7 for 10–12 minutes. Turn out the broccoli mousses into the cooled pastry bases.

1 **Coating with aspic jelly** (the technical term for this is *chemiser*). Pour cool aspic carefully into the mould, making sure no air bubbles form. This will only be possible if the aspic itself is free of bubbles.

2 **Stand the mould in iced water.** The water should come almost to the top of the mould. Leave the aspic until it begins to set – the length of time needed for this will depend on the temperature of the liquid aspic.

3 **Pour off the aspic:** it should leave behind an even layer of aspic 2–3 mm/about ⅛ in thick. If the layer is too thin refill the mould with liquid aspic and return to the iced water.

Smoked Fish Mousse

Mousse de poisson fumé

Smoked salmon mousse
150 g/5 oz smoked salmon fillet
100 ml/4 fl oz fish velouté
salt and freshly ground white pepper
5 leaves gelatine
5 tablespoons beef stock
100 ml/4 fl oz whipped cream
Smoked trout mousse
150 g/5 oz smoked trout fillets
100 ml/4 fl oz fish velouté
salt and freshly ground white pepper
5 leaves gelatine or 10 g/⅓ oz powdered
gelatine
5 tablespoons beef stock
100 ml/4 fl oz whipped cream

light fish aspic for coating
1 (56.8-g/2-oz) jar caviar
1 1-litre/1¾-pint mould

Cut up the smoked salmon and purée slowly in a blender with the velouté. Push through a fine sieve and season. Soften, then squeeze out the gelatine, dissolve it in the hot stock and add to the purée. Before the mixture sets, whisk in about a quarter of the whipped cream and then fold in the rest with a wooden spoon.

Prepare the trout mousse in the same way.

Coat the mould with the fish aspic and leave to set in the refrigerator. Fill first with the salmon mousse. Make a hollow along the centre and fill with caviar, leave to stand for a while and then add the trout mousse. Bang the mould repeatedly on a damp cloth to prevent air gaps. Smooth the top and leave to stand in the refrigerator. Cover the top with fish aspic and allow to set.

To turn out the mousse, dip the mould into hot water for a few seconds, slide the mousse carefully onto a flat dish and serve with caviar.

This smoked fish mousse with caviar filling is a real luxury coated in a delicate fish aspic. The coating of aspic not only protects the mousse and keeps it fresh, but should also bring out its flavour. So it is important for the flavours of the mousse and its coating to harmonise well, but the flavour of the aspic should not dominate that of the mousse.

Carrot Mousse

Mousse de carottes

150 g/5 oz carrots
100 ml/4 fl oz chicken velouté
3 leaves gelatine or 7 g/¼ oz powdered
gelatine
3 tablespoons beef stock
salt and ground white pepper
100 ml/4 fl oz whipped cream
light aspic made with chicken stock and
sherry or white wine, for coating
6 100-ml/4 fl oz moulds or cups of similar
size

Boil the carrots until soft, then dice and
slowly purée them in the blender with the
chicken velouté. Push through a fine sieve.
Soften the gelatine in a little cold water,
squeeze out well and dissolve in the hot
stock. Whisk into the carrot mixture, season
and check seasoning. Before the mixture
begins to set whisk in about a quarter of the
whipped cream, then gradually fold in the
rest with a wooden spoon. Coat the moulds
with aspic and leave to set. Add the carrot
mousse before it begins to set, smooth the
top and leave to set in the refrigerator. If
you use fluted moulds the aspic layer will
need to be slightly thicker; they will also
need warming for longer if they are to turn
easily out of the moulds, which will mean
losing some of the aspic.

Turn out the mousses and garnish with a
blanched parsley leaf and a slice of carrot.
Serve with a tomato and green peppercorn
sauce. *Serves 6.*

Goose Liver Mousse

Mousse de foie gras

150 g/5 oz fattened goose liver
¼ teaspoon pâté salt
white pepper
1 tablespoon Armagnac
2 tablespoons port
7 g/¼ oz butter
5 tablespoons jellifying chicken stock
5 tablespoons chicken velouté
2 leaves gelatine
2 tablespoons beef stock
100 ml/4 fl oz whipped cream
Muscatel aspic for coating
6 slices truffle
6 100-ml/4-fl oz moulds

Cut the prepared goose liver into thick
slices, season and cover with the Armagnac
and port. Leave to marinate in the
refrigerator for at least 2–3 hours. Wipe the
liver dry, fry until semi-cooked in the butter
and drain on kitchen paper. Reduce the
chicken stock and marinade to a thick liquid
and strain over the liver. Push the liver and
velouté through a fine sieve. Dissolve the
softened gelatine in the hot beef stock.
When the liver mixture is at room temperature whisk in the gelatine mixture. Season
and check the seasoning. Before the mixture
begins to set, whisk in about a quarter of the
whipped cream and then gradually fold in
the remainder with a wooden spoon. Coat
the moulds with aspic, place a slice of truffle
in the base of each and leave to set. Fill the
moulds with the goose liver mousse and
leave to set in the refrigerator.

Turn out the mousses and serve with
sliced kiwi fruit, sprinkled with pink
peppercorns. *Serves 6.*

Individual mousses are more time-consuming to make for each mould has to be coated with aspic. But
they look very attractive and in their aspic coating will keep fresher longer. Instead of small moulds
you can use cups, but they must taper towards the base so that they turn out easily.

Ham Mousse

Mousse de jambon

300 g/11 oz boiled ham
200 ml/7 fl oz veal velouté
salt and freshly ground white pepper
6 leaves gelatine or 15 g/½ oz powdered
gelatine
6 tablespoons beef stock
250 ml/8 fl oz whipped cream
white wine aspic for coating
6 100-ml/4-fl oz moulds, or cups of the
same size

Cut up the ham, mince then purée it in a blender with the velouté. Push through a sieve and season. Soften and squeeze out the gelatine, dissolve in the hot stock and add to the purée. Before the mixture sets whisk in about a quarter of the whipped cream and then gradually fold in the remainder with a wooden spoon. Coat the moulds with aspic and leave to set. Fill with the ham mousse, smooth the tops and leave to set in the refrigerator. Cover the tops with aspic and leave to set.

Turn out the mousses and serve with an asparagus sauce. *Serves 6.*

Tomato Mousse

Mousse de tomates

225 g/8 oz peeled, deseeded and
diced tomatoes
3 tablespoons tomato ketchup
2 tablespoons tomato juice
3 tablespoons tomato paste
salt, sugar and cayenne pepper
2–3 leaves gelatine or
4–6 g/¼ oz powdered gelatine
3 tablespoons hot beef stock
250 ml/8 fl oz whipped cream
white wine aspic for coating
6 100-ml/4-fl oz moulds, or cups of the
same size

Strain half the tomato flesh through a fine sieve, add the tomato ketchup, tomato juice and tomato paste and season with salt, sugar and cayenne. Soften the gelatine, squeeze out, dissolve in the hot stock and whisk into the tomato mixture. Before the mixture sets whisk in about a quarter of the whipped cream and then gradually fold in the remainder with a wooden spoon. Finally, fold in the remaining diced tomato. Coat the moulds with aspic and leave to set. Fill with tomato mousse, smooth the tops and leave to set in the refrigerator. Cover with some more aspic and leave to set until firm.

Turn out the mousses and serve with a salad of prawns, tomatoes and asparagus tips. *Serves 6.*

King Prawn Mousse

Mousse de crevettes

300 g/11 oz king prawns, boiled and
shelled
200 ml/7 fl oz fish velouté
salt and freshly ground white pepper
6 leaves gelatine or 15 g/½ oz powdered
gelatine
6 tablespoons hot beef stock
250 ml/8 fl oz whipped cream
light fish aspic for coating
2–3 tablespoons chopped dill
6 100-ml/4-fl oz moulds, or cups of the
same size

Purée the king prawns and velouté in a blender. Push through a sieve and season. Soften the gelatine, squeeze out, dissolve in the hot stock and stir into the prawn purée. Before the mixture sets whisk in about a quarter of the whipped cream, then gradually fold in the remaining cream with a wooden spoon. Coat the moulds with aspic, sprinkle with dill and leave to set. Fill with the prawn mousse, smooth the tops and leave in the refrigerator to set.

Turn out the mousses and serve with a lemon sauce. *Serves 6.*

Timbales or cup moulds

This term covers a whole range of creations which resemble pâtés in some way, but it also covers other dishes which have little in common with them. Originally the term referred to shortcrust pies in the shape of a small kettle drum (*timbale* in French). They were usually baked blind, that is, without their filling and then filled with some kind of stew. They were usually big enough to serve 4–6 people. Over the years the kettle drum shape changed to a cup shape and became smaller to serve one or two. These smooth or fluted moulds were thinly lined with pastry (shortcrust is best), filled with dried peas, covered with a pastry lid and baked. The lid was removed while still hot, the pie was filled, and the lid replaced before serving hot. But that is only one of many possibilities. Timbales can also be baked with the filling and served hot with a sauce or cold as individual hors d'oeuvres. Many fine timbale recipes use pasta dough, egg pancakes or macaroni arranged carefully in the mould as a casing.

Today, at least with individual timbales, the pastry is often omitted altogether and the moulds are lined with a fine forcemeat. They are filled, sealed with more forcemeat and poached standing in a water bath before being turned out of the mould.

Partridge Timbale with Morels in Cream

Timbale de perdreaux aux morilles à la crème

4 partridges, each weighing about 200 g/7 oz
6 juniper berries, crushed
1 clove garlic, crushed
grated orange and lemon rind
7 g/¼ oz pâté salt
2 egg whites, lightly beaten
75 g/3 oz flour panada
400 ml/14 fl oz whipped cream
20 g/¾ oz dried morels
200 ml/7 fl oz partridge or game essence
200 m/7 fl oz cream
salt and freshly ground white pepper
1 heaped tablespoon finely chopped chives
butter for greasing
4 200-ml/7-fl oz timbale moulds, or cups of the same size

Bone the partridges. Cut the carefully trimmed meat, to give about 350 g/12 oz, into strips and sprinkle with the crushed juniper berries, crushed garlic, orange and lemon rind and pâté salt. Cover with cling film and chill. When the meat has had time to absorb the flavour of the seasoning mince twice through the finest blade of the mincer. Over ice, gradually beat in the lightly whisked egg whites and then the sieved panada. Push the forcemeat through a sieve, beat in the whipped cream a spoonful at a time and continue beating until it is fully incorporated and the forcemeat smooth and silky.

Leave the dried morels in water to swell slightly, thoroughly wash to remove any dirt and then soak in fresh water. Boil for about 25 minutes in the steeping water and partridge essence, drain, leave to cool and chop. Reduce the cream until thick, strain into the morel juice and season. Check the seasoning. Add the morels and chives, stir in and leave to cool. Grease the timbale moulds or cups generously with butter and cover the bases and sides evenly with about three-quarters of the forcemeat. This is quite easy with a piping bag and plain nozzle. Pipe a spiral of forcemeat over the base and up the sides of each mould and smooth flat with a round-bladed knife. Fill with the stewed morels and cover with the remaining forcemeat.

Cook for about 15 minutes in a water bath, regulating the oven so that the water remains at a gentle simmer. If you use cups allow an extra 5–6 minutes.

Pistachio Timbale with Sautéed Pheasant

Timbale de pistaches au sauté de faisan

350 g/12 oz lean pork
salt and white pepper
2 egg whites
75 g/3 oz flour panada
100 g/4 oz shelled pistachios
100 ml/4 fl oz milk
200 ml/7 fl oz whipped cream
200 ml/7 fl oz cream
200 ml/7 fl oz pheasant essence
100 g/4 oz lean pheasant meat
1 tablespoon oil
butter for greasing
4 200-ml/7-fl oz timbale moulds

Cut the trimmed pork into strips and season it. Mince twice through the finest blade of the mincer. Gradually beat in the lightly whisked egg whites and then the strained panada. Purée the pistachios with the milk in a blender and work into the forcemeat. Push the forcemeat through a fine sieve and beat in the whipped cream a spoonful at a time.

To make the filling, reduce the cream until thick, then strain it through a sieve into the hot pheasant essence and season. Dice the pheasant meat and seal it in oil. Remove from the pan, drain and add to the sauce. Stir in well and leave to cool. Coat the buttered timbale moulds with about three-quarters of the forcemeat. Fill with the sautéed pheasant and cover with the remaining forcemeat.

Cook in a water bath for about 15 minutes, regulating the heat so that the water remains at a gentle simmer. *Serves 4.*

Salmon Timbale with Frog's Legs

Timbale de saumon au sauté de cuisses de grenouilles

350 g/12 oz salmon fillet
salt and white pepper
2 egg whites, lightly beaten
75 g/3 oz flour panada
400 ml/14 fl oz whipped cream
15 g/½ oz diced shallots
20 g/¾ oz butter
7 pairs frog's legs
3 tablespoons white wine
250 ml/8 fl oz veal stock
250 ml/8 fl oz cream
lemon juice
butter for greasing
4 200-ml/7-fl oz timbale moulds

Cut the salmon into strips, season and chill. Mince twice through the finest blade of the mincer and work in the lightly beaten egg white and then the sieved panada. Push the forcemeat through a sieve and add the whipped cream a spoonful at a time.

Glaze the diced shallots in the butter, fry the frog's legs, add the wine and stock and simmer for 8 to 10 minutes. Bone the frog's legs and cut them into small pieces. Reduce the stock by about three-quarters and strain. Reduce the cream until thick, strain into the stock, add the frog's legs and season with salt and lemon juice. Coat the moulds with the forcemeat, add the filling and cover with the remaining forcemeat. Cook in a water bath for about 15 minutes, regulating the oven so that the water remains at a gentle simmer. Serve the salmon timbales on a bed of steamed spinach. *Serves 4.*

Pike Timbale with Prawns in Dill Sauce

Timbale de brochet aux crevettes en sauce à l'aneth

15 g/½ oz butter
2 sliced shallots
350 g/12 oz pike fillet
salt and ground white pepper
generous pinch each of nutmeg and
English mustard powder
2 egg whites, lightly beaten
75 g/3 oz flour panada
400 ml/14 fl oz whipped cream
300 ml/½ pint cream
1 tablespoon lemon juice
150 g/5 oz peeled prawns
2 tablespoons chopped dill
butter for greasing
4 200-ml/7-fl oz timbale moulds

Melt the butter, glaze the shallots without allowing them to colour and leave to cool. Remove any bones from the pike fillet, cut into strips, season with salt, pepper, nutmeg and mustard, sprinkle with the shallots and chill. Mince twice through the finest blade of the mincer. Gradually beat in the lightly beaten egg whites and then the sieved panada. Push the forcemeat through a fine sieve and beat in the whipped cream a spoonful at a time.

Reduce the cream until thick, strain, season with salt, pepper and lemon juice, add the prawns and simmer for a few minutes. Finally add the dill and leave to cool. Grease the timbale moulds generously with butter. Cover the bases and sides with about three-quarters of the forcemeat, fill with the prawn mixture and cover with the remaining forcemeat. Cook standing in a water bath for about 15 minutes with water at a gentle simmer.

Smoked Salmon Timbale with Mussels

Timbale de saumon fumé aux moules

200 g/7 oz smoked salmon fillet
150 ml/¼ pint whipped cream
15 g/½ oz diced shallots
1 teaspoon butter · 50 ml/2 fl oz cream
150 g/5 oz bottled mussels
1 tablespoon freshly grated horseradish
salt and white pepper · butter for greasing
4 150-ml/¼-pint timbale moulds

Use only tender, best quality smoked salmon, to give the forcemeat a delicate flavour. Finely dice the salmon, chill

thoroughly and purée in a food processor. Over ice, gradually beat in the whipped cream.

Glaze the diced shallots in the butter. Reduce the cream until thick and strain over the shallots. Add the mussels and horseradish, season, stir well and leave to cool. Generously grease the timbale moulds with butter and cover the bases and sides with about three-quarters of the forcemeat. Fill with the mussel mixture and cover with the remaining forcemeat.

Cook in a water bath for about 15 minutes with water at a gentle simmer. *Serves 4.*

Fish forcemeats for individual timbales have one great advantage, they make a very light and airy hors d'oeuvre with great possibilities for variation. Unfilled fish or shellfish timbales are served with a suitable sauce. Hollow timbales can be filled with a forcemeat of the same fish or with prawns as in the Pike Timbale recipe on this page.

Broccoli Timbale with Walnut Sauce

Timbale de brocoli à la sauce aux noix

300 g/11 oz broccoli, cleaned
15 g/½ oz butter
200 ml/7 fl oz chicken stock
salt, white pepper and nutmeg
2 eggs
3 tablespoons cream
butter for greasing
4 150 ml/¼-pint timbale moulds

Cut the broccoli into small pieces and braise until soft in the butter, stock and seasoning. Purée, strain though a sieve, beat in the eggs and cream and check seasoning. Transfer the purée to the buttered moulds and cook for about 20–25 minutes in a moderately hot oven, 200 C, 400 F, gas 6. *Serves 4.*

Carrot Timbale with Herb Sauce

Timbale de carottes à la sauce aux herbes

575 g/1¼ lb carrots, cleaned
20 g/¾ oz butter
200–250 ml/7 8 fl oz chicken stock
salt, sugar and nutmeg
3–4 eggs
75 ml/2½ fl oz cream
butter for greasing
4 150 ml/¼-pint timbale moulds

Cut the carrots into small pieces and braise in the butter, stock and seasoning. Purée, strain through a sieve, beat in the eggs and cream and check seasoning. Transfer to the buttered moulds and cook in a moderately hot oven, 200 C, 400 F, gas 7 for about 20–25 minutes. *Serves 4.*

Cauliflower Timbale with Spinach Sauce

Timbale de chou-fleur à la sauce d'épinards

300 g/11 oz cauliflower, washed
15 g/½ oz butter
200 ml/7 fl oz chicken stock
salt and nutmeg
2 eggs
3 tablespoons cream
butter for greasing
4 150-ml/¼-pint timbale moulds

Braise the cauliflower in the butter, stock and seasoning until soft. Purée, strain through a sieve, beat in the eggs and cream and check seasoning. Transfer to the buttered moulds and cook in a moderately hot oven, 200 C, 400 F, gas 6 for about 20–25 minutes. *Serves 4.*

Prawn Parfait

Parfait d'écrevisses

450 g / 1 lb prawn meat
1 teaspoon salt
freshly ground white pepper
1 egg white
50 g / 2 oz flour panada
100 ml / 4 fl oz single cream
200 ml / 7 fl oz whipped cream
2 tablespoons chopped dill
butter for greasing
1-litre / 1¾-pint pâté mould
light fish aspic and chopped dill to finish

Cut half the prawn meat into pieces, sprinkle with the seasoning and chill. Mince twice through the finest blade of the mincer. Over ice beat in the lightly whisked egg white and then the sieved flour panada,

Chicken Parfait with Chicken Liver and Mushrooms

Parfait de volaille aux foies de volaille et cèpes

300 g / 11 oz lean chicken
pâté salt and white pepper
generous pinch of ground ginger
generous pinch of cardamom
1 egg white, lightly beaten
75 g / 3 oz flour panada
350 ml / 12 fl oz whipped cream
150 g / 5 oz chicken livers
150 g / 5 oz mushrooms, washed
1–2 tablespoons oil
butter for greasing
Madeira aspic
3 tablespoons chopped parsley
1-litre / 1¾-pint pâté mould

adding a little at a time. Push the forcemeat through a sieve and add the single cream and then the whipped cream a spoonful at a time. Finally stir in the dill.

Dice the remaining prawn meat and stir into the forcemeat. Grease the mould with butter and line with roasting film. Fill with the mixture and smooth the top. Bang the tin several times on a damp cloth, seal and cook for 40 minutes in a water bath, with the water at a gentle simmer.

Turn out the prawn parfait, cover with light fish aspic and sprinkle with dill.

Cut the chicken into strips, sprinkle with the pâté salt, pepper and spices and chill for at least 2–3 hours. Mince twice through the finest blade of the mincer. Over ice, first beat in the lightly beaten egg white and then gradually add the sieved panada. Push the mixture through a sieve and beat in the whipped cream a spoonful at a time.

Remove all skin and blood vessels from the chicken livers and cut into small pieces. Dice the mushrooms. Quickly fry the chicken livers and mushrooms separately in hot oil, drain and fold into the forcemeat. Line the buttered mould with roasting film, add the forcemeat and smooth the top. Fold the excess film over the forcemeat, cover the mould and cook, in a water bath, for about 40 minutes, with water at a gentle simmer.

When cool turn out the parfait, carefully

remove the film, cover with Madeira aspic, sprinkle well with parsley and cover again with Madeira aspic. Leave in the refrigerator to set and then arrange over a bed of diced Madeira aspic.

Pheasant Parfait with Foie Gras and Morels

Parfait de faisan au foie gras et morilles

1 kg/2 lb pheasant or other game bones and
trimmings
5 tablespoons oil
1 small carrot, coarsely chopped
1 onion, coarsely chopped
2 litres/3½ pints water
bouquet garni (½ parsley root, white of 1
leek, 1 piece celeriac, 1 bay leaf)
1 teaspoon salt
12 juniper berries, crushed
6 white peppercorns
1½ cloves garlic, crushed
150 g/5 oz trimmed pheasant meat
1 teaspoon pâté salt
grated rind of ½ orange and ½ lemon
1 egg white, lightly beaten
25 g/1 oz flour panada
175 ml/6 fl oz whipped cream
20 g/¾ oz dried morels
150 g/5 oz goose liver, marinated in
2½ tablespoons brandy
butter for greasing
500-ml/17-fl oz pâté mould

Roast the bones and pheasant meat
trimmings in the oil with the vegetables,
adding a little cold water from time to time.
Transfer to a saucepan and add the
remaining water. Bring to the boil, skim and
simmer for 2–3 hours. 45 minutes before the
end of the cooking time add the bouquet
garni, salt, 8 juniper berries, the peppercorns and 1 garlic clove. Strain through
muslin and reduce to about 750 ml/1¼ pints.

Remove any skin and ligaments from the
pheasant and cut into strips. Sprinkle with
the pâté salt, remaining juniper berries and
garlic and the orange and lemon rinds.
Mince twice through the finest blade of the
mincer. Over ice, beat in the lightly beaten
egg white a little at a time. Sieve the chilled
panada and gradually work into the
mixture. Sieve the mixture and beat until
smooth and silky. Work in the whipped
cream a spoonful at a time. Chill the
forcemeat thoroughly after each stage.

Soak the dried morels in water until they
begin to swell, wash thoroughly and soak in
500 ml/17 fl oz fresh water. Then boil in the
steeping water and an equal quantity of
pheasant stock for 25 minutes. Leave to
cool. Remove the morels from the pan and
reduce the liquid until thick. Cut the morels
into large pieces, return to the juice, bring to
the boil and leave to cool.

Cut up the goose liver and work into the
forcemeat with the morels and thick juice.
Grease the mould with butter, line carefully
with roasting film and fill with the
forcemeat. Fold over the excess film and
cover the mould.

Cook in a water bath for about 35
minutes with water at a gentle simmer.
Serve with a rose-hip sauce, delicately
flavoured with Armagnac.

Mushrooms on Spinach

100 ml/4 fl oz cream
200 g/7 oz mushrooms, sliced and braised
salt and white pepper
15 g/½ oz diced onion
20 g/¾ oz butter
250 g/9 oz spinach
nutmeg
2 tablespoons stock
4 individual tart cases
2 tablespoons Hollandaise sauce

Reduce the cream until thick, strain and bring back to the boil with the mushrooms. Season. Glaze the onion in the butter, add the spinach and cook for a few minutes, season with salt, pepper and nutmeg and add the stock. Fill the tart cases first with the spinach and then with the mushrooms. Cover with Hollandaise sauce. Brown under the grill. *Serves 4.*

Stewed Veal with Asparagus

200 ml/7 fl oz cream
4 tablespoons veal velouté
100 g/4 oz veal, braised and diced
75 g/3 oz mushrooms, cooked and diced
salt and white pepper
4 individual tart cases
12 asparagus tips, boiled
4 tablespoons Mornay sauce

Reduce the cream and strain into the velouté. Add the veal and mushrooms, warm through and season with salt and pepper. Fill the tart cases with the mixture, top each with 3 asparagus tips, and cover each with a tablespoon of Mornay sauce. Brown under the grill. *Serves 4.*

Salmon with Fried Egg

4 tablespoons mayonnaise
salt and white pepper
lemon juice
150 g/5 oz salmon fillet, cooked and diced
4 individual tart cases
4 fried eggs
4 heaped teaspoons mackerel caviar

Season the mayonnaise with salt, pepper and lemon juice, stir in the salmon and check seasoning. Fill the tart cases with the mixture, top each with a fried egg and garnish with the caviar. *Serves 4.*

Cheese and Bacon Tarts

20 g/¾ oz streaky bacon, fried, drained and crumbled
25 g/1 oz boiled ham, diced
25 g/1 oz Emmental cheese, diced
50 g/2 oz diced onion glazed in butter
4 individual tart cases
100 ml/4 fl oz cream
1 egg
1 egg yolk
1 tablespoon grated Parmesan cheese
salt
sweet paprika
1 teaspoon finely chopped chives

Mix together the bacon, ham, cheese and onion and arrange in the tart cases. Beat the cream with the remaining ingredients and pour over the ingredients in the tart cases. Bake for about 10 minutes in a hot oven, 220 C, 425 F, gas 7. *Serves 4.*

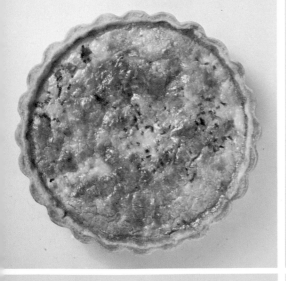

Goose Liver with Apple

8 slices fattened goose liver, weighing about 20 g/¾ oz each
salt and white pepper
flour
1 tablespoon oil
4 individual tart cases
8 slices apple, poached in 250 ml/8 fl oz cream
6 tablespoons Madeira sauce
12 white grapes, peeled and poached
1 thin rasher streaky bacon, cut into fine strips and fried

Season the goose liver with salt and pepper, dip in flour and fry each side in the oil. Line the tart cases with the apple slices, add the goose liver, cover with Madeira sauce and garnish with the grapes and bacon. *Serves 4.*

Mussels in Cream

15 g/½ oz diced onion
15 g/½ oz butter
20 g/¾ oz diced celery
20 g/¾ oz diced carrot
a little white wine
200 ml/7 fl oz cream
250 g/9 oz bottled mussels
1 teaspoon each chopped dill and parsley
salt and white pepper
4 individual tart cases

Glaze the onion in the butter, add the celery and carrot and glaze them also, add the wine and braise for a few minutes. Reduce the cream and strain in the vegetables. Add the mussels and herbs, season and warm through. Transfer the mixture to the tart cases. *Serves 4.*

Artichoke Tarts

65 g/2½ oz artichoke hearts
2 tablespoons béchamel sauce
salt and white pepper
275 g/10 oz veal forcemeat
4 individual tart cases
truffle strips to garnish

Purée the artichokes and warm through in the béchamel sauce. Season with salt and pepper. Pipe a ring of veal forcemeat into the tart cases and fill the centre with the artichoke purée, then cover with the remaining forcemeat. Bake for about 8 minutes in a hot oven, 220 C, 425 F, gas 7. Garnish with strips of truffle. *Serves 4.*

Leek Gratin

8 tablespoons béchamel sauce
2 tablespoons grated Parmesan cheese
1 tablespoon whipped cream
100 g/4 oz leeks, chopped and braised
40 g/1½ oz streaky bacon in fine strips, fried until crisp
salt and white pepper
4 individual tart cases
65 g/2½ oz sliced Emmental cheese

Warm the béchamel sauce, fold in the Parmesan cheese, cream, leek and bacon and season. Line the tart cases with the cheese slices, cover with the leek mixture and brown under the grill. *Serves 4.*

Turbot Medallions

12 slices turbot, each weighing about 15 g/½ oz
6 tablespoons fish velouté
½ teaspoon chopped basil
salt and white pepper
a little white wine
4 individual tart cases
25 g/1 oz each carrot, celeriac and green of leek, shredded and lightly braised in butter and a little fish stock

Poach the turbot in fish stock. Warm the velouté and season with basil, salt, pepper and wine. Line the tart cases with the shredded vegetables, top each with 3 slices turbot and cover with basil sauce. *Serves 4.*

Macaroni with Madeira sauce

150 g/5 oz boiled macaroni
75 g/3 oz boiled ham, diced
100 g/4 oz sliced, braised mushrooms
1 tomato, peeled, deseeded and diced
4 individual tart cases
6 tablespoons Madeira sauce
1 tablespoon grated Emmental cheese

Mix together the macaroni, ham, mushrooms and tomato and transfer the mixture to the tart cases. Cover with the Madeira sauce, sprinkle with cheese and brown under the grill. *Serves 4.*

Chicken Tarts

100 ml/4 fl oz cream
2 tablespoons chicken velouté
100 g/4 oz finely diced cooked chicken
100 g/4 oz finely diced cooked mushrooms
salt and white pepper
175 g/6 oz chicken forcemeat
4 individual tart cases
4 teaspoons Hollandaise sauce

Reduce the cream and strain it into the velouté. Add the chicken and mushrooms and season. Pipe a ring of chicken forcemeat into the tart cases and bake for 8 minutes in a hot oven, 220 C, 425 F, gas 7. Fill the centre with the chicken and mushroom mixture, cover each with 1 teaspoon Hollandaise sauce and brown under the grill. *Serves 4.*

Chanterelle Tarts

15 g/½ oz diced shallots
20 g/¾ oz butter
200 g/7 oz small canned chanterelles
salt and white pepper
400 ml/14 fl oz cream
1 tablespoon chopped parsley
8 quail breasts, fried
reduced quail stock
4 individual tart cases

Glaze the shallots in the butter, add the drained chanterelles, cook for a few minutes and then season. Reduce the cream until thick, strain and add the chanterelles and parsley. Season. Brush the quail breasts with the reduced stock. Fill the tart cases with the chanterelles, and top with the quail breasts. *Serves 4.*

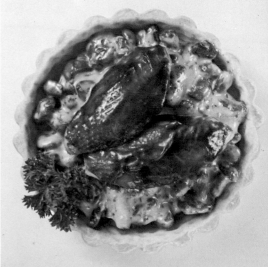

Bouchées, Patties and Vol-au-vents

This is a chapter on puff pastry pies, even though they were not all originally made in this type of pastry. But today they all have something in common. They are baked as pastry cases, that is, blind, and filled with a hot filling before serving. There are also more recent recipes with cold fillings, but puff pastry is in fact much more suitable for hot fillings. It has a better flavour hot than cold, especially if not made entirely with butter. When hot it is flaky and light and entirely suited to its warm filling.

Bouchées, as the name implies, were originally small – almost miniature – pies, which could be eaten at one mouthful. (The French word *bouche* means mouth, i.e. mouthful.) These are still made for special occasions, but have unfortunately been largely replaced by the somewhat larger individual patties. It is much easier to make one patty per person for an hors d'oeuvre or entremet, and the larger size means less chopping for the filling. So the term 'Bouchée' on a menu must not be taken too literally, and you must be prepared to eat them with a fork. Regardless of whether you choose to make bouchées or patties, both are the quickest to make of the pâté family. The pastry cases can be baked well in advance, freeze well (although freezing is not always necessary) and when warmed through are as crisp and tasty as they are when freshly made. You can also buy them ready made from the baker or from a supermarket. But ready-bought cases do not have that special all-butter flavour.

To save time you can also use ready-bought fillings, which are available in a variety of qualities and prices. But of course this would not suit the tastes of a real gourmet.

Patties are small puff pastry pies which are rather more difficult to define, but they too have their history. They are thought to have originated in the medieval courts of Les Baux and Orange in Provence. It is certainly true that the troubadours appreciated good food and in this land of milk and honey with its wealth of vegetables, meat and fish there was every opportunity for culinary discoveries of this kind. The edible patty case used to be made with shortcrust pastry, baked blind and covered with a pastry lid which helped keep the delicate filling warm. But there were also recipes which used potato dough, a dough from groats or pasta dough. These patties are closely related to the filled timbales. Weber's cookery lexicon of 1911 even gives a quick method of making a patty of this type: 'Grate the crust off a small roll, cut across the centre, remove the bread from the inside of the roll and fry in lard.' Today puff pastry patties are often made without a lid. They are baked in a wide range of sizes and shapes, ranging from the small individual patty to a large flan. Round, oval or square, any shape is possible and so of course is any filling, provided it is delicious and warm.

The story of the invention of the vol-au-vent entirely merits the word 'story'. Like many other inventions in the history of cooking, they are attributed to the famous French chef, Carême. He was the first to try making a patty with puff pastry instead of the traditional shortcrust. When his assistant opened the oven he is said to have shouted, 'Maître, il vole au vent' ('Master, it's flying into the air'). For the flat pastry had risen into a large dome. The master chef and the words of his assistant are still commemorated today in the name *vol-au-vent*, for the English equivalent of patty case comes nowhere near the descriptive quality of the French term. Puff pastry is a highly individual piecrust, which takes a long time to prepare and whose use is almost entirely restricted to the unpretentious bouchée or patty. But they can also be a great showpiece on any table and, with the right filling, a great delicacy.

Today, even the filling has become a matter of some debate with nouvelle cuisine turning its back on the rich sauces which complement the ingredients of the filling so well. It is, of course, possible to make new-style fillings for patties, but these omit the béchamel sauce or velouté. Just think of the great classic garnishes (the garnish in this case is the main ingredient bound by the sauce) such as Mirabeau or Financière. We don't have to stick to these classic fillings, but for puff pastry patties only the best is good enough.

A fine lobster filling which can be used in puff pastry patties of any shape or size, from bouchées to vol-au-vents. This delicate pastry is the best for these fine sauces.

1 **First cut out the rings.** Roll the puff pastry to 6–7 mm/⅓ in thick and cut into rings with a sharp 7-cm/2¾-in cutter and a 4.5 cm/1¾-in cutter. Roll out the remaining pastry to about 2 mm/⅛ in thick and cut out bases to match.

2 **Transfer to a baking sheet** moistened with water. Brush the rings with egg yolk, avoiding getting any egg on the sides. Place the side with the egg yolk onto the base and press down gently.

Puff Pastry Patties

Success in baking bouchées, and particularly the larger patties and vol-au-vents, depends primarily on the quality of the puff pastry. It must rise evenly. Ready-bought pastry rarely rises crookedly for, in the first instance it contains a highly stable mixture of fats and secondly it is turned mechanically. This guarantees even rolling with pastry layers of even thickness, and these are essential if it is to rise evenly during baking.

For small quantities you can buy frozen puff pastry in a block (good for rolling) or in ready-rolled rectangular sheets. These are too thin to use for large patties and should be used for nothing larger than small bouchées. But if you stick two sheets of pastry together with egg white or water and roll them quickly together with the rolling pin, this gives pastry of the right thickness. Halve the rectangle of pastry and cut to size with a sharp knife to give square patties. These have the advantages of greater stability for they tend to rise more evenly in baking and they also use all the pastry. If you want a pastry made with butter you will have to make your own, sticking strictly to the basic rules (pages 14–15). In addition, the butter puff pastry must be worked when it is as cool as possible, for butter becomes softer much quicker than vegetable fats, and is therefore slightly more difficult to handle.

When, using puff pastry, whether home-made or frozen, there are a few essential points which must be followed to give good results.

● Never roll out the pastry in one direction only, but where possible roll alternately from left to right and then from top to bottom. If the pastry is rolled in one direction only your round patty will be oval in shape when you take it from the oven.

● Puff pastry, especially when made with all butter, should be as cool as possible for handling. Ideally it should be rolled on a sheet of marble in a cool room. It is a good idea to open a window if the weather is cool or to cover the worktop with a cloth and ice-cubes.

● Always roll the thick rings first. They have to rise most and should be cut out while the pastry is still perfect. Use sharp cutters to prevent squashing the edges of the pastry together.

● Left-over pastry is good enough for the bases. Keep them thin to leave room for a lot of filling. If you use re-rolled leftovers they will not rise so much.

● Go carefully with the egg yolk! When brushing with egg yolk or putting the patties together do not allow any egg yolk to run down the sides. The pastry will stick together where there is any egg yolk and prevent even rising.

● Before baking puff pastry needs to stand for at least 15 minutes in a very cool place. This allows the pastry to settle and makes for more even rising in the oven.

● Damp the baking sheet with water, but do not grease it. The pastry itself contains enough fat to prevent sticking. The water turns to steam in the hot oven and helps the pastry rise. You can increase the steam by splashing half a cup of water into the oven and immediately closing the door. This will increase the amount of steam considerably.

● Puff pastry needs uninterrupted heat if it is to rise. Never open the oven door during the first 5 minutes of baking. This could

3 **Prick with a fork** to prevent any air bubbles forming in the base during baking. Brush the tops of the rings with egg yolk, again making sure not to get any egg yolk down the sides.

4 **Rolls of foil for even rising.** Professional chefs use metal tubes, but aluminium foil folded double or triple is almost as good. They should fit closely to the inside edge of the pastry.

5 **To make the lids** roll any left-over pastry to 2–3 mm/⅛ in thick. Cut out with a plain or fluted 6-cm/2½-in cutter. Brush with egg yolk and lightly mark a diamond pattern in the pastry with a fork for decoration.

make the steam condense and affect the rising of the pastry.

● The oven should be set to at least 220 C, 425 F, gas 7. It is advisable to have the oven hotter still, at 240 C, 475 F, gas 9, for the first 5 minutes. This will make the pastry rise quicker. Then reduce the heat to 220 C, 425 F, gas 7. This will prevent the patties either falling or burning.

● Small pastry lids need a much shorter baking time. So remove them from the oven earlier, unless you are baking them on the same baking sheet as the patties.

Puff pastry cases are in a manner of speaking an edible container for a variety of hot dishes. They rightly deserve their popularity as the round vol-au-vents or bouchées. Less familiar are the variously shaped patties. These can be square, round, oval or baked in a variety of other shapes.

The main thing once more is to obey the basic rules of the game, and then there is no reason why you shouldn't be able to make successful patties in flower or fish shapes.

Puff pastry is best frozen after baking. It is a good idea to make the filling in advance too and to freeze it in suitable sized portions. Then you can make an excellent hors d'oeuvre in a matter of minutes. But baked pastry cases will also keep for a long time out of the fridge, providing they are kept in a dry room and away from strongly flavoured foods. Puff pastry is very sensitive to other flavours, but you can overcome this problem by wrapping tightly in foil.

Lobster Filling

Ragoût d'homard

100 ml/4 fl oz oil
550 g/19 oz lobster and prawn shells
150 g/5 oz diced carrot and onion
4 tablespoons brandy
100 g/4 oz tomato paste
1 litre/1¾ pints fish stock
1 piece each celery and leek
¼ onion
¼ bay leaf
1 sprig thyme
20 g/¾ oz each flour and butter, worked together
a little salt and cayenne pepper
200 g/7 oz cooked lobster meat
100 g/4 oz cooked mushrooms

Heat the oil and sauté the lobster and prawn shells, add the carrot and onion and continue frying. Add the brandy, stir in the tomato paste and add the stock. Add the leek, celery, onion, herbs, salt and cayenne and simmer for 20 minutes. Then strain through a sieve.

Reduce the lobster stock by half, bind with the flour and butter mixture and season to taste. Strain, add the lobster and mushrooms and warm through without allowing to boil. *Serves 4.*

Bouchées à la reine

150 g/5 oz fresh mushrooms
3 tablespoons lemon juice
250 ml/8 fl oz chicken velouté
150 ml/¼ pint cream
salt and white pepper
1 teaspoon Worcestershire sauce
175 g/6 oz cooked veal, diced

Wash and trim the mushrooms. Bring a little water to the boil with 2 tablespoons of the lemon juice and braise the mushrooms for 5 minutes. Drain and cut into quarters.

Bring the chicken velouté to the boil and add the strained, reduced cream. Simmer until the sauce thickens, stirring continuously. Season the sauce with salt, pepper, Worcestershire sauce and the remaining lemon juice. Add the mushrooms and veal, warm through but do not allow to boil. *Serves 4.*

Basic White Sauce

Velouté

20 g/¾ oz finely chopped onion
40 g/1½ oz butter
50 g/2 oz flour
1.5 litres/2¾ pints defatted cold stock
(veal, chicken, fish or vegetable)
500 ml/17 fl oz cream
salt and white pepper

Normally veal stock is used to make the sauce as this goes well with most flavours. But for best results use the original stock, i.e. for a chicken filling use chicken stock.

1 **Make a roux (butter and flour liaison).** Glaze the finely chopped onion in the melted butter. Sprinkle with flour and stir in quickly. Cook for 5 minutes, stirring continuously.

2 **Add the stock.** Add the cold stock a spoonful at a time, whisking in with a balloon whisk. Bring to the boil, scraping the bottom of the pan continuously to prevent lumps forming and the sauce sticking to the pan.

Scampi Patty

Croustade de langoustines

65 g/2½ oz butter
300 g/11 oz shelled scampi or king prawns
25 g/1 oz finely chopped shallots
1 tablespoon flour
500 ml/17 fl oz chicken stock
½ teaspoon salt
a generous pinch each cayenne pepper
and ground ginger
250 ml/8 fl oz cream
1 egg yolk
2 tablespoons chopped dill
8–10 asparagus tips, freshly boiled or
canned
300 g/11 oz puff pastry

Melt the butter, quickly seal the scampi or king prawns, remove from the pan and drain on kitchen paper. Glaze the shallots in the remaining butter. Sprinkle with flour and cook for a few minutes. Dilute with the chicken stock and reduce to about 250 ml/8 fl oz. Season with salt, cayenne and ginger and pass through a sieve. Reduce the cream until thick and also sieve into the sauce. Bind with the egg yolk. Add the dill, scampi and asparagus tips and heat through, without allowing the mixture to boil. Transfer to the warm pastry case. The patty, that is the puff pastry case, requires a base 2 mm/⅛ in thick and 23 cm/9 in. in diameter and a ring 6–8 mm/about ⅓ in thick. The rim will rise perfectly if you roll out the pastry to the right size and then cut out the ring. You will need 500 g/18 oz pastry for this method. You will need 150 g/5 oz pastry for the ring and more or less the same quantity for the base. A second method uses less pastry: roll out 300 g/11 oz puff pastry until 38 cm/15 in in length and 6–8 mm/about ⅓ in thick. Then cut 2 strips 2.5 cm/1 in wide. Press the remaining pastry back into a ball and roll again to make the thin bases. Arrange the thin strips around the base to make a rim and press the ends firmly together. Fold a piece of aluminium foil over several times to give extra strength, shape the 5 cm/2 in wide strip into a ring and line the rim of the patty. Brush the top of the ring with egg yolk and leave to stand for at least 15 minutes. Bake in a hot oven, 220 C, 425 F, gas 7 for 15–20 minutes. After baking loosen the foil immediately from the rim and remove.

3 **Skim the velouté.** Simmer the sauce for 30 minutes. The scum which rises to the surface removes all impurities from the sauce and must be removed continuously until it no longer forms.

4 **Strain the cream into the velouté.** In a separate pan reduce the cream until thick, stirring continuously, and then strain into the velouté through a hair sieve to catch any lumps. Simmer for a further 15 minutes.

5 **Strain the velouté through muslin.** When thick pour the velouté into a basin lined with muslin. Lift the cloth, twisting both ends to allow the velouté to drain through.

Vegetable Filling

Ragoût de légumes

6–8 medium-sized dried morels
250 g/9 oz peas, about 100 g/4 oz when
shelled
salt
100 g/4 oz small young carrots
pinch of sugar
100 ml/4 fl oz cream
250 ml/8 fl oz chicken velouté
freshly ground white pepper
100 g/4 oz asparagus tips, freshly boiled
or canned

Soak the morels in cold water, wash
thoroughly and soak again in fresh water.
Bring the steeping water (without the
morels) to the boil, then add the morels and
simmer gently over a low heat for 20–25
minutes. Shell the peas and cook in a little
salted water for about 15 minutes. Trim the
carrots and cook in water with a little salt
and sugar for about 20 minutes. Drain the
morels and vegetables, catching the stock in
a basin. Reduce 2 tablespoons of the
vegetable stock with the cream to half the
quantity, stirring continuously. Add the
chicken velouté and simmer until the sauce
thickens, stirring continuously. Season with
salt and pepper. Add the morels, peas,
carrots and asparagus and heat through
without allowing to boil. *Serves 4.*

Chicken Filling

Ragoût de poulet

6–8 medium-sized dried morels
250 ml/8 fl oz chicken velouté
scant 150 ml/¼ pint cream
1 teaspoon Worcestershire sauce
2 teaspoons lemon juice
salt and freshly ground white pepper
350 g/12 oz cooked breast of chicken

Soak the morels in cold water, wash
thoroughly and soak again in fresh water
until soft. Bring the steeping water to the
boil, add the morels and braise over a very
low heat for 20–25 minutes. Drain thoroughly and chop. Bring the chicken velouté
to the boil. Reduce the cream until thick,
stirring continuously. Strain into the velouté and simmer until thick, stirring
continuously. Season with Worcestershire
sauce, lemon juice, salt and pepper. Chop
the chicken and add to the sauce with the
morels. Heat through without allowing the
mixture to boil. Garnish with lemon
wedges. *Serves 4.*

This filling is a sort of basic recipe and can
be used with other types of poultry; turkey,
pigeon or guinea-fowl for example. Nor
need you stick to morels: button, field or flat
mushrooms go just as well with poultry.

Sweetbread Filling

Ragoût de ris de veau

400 g/14 oz sweetbreads
white of 1 leek
1 onion, stuck with 2 cloves
1 bay leaf
40 g/1½ oz butter
5–6 tablespoons port
250 ml/8 fl oz reduced veal stock
25 g/1 oz shallots, finely chopped
250 ml/8 fl oz cream
salt and white pepper

Leave the sweetbreads in a bowl under cold
running water until they are completely
white. Remove the skins. Transfer to
lukewarm water, bring to the boil, pour off
the water and transfer to cold water. Bring
to the boil once more in fresh salted water.
Cut up the leek and, when the liquid has
boiled, add to the pan with the onion and
bay leaf. Simmer for 5 minutes. Leave the
sweetbreads to cool in the stock. Remove
any remaining skin and break into small
pieces. Fry quickly in 25 g 1 oz butter over a
high flame. Add 4 tablespoons port,
150 ml/¼ pint veal stock and reduce by half,
stirring continuously. Meanwhile glaze the
shallots in the remaining butter, add the
remaining port and veal stock and simmer
for a while. Add the reduced, strained cream
and reduce until the sauce thickens, stirring
continuously. Season with salt and pepper.

Strain sauce and check seasoning, add the
sweetbreads, warm through once more
without allowing the mixture to boil.
Garnish with parsley. *Serves 4.*

Prawn Nantua Filling

Ragoût d'écrevisses Nantua

150 g/5 oz cooked sweetbreads
75 g/3 oz fresh mushrooms
flour
40 g/1½ oz butter
250 ml/8 fl oz fish velouté
2 tablespoons prawn butter
salt and freshly milled white pepper
2 teaspoons lemon juice
75 g/3 oz veal forcemeat with diced
truffles
150 g/5 oz boiled, shelled prawns
strips of truffle to garnish

Break the sweetbreads into small pieces. Trim and quarter the mushrooms. Dip the sweetbreads and mushrooms in flour and fry quickly in hot butter over a high flame. Drain thoroughly on kitchen paper. Bring the fish velouté to the boil and whisk in the prawn butter. Season with salt, pepper and lemon juice. Take some of the veal forcemeat in the palm of your hand and shape into small balls with a teaspoon. Simmer the balls in water for about 5 minutes. Drain and add to the sauce with sweetbreads, mushrooms and prawns. Heat through without allowing the mixture to boil. Garnish the filled patties with strips of truffle. *Serves 4.*

If preferred the veal forcemeat can be replaced with small balls of lobster forcemeat.

King Prawn Filling

Ragoût de crevettes roses

8 fresh king prawns (about 250 g/9 oz)
salt
½ stem each dill and parsley
75 g/3 oz small mushrooms
about 3 tablespoons lemon juice
250 ml/8 fl oz fish velouté
1 tablespoon prawn butter
freshly ground white pepper
generous pinch cayenne pepper
pinch of sugar
dill to garnish

Wash the king prawns thoroughly under cold water. Bring a little water to the boil with salt and the herbs and braise the prawns for about 10 minutes. Wash the mushrooms. Bring a little water to the boil with 1 tablespoon of the lemon juice and braise the mushrooms in it for about 5 minutes. Remove the prawns from the liquid, shell and cut into pieces. Bring the fish velouté to the boil and whisk in the prawn butter. Season with salt, pepper, cayenne pepper, the remaining lemon juice and sugar. Add the prawns and drained, halved mushrooms and heat through without allowing the mixture to boil. Garnish with dill.

For special occasions add 75 g/3 oz lobster forcemeat in small balls. *Serves 4.*

Scallop Filling

Ragoût de coquilles Saint-Jacques

350 g/12 oz scallops
50 g/2 oz onion, finely chopped
50 g/2 oz butter
1 teaspoon curry powder
3 tablespoons sherry
generous 250 ml/8 fl oz cream
1–2 teaspoons chilli sauce
2 teaspoons mango chutney
salt
flour
1 banana
chopped pistachios and slices of
pimiento to garnish

Scallops without the roe are easiest to find frozen.

Thaw and drain the scallops, if frozen. Glaze the finely chopped onion in 20 g/¾ oz of the butter, stir in the curry, dilute with the sherry and bring to the boil. Add the reduced, strained cream, season with chilli sauce, mango chutney and salt and reduce to a thick sauce, stirring continuously. Meanwhile wipe dry and chop the scallops, dip in flour and fry in 15 g/½ oz butter. Strain the sauce through a sieve, check seasoning, add the scallops and warm through. Peel and slice the banana, coat lightly in flour and quickly brown in the remaining butter. Fold gently into the scallop mixture. Garnish with chopped pistachios and slices of pimiento. *Serves 4.*

Prawn and Dill Filling

Ragoût d'écrevisses à l'aneth

500 g/18 oz asparagus
1.5 litres/2¾ pints water
salt
pinch of sugar
2 tablespoons lemon juice
100 g/4 oz fresh mushrooms
250 ml/8 fl oz fish velouté
freshly ground white pepper
1 tablespoon chopped dill
200 g/7 oz boiled, shelled prawns
dill to garnish

Peel the asparagus from the tips down-wards, cut off the woody stems and tie together with a cotton thread. Bring the water to the boil with the salt, sugar and 1 tablespoon lemon juice and cook the asparagus for 20–30 minutes, depending on thickness. Remove from the pan, drain and cut off 8 tips. (You can use the liquid as the basis for a soup, adding the rest of the asparagus, finely chopped.) Wash the mushrooms. Bring a little water to the boil with half the remaining lemon juice and braise the mushrooms in it for 5 minutes. Drain and halve. Bring the fish velouté to the boil, season with salt, pepper and the rest of the lemon juice, stir in the dill, check seasoning, add the prawns, asparagus and mushrooms and warm through without allowing the mixture to boil. Garnish with dill. *Serves 4.*

Snails in Riesling Sauce

Ragoût d'escargots

3 dozen canned snails
100 g/4 oz fresh mushrooms
25 g/1 oz shallots, finely chopped
15 g/½ oz butter
1 tablespoon brandy
150 ml/¼ pint German Riesling
2 tablespoons snail juice (from the can)
250 ml/8 fl oz plus 1 tablespoon cream
1 clove garlic, finely chopped
salt
1 teaspoon chopped herbs (thyme, basil
and marjoram)
1 teaspoon chopped parsley
freshly ground white pepper
1 egg yolk

Drain the liquid from the snails into a bowl. Wash the mushrooms and cut off the stems. Finely chop the shallots and glaze in the butter. Add the snails and mushroom heads and cook for a few minutes. Add the brandy, bring to the boil and then add the Riesling and 2 tablespoons snail juice. Reduce by half, stirring continuously. Add the reduced, strained cream and reduce to a thick sauce, stirring continuously. Crush the garlic with a little salt. Season the filling with the garlic, herbs, salt and pepper. Beat the egg yolk into the extra tablespoon of cream and use to thicken the sauce. Do not allow the mixture to boil after this point. *Serves 4.*

Open Mushrooms with Sweetbreads

Ragoût de cèpes au ris de veau

25 g/1 oz shallots, finely chopped
40 g/1½ oz butter
1 tablespoon brandy
1 tablespoon Madeira
250 ml/8 fl oz reduced veal stock
150 ml/¼ pint cream
salt and white pepper
250 g/9 oz cooked sweetbreads
flour
200 g/7 oz flap mushrooms
1 teaspoon chopped parsley
slices of truffle to garnish

Glaze the shallots in a little of the butter. Add the brandy and Madeira, then the veal stock and reduce by half, stirring repeatedly. Reduce the cream until thick, strain into the sauce and reduce until thick, stirring continuously. Season with salt and pepper. Meanwhile cut 4 slices of sweet-bread and keep to one side for the garnish, then break the remaining sweetbreads into pieces. Dip in flour. Braise the mushrooms in the remaining butter, add the sweet-breads and cook for a few minutes. Add to the sauce and warm through without allowing the mixture to boil. Sprinkle with parsley and garnish with sliced sweetbread and truffle. *Serves 4.*

Large Vol-au-Vent Case

Vol-au-vent

If you follow the basic rules for puff pastry this is nowhere near as difficult as it looks. To make a 30-cm/12-in diameter vol-au-vent case (inclusive of rim) you will need about 575 g/1¼ lb puff pastry. You should use new pastry for the base, top and rim with the original layers of pastry still intact, but offcuts can be used for the decoration. After working this pastry together into a ball you should, however, leave it to stand for a few minutes. Leave the assembled vol-au-vent case to stand in the refrigerator for 30 minutes before baking in a hot oven, 220 C, 425 F, gas 7.

1 **Line a dome shape** (in this case a bombe mould) with aluminium foil, pressing the foil as smoothly as possible to the mould. Fill lightly with shredded cellophane and fold over the excess foil.

2 **Roll out a sheet of pastry 2 mm/⅛ in thick.** Place the foil dome on the pastry. With a pastry wheel or knife cut around the dome leaving a rim of 5–6 cm/about 2 in wide. Brush with egg yolk.

3 **Cover with the pastry lid.** It should be rolled to 3-mm/⅛-in thick. Fold in half or, simpler still, roll around the rolling pin to prevent tearing. Press gently into shape over the foil dome.

4 **Cut off any excess pastry** to leave a rim of about 5 cm/2 in. Before cutting press the two sheets of pastry firmly together with your thumbs to make sure they stick well together. Smooth out any creases.

5 **Decorate the case.** Roll out the leftover pastry to 1 mm/1/16 in thick and cut into tapering strips with either plain or fluted edges. Brush the top of the case with egg yolk and decorate with the strips. Cover the extreme top with 3 rounds of pastry, cut to varying sizes.

6 **Make the rim.** Roll fresh pastry and cut a long strip about 6 cm/2½ in wide and 2 mm/⅛ in thick, then cut to length. Brush the rim of the case with egg yolk and place the strip around the rim, pressing the ends firmly together.

7 **Trim the rim; it can be either plain or fluted.** You have three layers of pastry one on top of the other here, which can be cut into semi-circles with a cutter or plain with a knife. If preferred you can cut notches around the rim with a sharp knife.

8 **Cut the lid off the case,** holding the case firmly with the other hand. Hold a cutter over the opening; it should be slightly larger than the opening. This will allow you to remove the foil and shredded paper without damaging the pastry case.

Pies: the English Pâtés

England, with its old English pies, is quite a special case. English cooks usually refer to basin pies, either completely encased in pastry or with just a pastry lid, as puddings, and these feature as one of the favourite national dishes. As they are usually cooked in water – especially when made with suet pastry – the term pudding is most appropriate. But there are also a large number of pies which are baked in the oven. Let us concentrate for the moment on pies, which are popular not only in Great Britain but throughout the whole Anglo-Saxon world. To present the full picture we must mention that we possess numerous sweet pie recipes to complement our savoury pies.

According to English belief the pie was invented around the fifteenth century. But many would claim that the Ancient Romans had a hand in their invention when they conquered southern England and left behind many of their eating and cooking habits. It has been proved that these included the art of pie-making. But one fact is certain: over the centuries English cooks and housewives have perfected the art. Recipes have been handed down from generation to generation with continual refinements. English settlers took the tradition with them to the New World and today traditional pies, albeit with slight variations, are as popular in the eastern United States as in the mother-country.

They can be baked in either pie moulds or basins. For many pies the baking tin is lined with pastry, filled with the filling and topped with pastry. Or you can fill the dish with the filling alone and top it with a pastry lid. Sweet and savoury pies are easily distinguished in England, for traditionally the top of a savoury pie is decorated whereas sweet pies come without decoration.

When a visitor to Great Britain takes a stroll around an average supermarket, he will find all kinds of pies on sale. This could give the impression that pies are an important basic foodstuff for us British. This is not the case, of course, but the wide choice available does show the popularity of these dishes. Unlike France, pies are thought of as an everyday dish, as good, wholesome food. In certain respects this is correct. Mass-produced pies such as steak and kidney pies, chicken pies, Cornish pasties, pork pies and veal and ham pies, are eaten as fast-food by millions of working people who have neither the time nor the inclination to cook for themselves. But it would be wrong to assume that today's savoury pies are of poorer quality or less tasty than the penny pies of the nineteenth century or the pies sold at the Pie Corner near Smithfield meat market during the reign of Elizabeth I.

Of course the flavour of mass-produced pies cannot compare with home-made pies. In the Duchy of Cornwall in south-west England Cornish pasties, for example, can vary considerably in flavour despite the fact that they rely upon relatively simple ingredients such as meat, potato, seasoning and stock. But alongside such homely dishes there are also very special pies filled with rump steak and oysters. The basic rules of pie-making still apply for both homely and special pies; a good dish can only be made with the best ingredients.

Whereas in France the taste for pies was almost entirely restricted to the nobility prior to the nineteenth century, in the history of the British Isles puddings and pies were enjoyed by both rich and poor alike. Of course in Britain – as anywhere else – these varied considerably between rich and poor. The rich ate venison, partridge or even lark pies while the poor had to content themselves with far less expensive ingredients. For special court banquets pies were made in the north of England of such a size that they could not be transported by road but were sent south to London by sea. They created monstrosities, like those produced even earlier in France, with pastry which had to be malleable and was therefore inedible. The only consideration was for them to look attractive.

At one time pie moulds or basins were not used in Great Britain. The filling was surrounded with pastry, pressed into shape by hand and then baked on a baking sheet in the oven. But now it is becoming increasingly common for cooked or uncooked fillings, meat or otherwise, to be served in a dish. The dish may be lined with pastry in some cases, but the pie is always completed with a pastry lid before baking or steaming.

A recent innovation is the ovenproof pudding basin which is lined with suet, filled and covered with pastry. These pies are usually steamed like puddings. Although potatoes have been eaten in England since the sixteenth century when Sir Walter Raleigh brought them back from America, they were unpopular at first and of little commercial value. But their popularity increased when it was discovered that they could be used to great advantage in pies.

People began covering pies with a layer of mashed potato and also including it in the filling.

Steak and Kidney Pie

Illustrated on page 154

This is the oldest and best loved of all the English pies. It is equally traditional when made as Steak and Oyster Pie: for this simply replace the kidney with 8–12 oysters.

675 g/1½ lb lean rump steak
200 g/7 oz lamb's kidney
100 ml/4 fl oz port
25 g/1 oz beef dripping
150 g/5 oz diced onion
25 g/1 oz flour
400 ml/14 fl oz beef stock
½ teaspoon dried mixed herbs
1 teaspoon salt
freshly ground white pepper
1 teaspoon sugar
500 g/18 oz suet pastry (page 14)
1 egg yolk for brushing
1-litre/1¾-pint pie dish

Cut the rump steak into 2.5-cm/1-in cubes. Soak the kidneys thoroughly in water, remove the fat and cut into cubes also. Heat the port, flambé it and reduce by half. Heat the beef dripping in a large frying pan, brown the meat and kidney in several batches and remove from the pan. Glaze the onion in the remaining fat, sprinkle with the flour and cook for a few minutes. Return the meat and kidney to the pan and dilute with one-third of the port and stock. Bring to the boil, stirring continuously, add the remaining port and stock, bring back to the boil and add the herbs, salt and pepper. Over a moderate heat cook for 1½–2 hours until the meat is tender. Check seasoning. Bring the sugar to the boil with a little water, stir into the meat and leave to cool.

Roll out the pastry to 3–4 mm/⅛ in thick, cut a strip about 1.5 cm/¾ in wide and arrange around the lip of the dish. Carefully fill the dish with the meat. Brush the pastry rim with egg yolk, top with a pastry lid and press the edges firmly together. Cut off any excess pastry, work into a ball and use for decorations for the pastry lid, which you have previously brushed with egg yolk. Brush the top of the pie again with egg yolk and make an opening to allow the steam to escape.

Bake for about 25 minutes in a hot oven, 220 C, 425 F, gas 7.

Chicken Pie

1 chicken, weighing about 1.5 kg/3¼ lb
75 g/3 oz coarsely diced onion
1 clove
salt
60 g/2½ oz crustless white bread
milk
1 egg
½ teaspoon chopped thyme
½ tablespoon chopped parsley
nutmeg and white pepper
150 g/5 oz sliced pork fat
2 hard-boiled eggs, sliced
300 g/11 oz puff pastry
1 egg yolk for brushing
1-litre/1¾-pint pie dish

Bone the chicken and keep the leg and breast meat and the liver to one side.

With the remaining meat, bones, onion, clove, salt and 1 litre/1¾ pints water, make a stock. Reduce to 300 ml/½ pint and strain.

Thinly slice the bread, soften it in a little milk and squeeze out well. Coarsely chop the chicken leg meat and liver, about 250 g/9 oz, and mix with the bread, egg, herbs, salt, nutmeg and pepper. Slice one of the chicken breasts and use to line the base of the dish. Cover with the pork fat and then cover with half the filling. Arrange one hard-boiled egg over the filling, top with the remaining filling and then with the remaining egg and sliced chicken breast. Cover the dish with puff pastry, glaze with beaten egg yolk and make an opening to allow the steam to escape. After baking pour the hot stock into the pie through a funnel.

Bake for 55–70 minutes in a moderate oven, 180 C, 350 F, gas 4.

Squab Pie

4 pigeon breasts
300 g/11 oz dessert apples
150 g/5 oz thin rashers streaky bacon
juice of ½ lemon
25 g/1 oz caster sugar
1 teaspoon cinnamon
salt and white pepper
75 g/3 oz butter
350 g/12 oz puff pastry
1 egg yolk for brushing
100 ml/4 fl oz cream
1-litre/1¾-pint pie dish

Thinly slice the boned pigeon breasts. Peel, core and thinly slice the apples. Line the dish with bacon rashers, add a layer of apple, sprinkle with lemon juice, sugar and cinnamon. Cover with half the pigeon breasts, season with salt and pepper and dot with butter. Add a second layer of apple and pigeon breast and season. Dot with butter and top with the remaining bacon.

Cover with a pastry lid, decorate with any left-over pastry and make an opening for the steam to escape. Glaze with egg yolk. After 35 minutes baking pour the heated cream into the pie through a funnel. Bake for about 50 minutes in all, 15 minutes in a hot oven, 220 C, 425 F, gas 7, then at 180 C, 350 F, gas 4, until cooked. *Serves 4.*

One of the traditional pies and a favourite lunch dish. The chicken pie can also be eaten cold. There are several variations on this recipe and it is often adapted to use up any left-overs, but of course cannot compare with the original recipe.

Squab Pie, an interesting recipe which combines the smoky flavour of the bacon with pigeon, apple and sugar. It is said to have originated in the Middle Ages when combinations of such ingredients were quite common. Squab is West Country dialect for pigeon.

Eel Pie

1.5 kg/3 lb eel
root vegetables (1 carrot, a little parsley
root, leek and celery)
1½ teaspoons salt
freshly ground pepper
freshly grated nutmeg
flour for dipping
75 g/3 oz butter
100 g/4 oz diced shallots
150 ml/¼ pint dry sherry
1 tablespoon lemon juice
2 tablespoons chopped parsley
500 g/18 oz suet pastry (recipe page 14)
or 400 g/14 oz puff pastry
1 egg yolk for glazing

It is advisable to get your fishmonger to kill the eels for you. To skin them, cut through the skin below the head. Hold the head firmly with one hand and with the other pull off the whole skin at one go. Gut and fillet the eel and cut the fillets into pieces 7–8 cm/about 3 inches in length. Boil the head, fins and skin with the root vegetables in about 1.5 litres/3½ pints water for 20 minutes. Defat the stock, strain into a fresh pan and reduce to 500 ml/17 fl oz.

Season the pieces of eel with a mixture of salt, pepper and a little nutmeg and dip in flour. Heat the butter in a frying pan and fry the eel for a few minutes over a high flame until sealed all over. Remove from the pan and keep to one side. Glaze the shallots in the frying fat. Add the sherry and lemon juice and return the eel to the pan. Cover with the lightly salted stock. Simmer over a gentle heat for 10 to 15 minutes.

Arrange the eel in layers in a pie dish. The square shape of the eel pieces makes a square dish preferable. Cover with the stock and sprinkle with the chopped parsley. Cover the pie with pastry. Brush the top with egg yolk, decorate and make an opening to allow the steam to escape. Even with a pie of this sort it is a good idea to use a funnel to prevent the liquid spilling onto the top.

Bake for 35 to 40 minutes in a moderately hot oven, 200 C, 400 F, gas 6. *Serves 4 to 6.*

Eel Pie Island Pie is the original name of this pie for it originated from a small island of the same name in the Thames. This island has been famous for its fine eel pies since the seventeenth century. Early recipes, like many other English pie recipes, include hard-boiled eggs. For the pie crust either suet or puff pastry can be used. But puff pastry should be kneaded to prevent it rising too much.

Stick a thin strip of pastry around the rim of the pie dish with water or egg white. In this country special pie dishes are used, but any ovenproof dish with a rim to which the pastry will stick can be used.

Cover the pie with pastry. Brush the strip of pastry with egg yolk. Roll up the pastry lid and unroll over the dish. Press the edges firmly together with the handle of a large spoon. Use any left-over pastry for decoration.

Steak and Mushroom Pudding

To make a real English suet pudding you will need a proper pudding basin, a basin with a lip around the top. The cloth is tied into place below this lip. Metal basins are unsuitable because they do not allow the pudding to expand sufficiently during cooking. A successful pudding also requires the steam which comes through the cloth. This recipe for 4 will fill a 1.1-litre/2-pint basin. The same method can be used for other fillings, steak and kidney for example. The ingredients are used uncooked and finally covered with stock.

675 g/1½ lb rump steak
200 g/7 oz fresh mushrooms, peeled and halved
150 g/5 oz diced onion
50 g/2 oz flour
150 ml/¼ pint beef stock
1½ teaspoons salt
½ teaspoon freshly ground pepper
lard for greasing
500 g/18 oz suet pastry

Remove any skin and gristle from the steak and cut into 1.5-cm/¾-in cubes. Mix the diced meat, mushrooms and onion in a bowl. Add the flour and toss to coat. Season the stock well with salt and pepper.

Grease the pudding basin, line with suet pastry and fill with the meat and mushroom mixture. Pour in the stock. Cover with pastry and press the edges firmly together or pinch between finger and thumb. Cover first with greased greaseproof paper and then, as shown in the illustrations, cover tightly with a cloth. Place a wire rack or an inverted plate in the base of a large saucepan, stand the basin on the rack and fill the pan with water to just below the cloth. Simmer gently over an even heat for 4 to 4½ hours, topping up the water as it evaporates. *Serves 4 to 6.*

1 **Roll out the pastry to 4–5 mm/¼-in thick.** Grease the basin lightly with lard and line with pastry leaving a 1 cm/½ in rim of pastry overlapping the top of the basin. Cut off excess pastry. Fill with the uncooked ingredients.

2 **Cover the filled dish with pastry.** First pour the stock over the filling and brush the pastry rim with egg yolk or white. Roll out the remaining pastry into a circle, place over the pudding and seal the edges firmly.

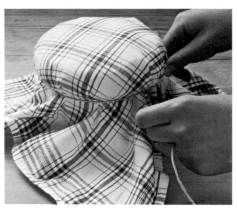

3 **Seal the pudding with a cloth.** Cut a round piece of greaseproof paper to fit the basin, grease and place over the pudding. Cover with the cloth and tie with string below the rim of the basin.

4 **Tie up the cloth.** Knot together the opposite corners on top of the pudding. It is essential that the string remains tight below the rim of the basin and the cloth remains firmly in place throughout the cooking time.

Veal and Ham Pie

500 g/18 oz flour
250 g/9 oz butter
1 teaspoon salt
2–3 tablespoons water
1 egg
butter for greasing
6 hard-boiled eggs
1 egg yolk for brushing
Madeira aspic to finish
1 30-cm/12-in long loaf tin

Veal and ham filling
675 g/1½ lb lean veal, diced
350 g/12 oz boiled ham, diced
2 tablespoons chopped parsley
5 tablespoons brandy
6 tablespoons chicken or beef stock
juice and grated rind of ½ lemon
1 teaspoon dried sage
2 teaspoons salt
freshly ground pepper

Work the butter, salt, water and egg into the flour to give a smooth dough.

Grease the loaf tin with softened butter. Roll about two-thirds of the pastry to 5–6 mm/¼ in thick and cut into a rectangle to fit the tin. Then line the tin with pastry. Mix together the ingredients for the veal and ham filling, add just under half of it to the tin and make a hollow along the centre. Cut the narrower end off the hard-boiled eggs so that they can fit closely together and arrange them in a row along the centre of the pie. Cover with the remaining filling, pressing it down as well as possible. Roll out the remaining pastry, cut to make a lid and cover the pie. Press the edges together with the handle of a wooden spoon. Decorate with cut-outs from the left-over pastry, make an opening to allow the steam to escape, insert a funnel and brush the pie with egg yolk. Bake for about 1¼ hours in a moderate oven, 180 C, 350 F, gas 4.

When cool top up the pie with Madeira aspic.

Serve the pie with a mustard sauce, made from mayonnaise and whipped cream, seasoned with mustard, salt and green pepper. There are many variations on this veal pie. For example, the eggs can be replaced with 8 to 10 bottled black walnuts. *Serves 8 to 10.*

1 **Place the eggs in a row over the filling.** Cut off the narrow ends to ensure that the eggs fit closely together and that every slice cut contains equal amounts of egg white and yolk. Fill the pie with the remaining filling, pressing down as firmly as possible.

2 **Make a wavy edge.** This looks attractive and also makes a good seal. Brush the rim of the pastry with egg yolk and cover with the lid. Cut to leave a 1-cm/½-in rim and press together with the handle of a wooden spoon.

Venison Pasties

500 g/18 oz boneless leg of venison
75 g/3 oz carrots, finely diced
75 g/3 oz celeriac, finely diced
50 g/2 oz onion, finely diced
rind of 1 lemon
1 bay leaf
1 sprig fresh thyme
5 juniper berries, crushed
3 tablespoons peanut oil
200 ml/8 fl oz vintage port
1 teaspoon salt
freshly ground pepper
2 tablespoons redcurrant jelly
675 g/1½ lb shortcrust pastry
1 egg yolk for glazing
40 g/1½ oz butter

Carefully remove all skin and gristle from
the venison and cut into 1-cm/½-in cubes;
make sure that they are no larger than this.
Place in a bowl and mix with the carrot,
celeriac and onion. Add the lemon peel, cut
into a spiral, the bay leaf, thyme and juniper
berries. Cover with the oil and port, cover
the bowl and leave to marinate in the
refrigerator for at least 48 hours.

Pour off most, but not quite all, of the
marinade. Remove the lemon peel, bay leaf,
thyme and juniper berries. Season with salt
and pepper and stir in the redcurrant jelly.
Roll out the pastry to 3–4 mm/¼ in thick
and cut into 8 18-cm/7-in rounds. Place 4 of
the rounds on a baking sheet and cover with
the meat mixture leaving the edges free.
Brush the edges with egg yolk. Cover the
pasties with the remaining rounds of pastry
and press the edges together with the prongs
of a fork. Brush the tops with egg yolk,
decorate with left-over pastry and make an
opening in the centre for the funnel. Bake
for 30 minutes in all, 5 minutes at 200 C,
400 F, gas 6 then at 180 C, 350 F, gas 4 until
cooked. After baking pour the warm butter
into the hot pasties through the funnel
opening. The pasties are best served hot,
possibly with a hot game sauce. *Makes 4.*

In England Venison Pasties are a luxury. They are usually made according to current international
cooking methods and thus are no different from French or German game pies. The pasties on this
page are something of an exception; they are typical home-made pasties, but no less tasty for all that.

160

Cornish Pasties

'The devil is afraid to come to Cornwall, for fear he should be baked into a pasty', so goes an English saying. In fact Cornish people are renowned for their pasties and are not fussy what goes into the filling. But a real Cornish pasty can be a great delicacy. Originally they always contained beef or lamb and potato. Sometimes a carrot or one other vegetable may be added. The pastry is usually a nice crumbly shortcrust, but Cornish Pasties can also be made with puff pastry or even yeast pastry. Recently pasties with mackerel filling have been introduced around the Cornish coast.

250 g/9 oz flour
salt
150 g/5 oz softened butter, diced
1 egg

Filling
150 g/5 oz lean beef or lamb, finely diced
150 g/5 oz potatoes, finely diced
1 shallot, finely chopped
1 teaspoon chopped thyme
4 tablespoons beef stock
salt and freshly ground pepper
1 egg yolk for brushing

Sieve the flour onto the work surface and make a well in the centre. Add the salt, soft diced butter and the egg. Gradually work in the flour and then work all the pastry ingredients together to give a smooth dough. Chill for 15–20 minutes until firm.

Mix together the meat, potato, shallots, thyme and stock and season with salt and plenty of pepper. Cut the pastry into 4 equal pieces and roll each into an 18-cm/7-in circle. Divide the filling over the centre of each round. Brush the edges with egg yolk. Fold the pastry over the filling and press the edges firmly together with a fork. Brush the tops with egg yolk.

Bake for 30–35 minutes in all, first for 10–15 minutes at 200 C, 400 F, gas 6, then at 190 C, 375 F, gas 5 until cooked. *Makes 4.*

They were the 'sandwiches' of the Cornish people, poor man's pie which could weigh as much as 1 kg/2 lb and which they took with them to work. Clever wives put their husband's initials in one corner so that they would be able to recognise their own half-eaten pasty, for they were usually big enough for two meals.

Pirozhki and Kulebyaka

A hearty 'Na zdorovye' to the thousands of different pies which go under the name of *pirozhki* in Mother Russia. A refined 'à votre santé' to the *coulibiac*, the elegant French relation of the original Russian *kulebyaka*. There are a wide variety of Russian pies, both large and small. The smaller varieties – served as an hors d'oeuvre or with soup or cocktails – are called *pirozhki* (*Piroggi* in Poland). The larger pies are called *pirog*, which is Russian simply for tart. Savoury, well-filled flans which are a meal in themselves. These include the great delicacy known as kulebyaka. The filling may be cabbage, which is preferred hot in Russia – or for special occasions fish, such as fresh salmon, and a delicate fish velouté. Sometimes they are filled country-style pasties made with yeast dough, or they may be made with a light brioche dough. They may be typically Russian or classically French with Russian origins.

Kulebyaka is one of the Russian national dishes, whereas the coulibiac is one of the best dishes that classic French cuisine has to offer. It is said to have been invented by the great Auguste Escoffier (1846–1935), based on an original Russian recipe, to honour a visit by the Russian ballet to Monaco. His was a real gourmet recipe which has remained a favourite over the years, made with salmon braised in wine, and the reduced stock mixed with fish velouté, egg yolk and seasoning and spread over the salmon, and left to cool. Escoffier then rolled brioche pastry until very thin to make a layer of fine pancakes. This was covered with a mixture of rice and hard-boiled eggs in a chicken sauce topped with a layer of salmon and further layers of pancake and rice mixture. The whole thing was wrapped in pastry, shaped into a loaf, decorated with pastry and baked to make the coulibiac. It was eaten warm with melted butter poured into the opening in the top. It is a complicated, time-consuming speciality admittedly, but worth the trouble. The taste is incomparably delicious.

But the Russian kulebyaka – which come in a host of variations – are less time-consuming, for they are made without the pancakes. There are no hard and fast rules about kulebyaka, the main thing is that it should contain plenty of salmon.

But there are also kulebyaka with cabbage filling, a special dish in country districts – and they are indeed special for, despite their modest filling and unpretentious method of preparation, they have a delicious flavour.

The many pirozhki which abound in Russia should not be looked on as the poor relation in the pie family. They amply repay closer attention.

Working from the outside inwards: first of all they are generally pasties made of yeast or shortcrust pastry, less frequently with puff pastry. The filling may be meat, fish, rice, egg or cabbage or any other suitable type of stuffing. For example there are Tvorogom *pirozhki* which have a curd filling. Or there are the delicious *chebureki*, fried pasties with a lamb filling. These were originally a Tartar dish, which they took with them from the Crimea to Central Asia. There are also *pyrishki* – bite-sized and delicious. These are usually made with yeast dough, occasionally with puff pastry, but always filled with meat or mushrooms, onion, cabbage or curds – and served with a clear chicken soup. In fact many types of pirozhki are traditionally served with soup, with the filling echoing the main ingredient of the soup. This means that with a fish soup you would only serve pirozhki with a fish filling.

And then there are *pelemeni*, boiled pasties, which are a cross between pasties, stuffed dumplings and ravioli. We cannot leave these without saying a little more about these walnut-sized meat balls wrapped in pastry. According to the original recipe they should be frozen, for they are Siberian pasties and in the Siberian winter freezing is no problem. They are cooked frozen in salted water. After draining they are sprinkled with chopped parsley or dill and eaten with soured cream or warm butter, and in many villages with a dash of vinegar too.

For many generations now Siberian peasant women have made pelemeni. The icy winters ensure that they keep for as long as necessary, so they were made in huge quantities and kept for use as required or to feed unexpected guests. For example, the farmers took a few pelemeni with them when they went out to cut hay for the cattle. And they helped fight off the gnawing hunger produced by the cold.

When a Russian describes someone as being an artist at making pirozhki, this is the highest praise that can be given. For they are almost as fond of pirozhki as they are of vodka. Of course the best thing is to have the two together if it can be arranged. And it can often be arranged, especially with the famous hors d'oeuvre table known as *zakouska* which precedes special celebration menus. This so-called hors d'oeuvre – adapted from Baltic cooking over 200 years ago – is so rich and delicious that many guests overeat and have no appetite left for their meal. This is due to the fact that zakouska is usually served in a separate room and guests – not knowing what is to follow on the dinner menu – happily eat their fill. Together with a variety of vegetable and fish dishes, kulebyaka and pirozhki are an essential feature of any zakouska. And this goes for the vodka too.

Russian Salmon Kulebyaka are the absolute tops among a host of Russian pies. Auguste Escoffier adapted this recipe and made it, under the name Coulibiac, a feature of classic French cuisine.

Russian Salmon Pasty

Kulebyaka

800 g / 1¾ lb salmon fillet, skinned
salt
freshly ground white pepper
3 tablespoons chopped dill
100 g / 4 oz butter
200 g / 7 oz onion, diced
150 g / 5 oz rice
250 ml / 8 fl oz meat stock
nutmeg
200 g / 7 oz cooked mushrooms, chopped
2 hard-boiled eggs
150 ml / ¼ pint fish velouté
1 tablespoon chopped parsley
brioche dough made with 500 g / 18 oz
flour
1 egg yolk mixed with 2 tablespoons
cream for brushing

Remove any bones from the salmon and cut into 1.5-cm/¾-in slices. Sprinkle with 2 teaspoons salt, pepper to taste and 1 tablespoon of dill and chill.

Heat 25 g / 1 oz of the butter, glaze 50 g / 2 oz of the diced onion, then add the rice and glaze it also. Add the meat stock, season with salt and nutmeg and cook in a preheated moderate oven, 180 C, 350 F, gas 4, for about 18 minutes until the rice is tender. Transfer the rice to a baking sheet, cover with buttered greaseproof paper and leave to cool.

Heat another 25 g / 1 oz of the butter, glaze the rest of the diced onion and leave to cool.

Mix the cool rice with this diced onion, mushrooms and eggs, velouté, the parsley, the rest of the dill and butter and check seasoning. Roll half the brioche dough into a rectangle and cover with a quarter of the rice mixture, leaving a 1.5-cm/¾-in rim. Continue with layers of marinated salmon and rice mixture, pressing each layer down gently. You should eventually have 4 alternate layers of rice and 3 of salmon. Roll out the remaining dough into a slightly larger rectangle. Brush the rim of the base with the egg and cream mixture, cover with the lid and press the edges firmly together. Cut off any excess pastry. Cut the left-over pastry into decorations, brush the top of the pie with egg and cream and add the decorations. Cut an opening, insert a funnel and brush the top of the kulebyaka once more with the egg and cream mixture to give a good brown finish after baking.

Bake for about 40–45 minutes in a moderately hot or hot oven, 200–220 C, 400–425 F, gas 6–7. *Serves 8.*

Russian Cabbage Pasty

Kulebyaka

1 kg / 2 lb white cabbage
200 g / 7 oz onions, diced
40 g / 1½ oz butter
250 ml / 8 fl oz water
3 hard-boiled eggs, chopped
3 tablespoons chopped dill
2 tablespoons chopped parsley
1 tablespoon salt
sugar
freshly ground white pepper
shortcrust pastry made with 575 g / 1¼ lb
flour
2 egg yolks for brushing

Quarter the cabbage, cut out the central stem and coarsely chop the leaves. Blanch the cabbage in a pan of boiling salted water for 5 minutes, drain through a sieve and leave to drain thoroughly. Fry the onions in the butter until golden. Add the cabbage, cover with the water and bake in a covered pan in a moderate oven, 180 C, 350 F, gas 4 for 30–40 minutes. When the cabbage is tender remove the lid to allow the liquid to evaporate. Drain the cabbage and leave to cool slightly. Mix in the chopped eggs and herbs and season with salt, sugar and pepper.

Roll out half the dough, fill with the cabbage mixture and cover with a lid, as in the recipe on the left.

Place the kulebyaka on a greased baking sheet and chill for about 15 minutes before baking in a hot oven, 220 C, 425 F, gas 7 for about 30 minutes. *Serves 8.*

If preferred you can fill the kulebyaka with red cabbage, replacing the dill with caraway.

The traditional loaf shape too can be varied, and the pasty made as a pie. The same quantities of pastry and filling are sufficient for a 25-cm/10-in pie plate. Line the plate with two-thirds of the pastry, add the filling and cover with the remaining pastry. Decorate, make an opening for the funnel and bake.

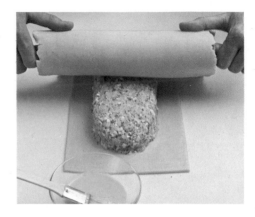

1 **Cut the 3–4 mm/⅛-in thick base** (about half the pastry) into a rectangle. Add the filling to make a loaf shape, leaving a 2.5-cm/1-in rim. Roll out the remaining pastry and, using the rolling pin to help you, transfer it to the pasty.

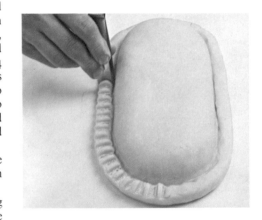

4 **Decorate the rim with a pastry crimper** or the prongs of a fork. Brush the rim with egg yolk so that the raised parts of the rim alone will brown during baking.

6 **Cabbage kulebyaka should come out of the oven brown and crisp.** Chill for at least 15 minutes before cooking to help the pasty keep its shape and prevent the seams splitting during baking. Serve with soured cream.

2 The edges, first brushed with egg yolk, must be firmly sealed. Shape the pastry over the filling and cut off any excess. Press the edges together with your thumbs or the handle of a spoon.

3 Brush the top of the rim with egg yolk and carefully fold over to make a roll of pastry all around the pasty. Make sure that the pastry does not tear. Gently press the pastry rim inwards with the tips of your fingers.

5 Decorate the pasty. Work the left-over pastry into a ball, re-roll and cut out your decorations with a knife or cutter. Arrange the decoration around the funnel opening and press into place. Brush the top with egg yolk.

Curd Tarts

Vatruzhki

300 g/11 oz flour
½ teaspoon baking powder
1 teaspoon salt
75 g/3 oz softened butter
3 eggs
250 ml/8 fl oz soured cream, plus 1
tablespoon
500 g/18 oz low-fat curd cheese
freshly ground pepper
1 teaspoon sugar
1 egg yolk for brushing

Sieve the flour and baking powder into a bowl, make a well in the centre, add ½ teaspoon salt and the soft butter and work in a little of the flour. Then add one egg and 250 ml/8 fl oz soured cream and beat with a wooden spoon to give a smooth dough. Shape into a ball, wrap in greaseproof paper and chill for at least 45 minutes.

To make the curd filling, pass the cheese through a sieve and stir in the remaining soured cream, eggs and salt, the pepper and sugar. Chill for at least 45 minutes.

Roll out the pastry to 2–3 mm/⅛ in thick and then cut it into equal quantities of 11.5–12 cm/4½ in and 10 cm/4 in rounds. Place 1–2 tablespoons of the curd mixture in the centre of each of the larger rounds and cover with a smaller round. Brush the edges with egg yolk. Fold up the edge of the lower round and pinch into small pleats. Brush the tops with egg yolk.

Bake for about 20 minutes in a moderately hot oven, 200 C, 400 F, gas 6. *Serves 6 to 8.*

Pirozhki

Pirozhki

There is no standard size for these small patties just as there is no standard pastry cutter. As a guide you can use the size given in old Russian cookery books which say 'cut to the size of a side-plate'. Pirozkhi can be made with shortcrust (page 12) or yeast pastry (page 15).Vatruzhki pastry with soured cream in the preceding recipe is excellent for pirozkhi. The quantities in the following filling recipes are for about 400–500 g/1 lb pastry. This is rolled to about 3 mm/⅛ in thick and cut into rounds or rectangles. Top with the filling and brush the rims with egg yolk. Fold over and seal firmly so that no filling can escape during baking. Press the edges together with a fork. Brush the tops with egg yolk and, if you are using yeast pastry, leave to rise thoroughly before baking. The baking time will depend on the size of the pirozhki, averaging about 15–25 minutes in a moderately hot oven, 200 C, 400 F, gas 6, depending on the filling.

Flap Mushrooms with Chicken

200 g/7 oz washed mushrooms
25 g/1 oz butter
200 g/7 oz cooked chicken
3 hard-boiled eggs
salt and pepper
chopped parsley

Braise the chopped mushrooms for a few minutes in butter. Mix with the diced chicken and egg and season.

Pork and Beetroot

250 g/9 oz minced pork
40 g/1½ oz diced shallots
40 g/1½ oz butter
100 g/4 oz boiled rice
150 g/5 oz cooked, diced beetroot
1 tablespoon chopped parsley
salt, pepper and caraway
250 ml/8 fl oz soured cream

Fry the minced pork and shallots in the hot butter, breaking up the meat with a fork. Mix with the rice, diced beetroot and parsley. Season with salt, pepper and caraway. Top the filling of each pirozhki with a teaspoon of soured cream.

Sauerkraut Filling

75 g/3 oz diced onion
60 g/2½ oz pork dripping
400 g/14 oz sauerkraut
salt
100 ml/4 fl oz white wine
1 tablespoon chopped dill
4 hard-boiled eggs, chopped

Glaze the onion in the hot dripping. Add the sauerkraut and braise for 20 minutes. Add the salt and wine, and braise for a further 10 minutes. Stir in the dill and chopped egg.

Herb Curds

250 g/9 oz curd cheese
1 egg
1 tablespoon soured cream
salt
3 tablespoons chopped herbs (parsley, dill, lovage, thyme)

Stir the curd cheese with the egg, cream, salt and chopped herbs.

Smoked Salmon Filling

50 g/2 oz diced onion
250 g/9 oz smoked salmon, cut into strips
1 tablespoon finely chopped dill
pepper

Mix the diced onion with the salmon, dill and pepper. Add salt only if necessary.

Ham and Rice Filling

50 g/2 oz butter
50 g/2 oz finely diced onion
1 clove garlic, crushed
250 g/9 oz boiled ham, diced
salt, pepper and chopped parsley
100 g/4 oz boiled rice

Heat the butter and glaze the onion and garlic in it. Add the ham and fry for a few minutes. Add salt, pepper and parsley and stir in the rice.

Lamb Filling

60 g/2½ oz finely diced onion
60 g/2½ oz chopped mushrooms
40 g/1½ oz butter
250 g/9 oz minced raw lamb
salt, pepper, garlic salt
2 hard-boiled eggs, chopped

Quickly glaze the onion and mushrooms in hot butter, stir into the minced lamb and season. Stir in the chopped eggs.

Pâtés from Around the World

Can anyone be familiar with all the pâtés that exist around the world? Can anyone know all their names? It is all but impossible to make even an approximate list. Regrettably, many will have to go unmentioned here, for our subject is an infinitely wide area in the world of cooking. Pâtés are found in South America and Finland, in China and Italy and in Germany too. All we can do is offer a brief look at some of these, starting with those which are baked or fried, and then going on to look at ones which are cooked in a variety of other ways, by steaming or cooking in soup, for they are all a form of pâté.

It is not known whether the Spanish conquistadors took the delicious pies known as *empanadas* with them to Latin America or whether they were a traditional Indian dish. But it is certain that these explorers succeeded in passing on some of their eating habits to the indigenous native population to produce a happy combination of native and Spanish cooking. There is no doubt about the Spanish origin of the Galician *empanada*, a local speciality whose wonderful flavour long ago conquered the hearts of gourmets throughout the length and breadth of Spain. In Santiago de Compostela they are made as both large and individual pâtés. The golden-brown piecrust hides a delicious meat or fish filling. Sometimes bread dough is used for the piecrust and sometimes *hojaldre*, a puff pastry made with pork lard. They are almost always cooked in a paella pan and are usually eaten cold rather than hot. Because the people of Santiago love their pies above all else they have even erected a monument to them in the middle of the cathedral which is dedicated to James the Apostle, the patron saint of Spain. Here a stylite is portrayed biting greedily into a typical Santiago pie (see photograph). In La Coruna, a coastal town on the northwest tip of Spain, live as every expert knows, the famous seafood empanada bakers. The sea provides an abundance of ingredients fresh from the net, fish and shellfish which other Europeans can only dream about. The empanadas eaten in Chile, Uruguay and Argentina do not vary greatly from the Spanish empanadas. They are among the most delicious speciality dishes of these countries and are usually served as an hors d'oeuvre, but are also popular as an entremets

Home cooking of the best possible kind is an empanada from Galicia. There the freshest fruits of sea and land are baked in pastry. This is a prime example of the many national pâtés which are often promoted to join the ranks of international cuisine.

or as a snack to be taken on journeys or picnics. They are usually filled with meat, mixed with raisins, olives, onion and vegetables. And they are often highly seasoned, with cayenne pepper for example, or chopped chillis.

In Finland too they know how to bake an excellent meat filling in pastry and these go by the almost unpronounceable name of *Lihamurekepiiras*. To suit the country's cold climate these are filling pies, with a lot of soured cream in the pastry. They are a close relative of the Russian pirozhki, and are usually served with more soured cream and cranberry sauce. But there are also a wide range of country-style pâtés which are baked for particular celebrations once a year, like the *Pâté de Paques du Berry*, a French Easter pâté with eggs baked into it, or the *Torta pasqualina*, an Italian Easter favourite.

Rissoles are usually made with 10-cm/4-in rounds of either shortcrust or brioche pastry filled with a *salpikon*, a fine stew, or less often with a forcemeat of some kind. And then comes the stage which gives rissoles their own individual character – they are deep fried in hot oil.

With pancake rolls, which can be enjoyed in Chinese restaurants throughout the world, we come to a close relative of the rissole. Here a dough, which may sound rather complicated at first, is made into small, thin pancakes, filled with all kinds of meat and vegetables, rolled and fried in fat. Experts claim that the best pancake rolls are made in Fukien on the south coast of China, and here too the best soya sauce is prepared, the essential accompaniment to pancake rolls. The wide variety of *dim sums*, steamed envelopes of pastry, which are made throughout the country, make China a promised land for many who love fine food. There is nothing unusual in a Chinese restaurant offering 50 different sorts of these savoury titbits on the same menu. This is a totally new experience for Europeans, but something which the Chinese take for granted.

But if you ask a Swabian or an Italian what they would prefer, it would certainly not be dim sums. Their favourite pâté-type dish would be *maultaschen*, triangles of pasta dough, filled with minced meat or ham, onion, spinach and seasoning which are boiled in stock. For the Swabians at least. Italians on the other hand, especially in Piedmont, swear by the ravioli, filled envelopes of dough which are eaten with tomato sauce and grated Parmesan cheese.

Empanadas, the Spanish pie

Empanadas are typical of many other types of national pâtés. Wherever they are made they have been adapted to suit the country and its local products. In northern Spain where the empanada originated recipes vary greatly from one region to another, or at

It is not only in their external appearance that empanadas are indistinguishable. Whether filled with potatoes, like these Colombian empanadas, or with best beef, the hotness of the chillies makes it difficult to distinguish.

least the fillings vary greatly. Some contain pork or vegetables or, as in the case of the *empanada Gallega*, chicken, onion and peppers. Or there are the fish and shellfish fillings found all along the Atlantic coast. They are usually baked to serve 4 to 6 and are a popular lunch or snack dish. But in South America empanadas are even more popular than in the mother country. The former Spanish colonies have introduced new varieties with new fillings and in new shapes. With a multitude of new products, vegetables and seasonings, each country with a Spanish population has produced its own specialities. Sometimes with extremely simple fillings such as vegetables or left-overs. But there are also extremely rich fillings, in Argentina for example, where best beef is seasoned with the best spices. *Empanada de horno* is one such speciality, whose filling includes hard-boiled eggs and olives.

Calamary Empanada

4 tablespoons olive oil
100 g/4 oz diced onion
2 cloves garlic, crushed
2 green or red peppers
3 peeled tomatoes
2 chilli pods
2 squid, weighing about 400 g/14 oz
250 ml/8 fl oz red Rioja wine
250 ml/8 fl oz fish stock or water
1–2 teaspoons salt
2 teaspoons sweet paprika
a little fresh rosemary, thyme and sage
500 g/18 oz mussels, in the shell
225 g/8 oz peeled fresh prawns
yeast dough made from 500 g/18 oz flour
2–3 sliced tomatoes
1 egg yolk for brushing

Heat the oil in a frying pan and glaze the onion and garlic. Cut the peppers into strips and add to the pan with the peeled tomatoes. Carefully remove the seeds from the chillis and finely chop them. Add to the vegetables and cook for about 10 minutes.

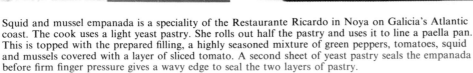
Squid and mussel empanada is a speciality of the Restaurante Ricardo in Noya on Galicia's Atlantic coast. The cook uses a light yeast pastry. She rolls out half the pastry and uses it to line a paella pan. This is topped with the prepared filling, a highly seasoned mixture of green peppers, tomatoes, squid and mussels covered with a layer of sliced tomato. A second sheet of yeast pastry seals the empanada before firm finger pressure gives a wavy edge to seal the two layers of pastry.

The cook believes, rightly enough, that sophisticated decoration would do nothing to improve the flavour and sticks to a simple criss-cross pattern made from thin rolls of pastry.

Clean the squid, removing the ink sack without damaging it, and take out the cuttle bone (you will use only the top of the head with the tentacles and tail which are cut into rings). Add the squid to the vegetables and then the red wine and stock. Season with salt, paprika and herbs. Braise for about 20 minutes over a moderate heat, adding more stock if necessary. Scrub the mussels thoroughly and boil for 5 minutes in salted water, then remove the shells. Stir into the filling with the prawns. Line the pan with pastry, add the filling, cover with sliced tomato and sprinkle with salt. Cover with pastry, decorate, glaze with egg yolk and leave to stand for 10 minutes before baking for 25–30 minutes in a moderately hot oven, 200 C, 400 F, gas 6. *Serves 6.*

Spanakópitta

300 g/11 oz flour
150 g/5 oz wholemeal flour
25 g/1 oz fresh yeast
200 ml/7 fl oz lukewarm water
1 egg
150 ml/$\frac{1}{4}$ pint olive oil
salt
1 kg/2 lb spinach
2 finely diced onions
1 clove garlic, crushed
a little pepper and nutmeg
2 sprigs dill, chopped
300 g/11 oz Feta cheese
1 egg yolk for brushing
1 30-cm/12-in round flan tin

Mix the flour and wholemeal flour in a bowl and make a well. Crumble the yeast into the well and dilute with the lukewarm water. Leave to stand for 10 minutes, then add the egg, 3 tablespoons olive oil and 1 teaspoon salt and work all the ingredients together to give a fine, uniform dough.

Wash the spinach, shake dry and chop, but not too finely. Heat the remaining oil in a large saucepan. Glaze the diced onions. Add the crushed garlic and spinach and braise for a few minutes until the spinach wilts. Salt lightly, for the cheese can sometimes be extremely salty, and season with pepper and nutmeg. Stir in the dill and crumbled Feta cheese.

Roll out two-thirds of the pastry, line the tin leaving a rim of about 1 cm/$\frac{1}{2}$ in. Prick the base several times with a fork and fill with the cooled spinach mixture. Brush the pastry rim with egg, roll out the remaining pastry and use to cover the pie. Pinch the edges firmly together and cut off any excess pastry. Brush the top with egg and use any left-over pastry for decoration. Make an opening in the centre to allow the steam to escape. Leave to rise for 15–20 minutes, then bake in a moderately hot oven, 200 C, 400 F, gas 6 for 40–45 minutes. *Serves 6.*

Spanakópitta is a vegetarian pâté from Greece, filled with spinach and sheep's milk cheese, highly seasoned with fresh dill. An excellent variation can be made with shortcrust pastry. But to fully appreciate the hearty flavour, use a yeast dough or, as in the recipe above, a wholemeal flour yeast dough. The Greeks use the same filling to make small pies which look just like the Indian samosa (page 173), and are also made by folding strips of pastry. These are called *spanakotrigona* and the pastry is similar to our pasta dough, made without eggs and rolled almost as thin as pasta dough. The pastry for Chinese pancake rolls is very similar and could be used instead. They are baked in the oven until brown and crisp.

Rissoles

These are an ideal snack for any sort of occasion, but are also a traditional starter. It is not certain how far back their history can be traced, but in French the term *rissoler*, to cook until brown (in fat) has been around for a long time. It is also associated with the French word *roussâtre* (reddish), which is fairly appropriate for, when cooked, rissoles do in fact have a reddish tint to them. The common factor among all rissoles is that they are deep fried, and they are usually similar in shape. They are made from rounds of pastry, folded over to a half-moon shape before coating with egg and breadcrumbs. There are fewer standard recipes for the fillings, for they can be varied in any number of ways, but it should be strong enough in flavour not to be masked by the fried pastry. They can be made with puff pastry but a shortcrust usually gives better results. Roll the pastry to about 3–4 mm/⅛ in thick and cut into 10–12-cm/4–4½-in rounds. Place 2–3 tablespoons of filling in the centre of each, brush the edges with egg yolk and fold over. Press the edges firmly together, coat in breadcrumbs and deep fry.

Curry Filling

2 tablespoons oil
50 g/2 oz diced onion
1 clove garlic, crushed
250 g/9 oz diced lamb
½ teaspoon salt
2 teaspoons curry powder
1 teaspoon tomato paste
½ bay leaf
100 ml/4 fl oz stock
1 cooking apple, diced

Heat the oil and glaze the diced onion. Add the garlic, lamb, salt, curry powder, tomato paste and bay leaf and fry, stirring from time to time. Add the stock and diced apple and cook for about 10 minutes. Leave to cool and use to fill the rissoles.

Samosa

250 g/9 oz flour
4 tablespoons oil
salt
scant 150 ml/¼ pint warm water
2 onions, finely chopped
2 teaspoons grated fresh ginger
1 clove garlic, crushed
1 fresh chilli, finely chopped
½ teaspoon crushed coriander
2 teaspoons curry powder
1 tablespoon tomato paste
1 tablespoon lemon juice
250 g/9 oz lean lamb, very finely chopped
scant 150 ml/¼ pint veal or beef stock
1 tablespoon coarsely chopped mint
oil for deep frying

To make the pastry, sieve the flour onto the worktop and make a well in the centre. Add 2 tablespoons of the oil and 1 teaspoon salt with half the water. Working round the mixture from the centre outwards, mix the ingredients together by hand. Gradually work in the remaining water, adding a little more if necessary. As with all water-based pastries the type of flour will determine the exact quantity of water needed. Knead the dough for about 10 minutes until completely uniform with the consistency of pasta dough. Cover with film and leave to stand for 1–2 hours.

Heat the remaining oil in a pan and glaze the onions. Add the ginger, garlic and chilli and cook for a few minutes before adding the coriander, curry powder, ¾ teaspoon salt, the tomato paste and lemon juice, and finally the very finely chopped lamb. Fry over a hot flame, stirring continuously. Add the stock, cover the pan and simmer over a low heat until all the liquid has evaporated. Sprinkle with the coarsely chopped fresh mint and leave to cool. Roll out the pastry and cut into strips, fill and deep fry the samosas in oil at 180°C/356°F.

Filling for *singaras*, a vegetarian variation:

Peel and dice 2 boiled potatoes. Mix with 2 tablespoons diced cooked carrot and season with 1 tablespoon lime juice, a finely chopped chilli pod, 2 teaspoons curry powder and a little cumin and salt.

Like all deep-fried pies, samosas, pies from India, are best served hot. Singaras are a vegetarian variation, which are made with a spicy potato filling. Both can be made with a ready-bought strudel or Chinese pancake pastry.

Fill the strips of pastry. Roll out the pastry thinly as for pasta and cut into strips 6 × 20 cm/2½ × 8 in. Place 1 tablespoon of cold filling at one end.

Fold the end of the pastry diagonally across the filling. Then fold over the other end and continue folding the pastry diagonally until you have used the whole strip. Stick the end in place with egg white.

173

Dim Sums, pies from China

Every day these small individual pâtés are eaten in their millions, and like most of the dishes of great Chinese cooking, they are little culinary masterpieces. They are filled envelopes of pastry which are steamed or deep-fried in fat like pancake rolls. They come originally from the old traditional cooking of Canton and the name can be translated either as 'what the heart desires' or as 'stopgap'. Both are appropriate. There are hundreds of recipes for dim sums and the wealth of Chinese cooking makes for a wide variety of fillings. There are also a number of different pastries. Dim sums are often served between the separate courses of a Chinese meal, but can also be served in many variations as a meal in themselves, usually served for the lunch diner in a hurry nowadays. Waitresses push trollies laden with steaming bamboo baskets from table to table. They open the lids one after another patiently listing the separate ingredients of each. These usually range from simple Chinese cabbage with pork to the refined mixture of mushrooms and prawns. But they are also sold on the streets by itinerant cooks who pile their three-wheeler bikes with large bamboo baskets. Each basket holds a different kind of dim sum with traditional fillings. Most types can be made at home, nor are they very difficult. Before steaming they will keep for 1–2 days in the refrigerator and can even be deep-frozen. The Chinese housewife can often buy the pastry ready-made, so that it only requires to be filled and cooked. For steaming you can't do any better than the traditional bamboo baskets. They are inserted into a large pan with water below the level of the internal sieve. The dim sums should not stand in water. Several baskets, covered at the top with a lid, can be cooked together. This is similar to the layered method of cooking which is used in modern pressure cookers. Of course it is hardly doing them justice to describe such peaks of Chinese cooking in the usual telegrammatic style of the recipe. But anyone who is used to handling food and possibly has a little experience in Far Eastern cooking, will know exactly how to proceed with the recipes for fillings which are given opposite.

A specialist in pancake roll pastry. The housewife doesn't need to concern herself with the time-consuming making of these rounds of pastry. But it is no easy matter even to cook them. It is a dough of flour, water and salt with a very low fat content, which may be lard or oil. The fat helps keep the pastry malleable so that it folds easily. The pastry is dipped into a frying pan for a few seconds and then removed, leaving behind an extremely thin layer of pastry. After a minute at the most it is cooked and removed from the pan with the speed and dexterity of a true artist, using only the fingers.

Siew Mai For about 20 pancakes make a dough using 100 g/4 oz flour, 1 egg and a pinch of salt. To make the filling scald 15 g/½ oz tongu mushrooms with boiling water, leave to steep for 30 minutes and then finely chop. Mix with 150 g/5 oz uncooked, shelled prawns, 75 g/3 oz pork fillet and 50 g/2 oz pork fat, all finely chopped. Add ½ tablespoon cornflour, and salt, pepper, sugar, monosodium glutamate and a little sesame oil. Cut the dough into thin 6-cm/2½-in squares, cover with the filling and squeeze together to leave an opening at the top. Steam for 8 minutes.

Fan Goa Pau These dim sums are made in the same way as Siew Mai, but have a different filling. Soak 2 tongu mushrooms, drain and chop the heads. Finely chop 40 g/1½ oz pork fillet, 25 g/1 oz water chestnuts (canned) and 75 g/3 oz uncooked prawns. Shred 75 g/3 oz Chinese cabbage and blanch. Mix these ingredients with 1 tablespoon chopped spring onion, ½ tablespoon chopped coriander leaves or parsley, ½ tablespoon cornflour, and salt, pepper, sugar, monosodium glutamate and a little sesame oil.

A selection of dim sums made by Mr. Li. Each type has its own shape, its own special pastry and its own particular filling. Mr Li is the chef at the Mayflower Restaurant on Singapore's Shenton Way and is known throughout the city for the best dim sums with the most varied fillings. At his restaurant you can choose between traditional recipes and refined new creations. The delicious fillings come wrapped either in a thin egg-pancake dough, delicate yeast pastry or a pastry made with lard and cornflour, which when steamed looks like frosted glass. As with many Western terrines or galantines, the wrapping is sometimes completely omitted even here, and the filling cooked in small balls.

Har Kau To make about 20 dim sums, mix 100 g/4 oz Chinese wheat flour with 25 g/1 oz cornflour, stir in 100 ml/4 fl oz boiling water, leave to cool slightly and then work in 1 teaspoon lard. For the filling finely chop 350 g/12 oz uncooked prawns, 25 g/1 oz pork fat and 100 g/4 oz bamboo shoots and mix with ½ teaspoon cornflour, ½ teaspoon sesame oil, and salt, pepper, sugar and monosodium glutamate. Use the mixture to fill thin 8-cm/3-in rounds of dough and press together at the top. Sprinkle with a little sesame oil and steam for 5 minutes.

Glossary and Ingredients List

A

Abatis
French term for poultry giblets.

Abats
general French term for offal.

Agnolotti
egg-pasta ravioli with meat and vegetable filling, served with meat sauce, butter, grated cheese. From Piedmont.

Alsace timbale
line moulds with goose liver purée, filling of goose liver, smoked tongue, mushrooms and truffles in Madeira sauce. Top with purée. Serve with Madeira sauce.

Armagnac
well-known brandy from south-west France. Contains at least 38 per cent alcohol and matures in oak casks. Its flavour is the ideal complement for meat pâtés.

Aromatics
seasonings such as roots, herbs or spices.

Artichoke
thistle-like vegetable from southern Europe.

Aspic
term for a meat or fish jelly.

Aspic jelly
clarified liquid from various basic ingredients allowed to set. Aspic jelly preserves, keeps forcemeat fresh longer, brings out flavour. Boil the carcass or bones of meat used for pâté with water and seasoning. It jellies easier if you include bones that contain a lot of gelatine – for example veal, or by adding gelatine. Aspic jelly can be used for coating or served diced with pâté. Usually flavoured with wine: Madeira, port, sherry, Tokai, Muscatel or strongly-flavoured white wine.

Aspic powder
ground gelatine, sometimes sold mixed with herbs.

Aubergine
(eggplant, *melanzane*), with lamb and herbs makes a good filling for hot pies.

B

Ballotines
small galantines of stuffed poultry legs which retain the original shape, poached in stock.

Beans
almost all varieties can be used for pâtés or included in pie fillings.

Béchamel sauce   *page 36*
white sauce made from flour, butter, milk or veal stock, and possibly herbs. A basic sauce, which can also be used to bind pâtés.

Beef marrow pâtés
line small brioche tins with shortcrust. Filling of moistened bread rolls, ground almonds, egg, egg yolk, beef marrow, salt, pepper, cayenne pepper. Bake and serve hot.

Beef and potato pie
English beef and potato pie. A precooked mixture of meat, potato, onion, stock and flour, placed in small oval dishes, covered with gravy, topped with mashed potato and browned under the grill.

Bénédictine
French herb liqueur.

Bindings for pâtés   *page 18*

Bouchées
puff pastry patties, usually baked blind before filling with fine forcemeat. Generally small enough to be eaten in one bite. Still feature in fine cuisine today but have been largely replaced by bigger vol-au-vents. Served as an hors d'oeuvre or entremets.

Bouchées à l'américaine
American-style patties. Served in puff pastry with a filling of lobster à l'américaine.

Bouchées à la bouquetière
puff pastry patties with mixed vegetable filling of carrots, turnip, peas, cauliflower, in a hollandaise sauce or fine cream sauce.

Bouchées à la chasseur
filling of game, mushrooms and truffles in Madeira sauce.

Bouchées à la dieppoise
puff pastry patties with a filling of prawns and mussels in white wine sauce.

Bouchées à la financière
puff pastry cases filled with cocks' combs, chicken kidney, sweetbreads, mushrooms, chicken meat balls, olives and sliced truffles in sauce financière.

Bouchées à la reine
a filling of mushrooms, chicken velouté with cream, diced cooked veal, Worcester sauce, lemon juice and seasoning in round puff pastry patties.

Bouchées Montgelas
puff pastry patties with a filling of foie gras, mushrooms, smoked tongue and truffles in Madeira sauce.

Bouchées Nantua
puff pastry patties with a filling of prawns, mushrooms and truffles in Nantua sauce.

Bouquet garni   *page 42*
bunch of herbs and spices, e.g. parsley, chervil, chives, tarragon, thyme, bay leaf, marjoram and onion, often tied in muslin. Ingredients are interchangeable. Used to season soups, sauces and stocks.

Broccoli
green cabbage vegetable, best suited for vegetable pâtés.

Burgundian lark pie
classic French pie, also named after chefs Rousette or Racouchot. Instead of the rare lark, the French now use farm-raised quail. The dish is lined with pastry, covered with thin rashers of pork fat, topped with 12 larks or 4 quail surrounded by forcemeat. The forcemeat is made from the gizzards, livers, lark innards, pork, pork fat, boiled ham, truffles, seasoning, with Madeira marinade (from the birds) lightly cooked in butter in a frying pan. The birds are covered with a layer of forcemeat and topped with a pastry lid.

C

Calf's brain pie
filling of calf's brains, mushrooms, butter, onion, cream, salt, pepper, lemon peel. Puff pastry cut into round, filled, folded over in half-moon, or made into long pie.

Carolines
choux pastry éclairs filled with foie gras.

Carrot mousse   *page 134*
carrots boiled until soft and puréed with chicken velouté.

Carrots
a popular vegetable for pâté fillings or as a mousse.

Cauliflower
used for vegetable pâtés or as ingredient for pie fillings.

Champagne rabbit pie
jelly from rabbit bones, calf's foot, onion, carrot. Cut good meat into pieces, marinate 48 hours in red Bouzy champagne. Mix rabbit meat with lean forcemeat. Flavour with champagne brandy. Line dish with pastry, add stuffing and rabbit pieces. Cover with pastry, bake. Top up with jelly when cool.

Champignons
(button mushrooms), the most popular mushrooms for pâtés and terrines.

Chanterelle tarts   *page 143*

Chanterelle terrine   *page 90*
terrine de chanterelles, fine veal forcemeat with chanterelles.

Chaudfroid sauce   *page 98*
the term chaudfroid applies generally to any dish which is prepared warm but eaten cold (*chaud* = warm, *froid* = cold).

Chebureki   *page 163*
fried pasties with lamb filling from Tartar cookery.

Cheese and onion pasties
small, English cheese and onion pies in tartlet
form made with cheese puff pastry. Filling is
made of cheese, onion, milk, bound with
cornflour and covered with puff pastry.

Cheese pirozhki
filling from eggs, butter, salt, pepper, grated
cheese. Cut rounds of shortcrust pastry, add
filling, fold over into half-moons. Brush with
egg yolk and bake.

Chicken liver mousse *page 132*
mousse de foies de volaille.

Chicken pie *page 156*

Citrus fruit
mainly orange and lemon (juice and peel)
used to season forcemeats and stocks. Lime
goes well with game meat and birds.

Cocks' combs
specially used for fillings (à la financière), for
bouchées or puff pastry patties.

Cognac
French brandy from Charente. Indispensable
for flavouring stocks or pâtés.

Confit d'oie *page 101*
speciality of south-west France where geese
are reared for foie gras, but popular
throughout France. Can also be made with
duck or turkey.

Corail
lobster roe, used to colour fish pâtés.

Cornish pasties *page 161*

Cou d'oie farci *page 126*
stuffed neck of goose.

Coulibiac
Escoffier's grand cuisine adaptation of the
large Russian pie filled with salmon, a rice
mixture and pancakes.

Country-style terrine
filling: meat, poultry or offal stuffings with
diced fat. Also known as Pâté de Campagne,
Terrine du Chef, Pâté de la Maison. Wrapped
in pork fat.

Cream mussel tarts *page 142*
in an onion-celery-carrot mixture.

Croustade à la financière
puff pastry pie with a filling of goose liver
poached in butter, cocks' combs, chicken
kidneys, truffles, finely-chopped and seasoned
with salt and pepper, all in a basic brown
sauce flavoured with brandy.

Croustade de langoustines *page 149*
a scampi tart.

Croûtes
a ready-made pie. Thick slices of white bread,
hollowed out, fried in butter and then filled.

Curd puff pastry
can be used instead of traditional puff pastry,
but has slightly sour taste. 250 g/9 oz flour, 1
teaspoon baking powder, 250 g/9 oz dried
curds, 250 g/9 oz finely chopped cold butter,
salt. Work together, chill and use as for puff.

D

Darioles gallic style
small pâtés made in moulds lined with aspic
jelly. Filling of cocks' combs, chicken kidneys,
mushrooms and truffles in mayonnaise, put
into the mould, covered in aspic jelly and
turned out.

Demiglace *page 93*
highly-flavoured brown sauce, reduced and
flavoured with Madeira. A basic sauce, a
gelatinous stock.

Dim sum *page 174*
Chinese titbits. Various fillings are wrapped in
pasta-like pastry and steamed in bamboo
baskets. Can also be boiled, braised or
steamed in stock. A teatime or cocktail dish.
Also served as a lunch dish in special
restaurants. Numerous variations.

Dim sum beef meat balls with ginger
small squares of pasta dough filled with beef
forcemeat, salt, soda (lightening), cornflour,
sugar, green pork fat, coriander leaves, fresh
ginger, seasoning, spring onion. Walnut-sized.

Dim sum char siew pau
steamed rolls of baking powder pastry with
pork filling, but often made with yeast dough.

Dim sum hoeng sai kau
pastry envelopes with coriander leaves. Rolled
lard pastry cut into rounds. Filling: tongu
mushrooms, prawns, pork, pork fat, bamboo
shoots, chopped, salted, seasoned with
coriander leaves.

Dim sum pockets with bamboo shoots
filled balls of dough, pressed together in
waves at the seams. Filling of prawns, pork,
pork fat, bamboo shoots, groundnut oil,
sugar, glutamate, sesame oil, cornflour,
chopped coriander leaves or chives.

Duck pie Amiens
jelly from giblets. Bone but do not skin duck.
Stuffing from liver, gizzard, streaky bacon,
mushrooms, seasoning, mainly bay leaf. Fry
in butter. Flambé with juniper spirit. When
cool mix with fried onion purée and beaten
egg. Line dish with pastry, add duck.
Surround with stuffing. Top with pastry,
bake. Fill up with giblet jelly.

Duckling terrine Nantes
small boned duckling with skin. Giblets boiled
to a jelly. Duck marinated in potato spirit
with mild fennel and fresh mint. Stuffing of
duck and chicken livers, pork, marinade. Line
terrine with pork fat, add duck stuffed with
filling and surround with stuffing. Cover with
aspic jelly when cooked.

Duxelles
thick, brown, mushroom-based sauce for
pouring over meat or poultry dishes or as
filling for puff pastry pies.

E

Easter patties Berry
served as starter to precede Easter lamb.
Marinate half pork and half veal in white
wine for 24 hours, then mince. Flavour with
brandy and nutmeg. Line a square tin with
pastry and fill with alternate layers of
forcemeat and hard-boiled eggs, ending with a
layer of forcemeat. Cover with pastry. Bake.
Serve at room temperature.

Eel
river fish used whole in pâtés or as outside
casing. It is used for pies in England.

Eel pie *page 157*

Eel terrine *page 78*
terrine d'anguille.

Empanada *page 170*
pie from Galicia. Case of pasta (bread dough)
or *hojaldre* (puff pastry) with filling of meat,
seafood such as scampi or prawns, or fish.
Almost always baked in a paella pan.

Empanada gallega
Spanish chicken pie. Filling of cooked
chicken, fried onion, garlic, peppers, ham,
tomatoes. Filling is spread on a round of
pastry, topped with a second round and
pressed together. Edges are turned upwards.
Baked and served hot or lukewarm.

Empanadas fritas
small envelopes of lard pastry, with filling of
beef, onion, garlic, peppers, cumin, olives and
hard-boiled egg. Half-moon shaped, deep-
fried in fat and served hot.

Entrées
(from the French for 'start') cold or hot hors
d'oeuvres. Most pâtés are served as an entrée.

F

Farce
forcemeat, finely chopped or puréed mixture
of meat, game, poultry, fish or vegetables.
Includes lightening or binding agents.

Fattened chicken
(poularde) young, fattened chicken with firm,
white flesh. Basis for good stuffings. Best
quality from France, e.g. Bresse or Landes
chickens.

Fattened liver
alternative name for foie gras.

Fish
for fish pâtés and terrines quality is very important. Specially recommended: pike, salmon, eel, pike-perch, trout.

Fish balls *page 37*
made from fish forcemeat and cooked in stock. Used as filling for vol-au-vents or bouchées.

Fish forcemeat *page 34*
made with fish fillet and bread or flour panada, with egg white and cream.

Fish stock
made with fish bones and offcuts, sliced onion, parsley, mushroom peelings, peppercorns. Boiled in water and white wine and strained. Used for poaching galantines and making sauces.

Fish velouté
basic white fish sauce.

Flour panada *page 36*
popular lightening agent for delicate meats such as poultry and veal, but also used for fish and vegetables. Basic recipe: 100 ml/4 fl oz milk, 25 g/1 oz butter, seasoning, 50 g/2 oz flour, 1 egg. Made like choux pastry and pushed through a sieve when cool.

Foie gras en brioche *page 106*
goose liver in brioche pastry.

Foie gras mousse *page 134*
mousse made from goose liver, marinated in Armagnac and port and lightly fried.

Frying fat
for deep-frying of pies. The fat should have a high burning-point, like oil or vegetable fats.

Fungi
most varieties can be used for pâtés. Often used in veal or poultry forcemeats.

G

Galantine de canard *page 118*
duck galantine, rolled pâté.

Galantine de canard sauvage *page 120*
rolled galantine of wild duck.

Galantine de coquilles Saint-Jacques *page 121*
scallop galantine.

Galantine de foie gras
goose liver galantine. Made from seasoned fattened goose liver, a forcemeat of liver offcuts, onion, salt, pepper, bay leaf, thyme, Madeira, pork, pork fat, reduced Béchamel sauce, breadcrumbs, egg and brandy. Lay smoked pork fat on foil or cloth, cover with forcemeat, dot with diced truffle, fat and pistachios. Top with goose liver. Roll. Poach in veal stock then cut into slices and glaze with aspic jelly.

Galantine de gibier à l'épicure
Italian game galantine. Filling of venison, hare, pork, pork fat (part diced and marinated in brandy) and marinade. Fold in marinated mixture. Spread forcemeat on tea-towel or foil, place venison breast in centre. Roll. Poach in stock of vegetables, thyme, bay leaf, cloves, peppercorns, red wine, salt, water and powdered gelatine. Make aspic jelly from stock and cover galantine.

Galantine de pigeon à l'ancienne
old-fashioned Dutch pigeon galantine. Filling of poultry livers poached in butter, pork and veal, with seasoning, Armagnac, Madeira, eggs, goose liver marinated in Madeira and diced truffles. Stuff the pigeons, and include breast meat marinated in Armagnac. Poach in bone stock. Cool, slice and cover with jelly.

Galantine de poulet *page 123*
chicken galantine.

Galantines
pâtés enclosed in boned meat, including skin. Filled with fine forcemeat. Cooked in an appropriate stock, e.g. duck in duck stock. A simpler and more usual modern method, after stuffing do not try to recreate original shape but roll to make a rolled pâté.

Game
excellent for pâtés, especially hare and game birds, for it is low in fat, high in protein and of good flavour. Can also be used frozen for pies, unlike other meats. It contains little liquid to be lost during thawing. For a fine forcemeat only the best is good enough.

Game stock *page 42*
made from game bones and offcuts, vegetables, first roasted in oil, tomato paste, water, bouquet garni of celery, leek, parsley, bay, thyme, shallots, garlic, juniper, peppercorns and salt.

Game terrine with truffles *page 54*
terrine de gibier aux truffes.

Gefillte fish
stuffed fish from Jewish cooking. One of the most famous international dishes. Classic method: skin fish (with bones) and fill skin with stuffing, trying to recreate the original shape. Simpler method: cook fish in a fish-shaped mould. Usually two freshwater fish are used, for example trout, bream, pike, carp. Stuffing: fish, onion, seasoning, egg, matzo flour. Cooked in fish stock which is then reduced to jelly and used for coating. Serve with horseradish.

Genoese vegetable pie
pastry filled with exotic vegetables in velouté and baked.

Goose liver
(foie gras), usually refers to fattened goose liver, which comes from 6 to 8-kg/13 to 18-lb geese, force-fed for 21 days, and weighs 700–1000 g/1½–2¼ lb. From grey Gascony or Périgord geese or white Alsace geese. Imported from the Eastern Bloc and Israel.

Goose liver and apple tarts *page 142*
fry seasoned and floured pieces of goose liver in oil and top with sliced apple.

Goose liver parfait
(parfait de foie gras), goose liver mixed with a pork forcemeat. Goose liver mousse is often referred to as parfait.

Guinea-fowl
(pintade), gives excellent meat for forcemeats.

H

Halibut pie
filling made from mushrooms, chopped green pepper, salt, pepper, thyme, nutmeg, ginger, fried in butter. Roll rectangle of puff pastry and cover with cool mushroom mixture. Top with halibut fillets, seasoned, fried in butter and cooled, and cover with mushroom mixture. Dot with butter. Fold over pastry, seal and bake. Serve with prawn sauce.

Ham mousse *page 135*
mousse de jambon.

Hare pâtés
are made from various recipes. The fillets are usually marinated and included whole.

Hare pie
hare cooked in butter, white wine, brandy and seasoning with glazed onions and mushrooms. Transferred to a pie dish, covered with seasoned gravy and puff pastry. Served hot with the remaining gravy.

Herbs *page 24*
pâtés and terrines are usually seasoned with dried herbs, but fresh herbs are substituted where they complement the dish. Fresh herbs can be used in fish pâtés and pies, aspics, sauces, hot patties.

Hure de sanglier farcie
stuffed wild boar's head. Highly complicated galantine, with a long tradition.

J

Jus
(French for stock) is a defatted meat juice. For forcemeats it is usually made with the bones and offcuts of the meat used.

K

Khatshapuri
Georgian cheese loaf, an unusual pâté in the shape of flans or loaves of yeast dough. Filled

with a mixture of mild camembert, chopped gouda, sheep's milk cheese, butter, egg and parsley.

King prawn mousse *page 135*
mousse de crevettes.

Kneaded pastry
one of the many terms referring to shortcrust, also known as pie pastry.

Kulebyaka *page 164*
Russian salmon or cabbage pies.

Kulebyaka with chicken
filling of chicken cooked in butter with salt and pepper. Chopped onion, sliced mushroom, chicken stock, chopped hard-boiled egg and parsley added. Spread over rectangle of yeast pastry, topped with fried pancakes, layers of stuffing and pancakes. Covered with pastry, sealed to make a loaf and baked.

L

Lamb galantine
stuffing of sliced calf's liver with fried onion, lamb, pork fat, eggs, seasoning, parsley, brandy, diced smoked tongue. Spread over boned shoulder of lamb. Roll and truss and poach in slightly gelatinous lamb stock.

Le poirat berrichon
pear pie from Berry region. Pears marinated in brandy, sugar and a little pepper. Line casserole dish with shortcrust pastry. Add drained pears, cover with pastry. Bake. Add marinade through steam opening. Serve chilled. Variation: use half apples, half quinces.

Leek tarts gratin *page 143*

Leverpostej
Danish liver pâté. Forcemeat of pork liver, pork fat, onion, eggs, puréed anchovy fillets, seasoning, béchamel sauce, whipped cream, meat stock. Transfer to mould lined with pork fat and cover with fat.

Lihamurakepiiras
Finnish pâtés. Shortcrust pastry with soured cream, filled with forcemeat of mushrooms, minced meat and cheese (Cheddar). Eaten with soured cream.

Liver pâté
all pâtés with liver as main ingredient. The absolute tops for gourmets: pâté de foie gras.

Livonian caldunis
filling of pork, suet, pepper, allspice, mace, salt. Pirozhki yeast dough thinly rolled, cut into rounds, filled, folded to half-moons. Cooked in boiling salted water. Served with brown butter and Parmesan.

Livonian salmon pirozhki
pastry of flour, water, egg, brandy and plenty of butter. Rolled as for pirozhki. Filling of rice mixture with slices of salted salmon, chopped onion and butter. Shape into pirozhki before baking.

Lobster
(langouste) delicately flavoured, expensive shellfish. Popular for parfaits and used in pieces in fish pâtés. Also used as filling for patties.

Lobster terrine with vegetables *page 84*
terrine de langouste aux légumes.

Lorraine boar's head pie
can also be made as a terrine. Forcemeat of fat belly pork, beaten egg, white cheese, plum brandy, seasoning. Included whole: boar's head meat marinated in Aligoté white wine and plum brandy and slices of boar's liver. Fold boar meat into forcemeat. Line dish with shortcrust pastry, top with stuffing, liver, more stuffing, then pastry lid. Decorate and bake.

Lorraine cheese tarts *page 142*
quiche lorraine.

Lorraine goose pâté
line dish with heavy, but smooth, shortcrust. Forcemeat of pork and veal, egg, breadcrumbs, plum brandy, seasoning. Top with goose, veal and breast of pork, all in pieces and marinated in Mosel wine. Then cover with pastry. Bake. Make jelly with goose offcuts and veal bones and pour into pie while still warm.

M

Macaroni tarts *page 143*
à la milanaise, filled with macaroni, ham and mushrooms.

Madeira aspic
extremely popular aspic for topping up pies or served diced with pâté.

Marinade
pâté ingredients used whole, or for the forcemeat, are often marinated for up to 3 days depending on the recipe. Basis of marinade is usually wine, mainly southern wines such as port, Madeira, sherry, but also red and white wine.

Maultaschen
speciality from Swabia. Rolled pasta dough is cut into rectangles and filled with minced meat or ham, onion, spinach and seasoning and folded into triangles – boiled in stock.

Meat forcemeat
meat filling for pâtés, pies or meat balls.

Meat jelly
clarified meat stock which jellyfies on cooling by addition of calf's feet or gelatine.

Mirabeau pies
puff pastry patties filled with sole, cooked in butter, broken into pieces and bound with anchovy sauce.

Mogador pâtés
once a speciality in the Parisian restaurant of the same name. Diced chicken and smoked tongue are bound with a chicken cream sauce and filled into patties with alternate layers of puréed goose liver, and served warm.

Montgelas filling
for vol-au-vents. Goose liver and smoked tongue are poached separately in Madeira and mixed with fried mushrooms and Madeira sauce.

Moorland sheep pie
filling made from moorland sheep, pork, pork fat, seasoning, reduced stock, with smoked tongue and ham – both diced. Line dish with pastry, add half filling. Top with pieces of leg or loin of lamb seasoned with special sauce from shallots, Kümmel liqueur, reduced stock and seasoning. Cover with remaining filling and pastry. Decorate.

Morels
after truffles the most popular fungus for pâtés and fillings.

Mousse *page 131*
one of the unusual pâtés. They are pâtés with aspic added, whose main ingredient may be a fine purée of vegetables, poultry, ham, game, chicken liver, fish or shellfish. Made with gelatine and whipped cream and turned out of the mould to serve.

Mousseline farce
forcemeat for mousse.

Mushroom tartlets *page 142*

Mushroom terrine *page 90*
terrine de cèpes.

N

Nantes patties
puff pastry patties filled with cooked seafood mixed with mushrooms fried in butter and fish velouté. Served with mushroom gravy.

O

Offal
innards, particularly of veal and lamb (can include beef – for example tongue), popular used in pieces in pâtés.

Offcuts
waste and odd pieces of meat produced when meat or fish is trimmed.

Onions *page 23*
for fine pies and terrines the more delicately
flavoured shallot is used, or possibly mild
seasoning onions. Yellow onions and garlic
are used where a stronger flavour is
appropriate. Red onions are milder and can
be used more freely. The same is true for
spring onions.

Ox tongue
smoked, popular diced in pâté fillings.

Oyster
delicately flavoured type of shellfish, made
into pâté or included whole.

Oyster pasties
braised oysters in rounds of shortcrust pastry,
shaped into half-moons and cooked in hot
butter.

Oyster pie
old English recipe. The oysters are cooked in
a stewed beef filling.

P

Panada *page 36*
used for lightening forcemeats. Can take the
form of a flour panada (like choux pastry) or
a cream béchamel sauce.

Pancake rolls *page 174*
thin pancakes of special dough, filled with
bean shoots, Chinese mushrooms, chicken,
pork, prawns, bamboo shoots and seasoning.

Paotze
small Chinese meat balls of pasta dough filled
with pork (like dim sum).

Parfait
term for fine forcemeats which include either
aspic or egg white and are poached in a bain
marie. Ideal basic ingredient: vegetables, also
fish and shellfish.

Parfait d'écrevisses *page 140*
prawn parfait.

**Parfait de faisan au foie gras
et morilles** *page 141*
Pheasant parfait with goose liver and
morels. Forcemeat: seasoned pheasant, egg
white, flour panada, whipped cream, pieces of
goose liver marinated in brandy, morels in
their juice.

**Parfait de volaille au foies de
volailles et cèpes** *page 140*
chicken parfait with chicken liver and flap
mushrooms

Parisian pie
1. Forcemeat of marinated pork, pork fat,
eggs, shallots, seasoning, thyme, bay. Fill
pastry-lined dish with alternate layers of
forcemeat and diced meat. 2. Marinate beef
fillet in white wine and brandy, shredded,

salted and flavoured with herbs and shallots.
Line mould with pastry, fill with balls of beef,
veal and panada forcemeats and cover with
beef fillet. Cover with pastry and bake.

Partridge
ideal meat for forcemeats. Breasts of young
partridge are good for using whole.

Pâté
French for pie or pâté.

Pâté d'alouettes
lark pâté. Bone birds, stuff with truffles and
goose liver. Roll into balls. Sieve sealed liver
to make a forcemeat. Line dish with pastry,
fill with forcemeat, stuffed birds and more
forcemeat. Cover with pastry. Top up with
jelly after baking.

Pâté de venaison *page 50*
venison pâté. Same recipe can be used for
antelope pâté.

Pâté d'artichauts *page 86*
artichoke pâté. Filling of veal and pork with
artichoke hearts. Bake in yeast dough.

Pâté de bécasses
woodcock pâté. Forcemeat of innards, lightly
fried chicken liver, woodcock legs mixed with
pork forcemeat. Stuff boned woodcock with
this forcemeat and the breasts. Truss. Mix
pork forcemeat with Madeira and pâté
seasoning. Fold in diced foie gras. Line dish
with pastry. Add woodcock forcemeat, stuffed
birds, pork and liver forcemeat. Cover with
pastry. When cold top up with aspic jelly
from woodcock bones.

Pâte brisée
French term for shortcrust pastry.

Pâté de caille *page 54*
quail pâté. Forcemeat of quail meat, pork,
pork fat, seasoning, quail stock, chopped
pistachios and truffle. Line tin with pastry and
fill with stuffing. Top with foie gras and fried
quail breasts. Cover with stuffing and pastry.

Pâté de chevreuil *page 48*
venison pie.

Pâté à la contade
original name of pâté de foie gras, named by
its inventor Jean-Pierre Clause after his
master, the Maréchal de Contade.

Pâté à la corniaule
takes its name from the Corniaule area near
Vichy. A pâté made from kid served on 23
April for the feast of St George. Kid is
marinated for 24 hours in local wine (from
gaillard noir grapes) with wild thyme, juniper
berries, onion and garlic. Forcemeat of kid's
liver, pork fat, wood mushrooms, salt,
seasoning, shallots, lightly fried in butter. Use
reduced white wine to make forcemeat
smooth. Stir in egg yolk. Line a dish with
pastry, add stuffing and kid meat, cover with
pastry and bake.

Pâté d'escargots *page 85*
snail pâté. Forcemeat of fried, sliced shallots,
white bread, egg white, single and whipped
cream, veal, thyme, marjoram, seasoning.
Halve snails (tinned) and fry in butter with
shallots. Make stock with Pernod, brandy,
veal stock, snail liquid, seasoning, and reduce.
Fold into forcemeat with snails. Line tin with
pastry, add filling and pastry lid.

Pâté de faisan en croûte
filling of pheasant meat (marinated and fried)
with pork, pork fat, goose liver and meat
glaze. Line oval tin with pastry, cover with
slices of fat and the stuffing. Fill with
marinated breast meat, pheasant and chicken
liver, halved truffles and strips of pork fat.
Cover with fat, more stuffing and pastry. Top
up with Madeira jelly after baking.

Pâté de foie gras *page 101*
goose liver pâté. Invented by Jean-Pierre
Clause in 1762. Fattened goose liver from
Alsace was wrapped in pastry and baked
without truffles.

Pâté de foie truffé *page 108*
truffled liver pâté. Stuffing of calf's liver,
pig's liver and pork. With diced, fried liver,
ham and truffles included.

Pâté de jambon *page 61*
ham pâté, pork forcemeat around a piece of
pork fillet.

Pâté de lièvre
hare pâté with a filling of hare and pork.
Includes hare fillets wrapped in pork fat.

Pâté de marcassin *page 50*
wild boar pâté with a stuffing of boar's leg
and pork loin.

Pâté de perdrix *page 53*
partridge pâté Filling of partridge legs, pork,
fat and seasoning with diced foie gras, truffles,
smoked tongue and pistachios.

Pâté de poularde, chaud ou froid *page 67*
chicken pâté, hot or cold. Served warm with
Madeira sauce, or cold topped up with
Madeira jelly.

Pâté de saumon *page 77*
salmon pâté. Forcemeat of salmon fillet, white
bread, egg white, cream, diced truffles.

Pâté de tartouffes
potato pâté. Pastry of flour, egg, butter, salt,
water. Line a pie dish. Alternate layers of
thinly sliced potato and onion (dotted with
lard and goose fat) and seasoned. Cover with
pastry, bake and serve hot.

Pâté de volaille au foie gras *page 69*
poultry pâté with goose liver. Forcemeat of
seasoned guinea-fowl, duck and pork fillet.
Includes fried guinea-fowl breasts and truffled
goose liver.

Pâté seasoning *page 22*
mixture of seasoning for all types of stuffings.

Patties
also croustades. Usually blind-baked puff or shortcrust pastry cases. Filled and served as starter or entremets. Once they always had a pastry lid but seldom nowadays. Size ranges from individual to large flans.

Patties capuchin
puff pastry patties filled with scrambled egg, braised sweetbreads and chopped truffle.

Patties à la Kaunitz
Austrian. Fry diced blanched sweetbreads and diced mushrooms in butter. Add diced truffles and balls of veal forcemeat. Bind with Madeira sauce. Transfer to hot puff pastry cases. Cover with pastry lid.

Patties nimois
filling of lamb and smoked bacon, chicken liver, basil and brandy. Fried and then lightly crushed. Serve in hot puff pastry cases.

Pelemeni *page 163*
a kind of pâté of egg-pasta dough with meat filling, cooked in salted water. Served hot with chopped parsley or dill, melted butter or soured cream. Originally from Siberia.

Peppers
mostly used in fillings for empanadas.

Perch
one of the best freshwater fish, equally good for forcemeats or used in fillets.

Petites terrines de champignons en couche *page 89*
individual mushroom terrines. Filling as for terrine de champignons à la maison, of veal or poultry. Cook in buttered moulds and cover with white or green chaudfroid sauce.

Petits pâtés de foie en brioche *page 107*
individual liver brioches. Filling as for terrine de foies de volaille. Line brioche tins with pastry, fill with forcemeat, top with pastry. Top up with port jelly when cold.

Pheasant
game bird, excellent for pâtés.

Pie case *page 151*
vol-au-vent.

Piecrusts *pages 10–17*

Pie alla ferrarese
line tin with pastry. Filling of mushrooms, fried sweetbreads, chicken, salt, pepper, wine, boiled short macaroni and stock, béchamel sauce, cheese and butter. Cover with pastry.

Pies *page 155*
English dish pies, usually with only pastry lid, less frequently with dish completely lined with pastry.

Pigeon terrine *page 73*
terrine de pigeon au basilic.

Pike
(brochet), the ideal fish for forcemeats. Can be used for pie fillings or fish balls.

Pirozhki
term covers a variety of Russian pâtés. Served with soup or as starter.

Pirozhki fillings *page 167*
flap mushrooms with chicken; pork and beetroot; sauerkraut; herb curds; smoked salmon; ham and rice; lamb.

Pirozhki Smolensk style
buckwheat groats, pre-roasted in a pan, seasoned and boiled until thick. Mixed with melted butter, finely chopped hard-boiled egg, chopped onion and parsley. Spread on squares of yeast dough, rolled and baked.

Pirozhki tworogom
pirozhki filled with herb curds.

Pistachios
fruit of pistachio tree is a popular ingredient for pâtés, partly for their lovely green colour.

Poisson en brioche *page 78*
fish pâté in brioche dough.

Pork
by far the most popular meat for pâté fillings. Pork is also added to most kinds of game to make the meat less dry.

Pork fat
for most terrines and pie fillings best quality green, i.e. fresh, pork fat is used, sometimes smoked. Can also be marinated. To line and cover terrines.

Pork pie
English pork pie. Pastry of flour, lard, water, eggs is scalded and covered with pork fillet forcemeat while still hot, rolled, brushed with egg yolk and baked. Topped up with pork jelly when cold.

Port
famous Portuguese wine, mainly used to flavour jellies.

Poultry liver
the liver (unfattened) of all types of poultry is a popular ingredient for forcemeats. If included in pieces in pâtés, it is usually diced and fried first.

Poultry pâté with goose liver *page 69*
Pâté de volaille au foie gras.

Poultry tartlets *page 143*
small tarts filled with cooked poultry and poultry forcemeat, covered with Hollandaise sauce and browned.

Poultry velouté
basic white poultry sauce.

Pudding *page 158*
English term also refers to steamed meat pies.

Puff pastry *page 16*

Punta di vitello ripieno *page 128*
Italian-style stuffed breast of veal.

Q

Quail
the smallest game bird of the field fowl family, also available from quail farms. For fine forcemeats and used in pieces (particularly breasts).

Queen patties *page 148*
the most popular of the puff pastry patties, filled with various fillings, but usually with ragoût fin.

R

Rabbit
popular for pies in both the domestic and wild varieties. As with hare the fillets are often included whole.

Ragoût de cèpes au ris de veau *page 152*
flap mushrooms with sweetbread and truffles.

Ragoût de coquilles Saint-Jacques *page 151*
scallop filling.

Ragoût de crevettes roses *page 151*
filling of king prawns and mushrooms.

Ragoût d'écrevisses à l'anèth *page 152*
prawn and dill filling.

Ragoût d'écrevisses Nantua *page 151*
Prawn filling Nantua.

Ragoût d'escargots *page 152*
snails in Riesling sauce with shallots and mushroom heads.

Ragoût d'homard *page 148*
lobster filling.

Ragoût de légumes *page 150*
vegetable filling of morels, green peas, spring carrots in chicken velouté with cream and asparagus tips.

Ragoût de poulet *page 150*
chicken filling of diced morels in chicken velouté with cream and cooked diced chicken breast.

Ragoût de ris de veau *page 150*
veal sweetbread filling of pieces of sealed sweetbread in a port-veal-stock-cream sauce with parsley.

Raised game pie
English game pie. Line pie mould with hot water pastry. Cover with slices of pork fat and filling of hare, rabbit and pheasant. Top with strips of fried pheasant breasts, rabbit and hare fillet. Brush with melted butter,

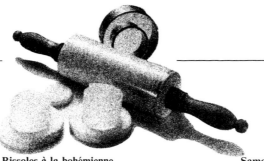

cover with pastry. Top up with aspic jelly after baking.

Rastegai
pâté with *vesiga*, the dried back tendon of the sturgeon. Sold in continental European delicatessens. *Vesiga* is soaked and cooked in meat stock, then finely chopped, mixed with chopped hard-boiled egg and fish velouté, transferred onto rounds of yeast pastry, shaped into half-moons and baked.

Ravioli
envelopes of Italian pasta in various shapes, filled with meat or vegetables and cooked in stock or tomato sauce. Served with grated Parmesan. A speciality of Genoa.

Ravioli alla genovese
envelopes of Italian pasta with filling of veal and pork, calf's brains and sweetbreads, egg, bread, Parmesan and turnip. Seasoning: nutmeg.

Red deer pie
prepared as for venison pie, the fillet being sealed and included whole.

Reduced stock
concentrated flavour which underlines the main flavour of fine pâtés and terrines. Made from offcuts of the main meat used, with root vegetables. Often diluted with wine. The stock is greatly reduced, and can then be added to forcemeat, or used to bring out the flavour of ingredients used whole – for example by brushing onto fillets.

Reims pie
marinate pork for 24 hours in champagne, little oil, seasonings and juniper berries. Cut into strips. Line tin with pastry. Fill with lean meat forcemeat bound with eggs. Cover with strips of meat and pastry lid.

Rice croustade capuchin
fry glazed onions and rice, and allow to swell in meat stock. Press into cup moulds and leave to cool. Cover in egg and white breadcrumbs and deep-fry. Remove centres and fill with scrambled egg and grated Parmesan.

Rillettes de porc
the original terrine recipe, preserved pork. French speciality. Chopped fat pork is fried in lard with onions, herbs and seasoning, chopped, boiled until soft, seasoned with paprika, mixed with liquid lard and bottled. Use to spread on bread.

Rissoles
rounds of shortcrust or brioche pastry, topped with forcemeat of meat, fish, poultry or shellfish, folded into half-moons and deep-fried.

Rissoles with beef marrow
filling of poached beef marrow, with Madeira sauce reduced until thick, in puff pastry. Coated in breadcrumbs and deep-fried.

Rissoles à la bohémienne
filling of goose liver and truffles bound with meat glaze. In brioche pastry.

Rissoles Cendrillons
Cinderella rissoles. Brioche pastry with filling of chicken and truffles in puréed goose liver. A totally undeserved name.

Rissoles à la chalônaise
chicken rissoles. Shortcrust filled with chicken, mushrooms and truffles in velouté sauce.

Rissoles Indian style
puff pastry with filling of lamb (fried), onion, flour, curry, tomato paste and chopped apple. Reduce the sauce.

Rissoles Lucy
with a filling of crushed, smoked sprats and blue-vein cheese.

Rissoles de poisson
fish rissoles. Seasoned minced fish in thick béchamel and egg yolk. Puff pastry, coated in breadcrumbs and deep-fried.

Rissoles Pompadour
tongue rissoles. Shortcrust filled with smoked tongue, mushrooms, truffles and meat glaze.

Rolled pâté   *page 116*
term for galantine with filling spread over boned poultry such as duck or pheasant and then rolled, with no attempt to keep the original shape. Quick method for making galantines.

Roman pies
batter made from 125 g/4½ oz flour, 8 fl oz milk, 1 tablespoon oil, salt, nutmeg. Traditional pie irons are heated in fat and dipped into the batter. Fry pies in fat until golden brown and fill with filling to taste.

Roux   *page 148*
binding agent for forcemeats.

Rub-in pastry   *page 13*
shortcrust, for which fat and flour are rubbed in to form crumbs before the other ingredients are added.

S

Salmon
(saumon), this almost boneless fish is ideal for pâtés either fresh or smoked. Equally good as a forcemeat or used in fillet form.

Salmon and fried egg tarts   *page 142*

Salmon terrine   *page 82*
terrine de saumon, with its truffled salmon stuffing, wrapped in salmon fillets, almost a galantine.

Salpiçon
(ragoût fin), meat, poultry, game, fish or vegetables, finely diced and bound with a little gravy. Used as bouchée or tart filling.

Samosa   *page 173*
savoury Indian pancakes. Flour-oil-water pastry cut into thin rounds (saucer-sized). Halve rounds, top with filling, press together into triangles. Filling of garlic, ginger, onion, oil, curry, minced beef or lamb, mint and coriander.

Sea trout
freshwater fish of the salmon family. Makes a particularly delicate fish pâté.

Seafood pie
American pie of chicken, scallops, oysters, fish, onion, celery, lobster and sherry. Covered with pie crust.

Seasonings   *page 19*

Shallots   *page 23*

Shepherd's pie
place cooked, minced lamb with onion, carrot and seasoning in dish. Top with mashed potato beaten with egg and egg white and seasoned. Flavour meat with plenty of mint, rosemary, marjoram and parsley.

Shortcrust or kneaded pie pastry   *page 12*
known as pâte brisée in France. Suitable for all crust pies. Basic recipe: 600 g/1¼ lb flour, 300 g/11 oz butter, 1 teaspoon salt, 8–12 tablespoons water, 1 egg.

Shortcrust with lard   *page 12*
basic recipe: 500 g/18 oz flour, 200 g/7 oz lard, 1 teaspoon salt, 100–200 ml/4–7 fl oz water.

Shrimps
made into fillings for pâtés, terrines, parfaits and timbales and also used whole. Also popular in vol-au-vents.

Singara   *page 163*

Smoked fish mousse   *page 133*
mousse de poisson fumé, with caviar filling.

Snipe
a much sought-after game bird for pâtés, but protected in some countries.

Spanakopitta   *page 171*
Greek pie with spinach and Feta cheese filling. Yeast pastry.

Spirits
used to flavour forcemeats. Added to stock, alcohol boiled out to leave the flavour.

Squab pie   *page 56*
English pigeon pie which ideally combines sweet and savoury ingredients.

Steak and kidney pie   *page 156*
the best-known of all the English pie recipes.

Steak and mushroom pudding   *page 158*
steamed suet pie.

Strasbourg goose liver pâté
a pâté de foie gras. Basically a terrine of truffled goose liver, marinated in Madeira and brandy, and goose liver forcemeat.

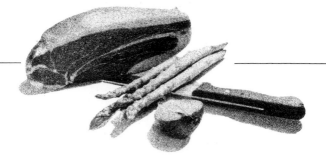

Suet shortcrust pastry *page 14*

Sulzpastete
German term for mousse.

Sweetbreads
popular offal for pies and also for patty fillings.

T

Tartar caldunis
mix tender, finely chopped beef with finely diced suet, season, add a little cold water. Chop with a knife. Cut low-fat pastry into thin rounds, fill, fold into half-moons. Boil in salted water or light stock.

Tartlets
small, blind-baked flans of shortcrust, occasionally puff or yeast, pastry. Filled with ragoût fin (salpiçon) and served hot. Or first lined with forcemeat, then baked and filled.

Tartlets Agnes Sorel
flans coated with chicken stuffing and baked. Filled with chicken, mushrooms and truffle in velouté with cream. Covered with chicken forcemeat and browned. Decorated with smoked tongue and truffle slices and a dash of Madeira sauce.

Tartlets aiglon
fresh goose liver, mushrooms braised in butter, half made into forcemeat, flavoured with brandy, mixed with egg yolk and egg white. In tarts, covered with forcemeat and browned.

Tartlets Argentueil
cooked chicken breast and boiled asparagus, puréed, seasoned, put into flan cases and decorated with buttered asparagus tips.

Tartlets Danoises
Danish flans filled with salmon purée, topped with mayonnaise, sprinkled with cheese and browned.

Terrine *page 39*
pâté without piecrust. The filling is cooked in terrines (porcelain or ceramic dishes), usually lined with thin slices of pork fat.

Terrine d'abatis d'oie *page 70*
duck giblet terrine. Forcemeat very low in fat content.

Terrine de brocoli *page 87*
broccoli terrine. Alternate layers of broccoli and celery forcemeat. Covered in chaudfroid sauce.

Terrine de campagne *page 60*
country-style terrine. Forcemeat of rabbit and pork, flavoured with herbs and brandy.

Terrine de canard *page 71*
duck terrine.

Terrine de canard au poitrine de canard truffée *page 72*
duck terrine with truffled breast of duck. A breast of duck is stuffed with truffles and included in the terrine.

Terrine de canard sauvage au foie de canard *page 59*
wild duck terrine with duck's liver. Filling of wild duck and pork with breast of duck included.

Terrine de champignons à la maison *page 88*
house-style mushroom terrine with veal filling.

Terrine de dindon truffé *page 72*
truffled turkey terrine with turkey and pork stuffing.

Terrine de faisan au foie gras *page 58*
Pheasant and goose liver terrine. Forcemeat of pheasant and pork with pistachios and diced truffles. Pheasant breasts and goose liver included in pieces.

Terrine de foie gras *page 120*
goose liver terrine.

Terrine de foie de veau *page 108*
calf's liver terrine. Filling as for pâté de foie truffé, but with pork to replace the pig's liver.

Terrine de foies de volaille *page 122*
poultry liver terrine with pork and pork fat.

Terrine de lapin *page 57*
rabbit terrine with forcemeat of rabbit and pork and back fillets of rabbit included whole.

Terrine de légumes au foie gras *page 87*
vegetable and goose liver terrine and a chicken stuffing.

Terrine maison aux haricots verts *page 65*
house-style terrine with green beans. Filling of pork, chicken breast and calf's liver.

Terrine de Nérac
line dish with smoked bacon and fill one-third full with a forcemeat of partridge, pork fat, chicken liver and Armagnac. Top with partridge breasts, fried and flambéed in Armagnac, slices of foie gras and truffle and cover with remaining filling and smoked bacon.

Terrine de pintade au ris de veau et morilles *page 74*
guinea-fowl terrine with sweetbreads and morels.

Terrine de pintadeaux *page 74*
terrine of young guinea-fowl. Filling of guinea-fowl and pork fillet, with guinea-fowl breast flavoured with Armagnac included whole.

Terrine de poisson du chef *page 77*
chef's own fish terrine. Filling of pike or turbot fillets; flap mushrooms, lobster claws, green beans, carrots, salmon trout and turbot included.

Terrine de poulet au foie de volaille *page 68*
chicken terrine with liver.

Terrine de ris de veau *page 63*
sweetbread terrine with filling of veal and pork.

Terrine de sanglier *page 52*
wild boar terrine.

Terrine de sanglier 'Rioja' *page 52*
wild boar terrine with game liver marinated in Rioja and Armagnac.

Terrine de sole au foie gras *page 81*
sole terrine with goose liver.

Terrine de truites arc-en-ciel et truites saumonées *page 80*
rainbow and salmon trout terrine.

Terrine de truites saumonées au parfait d'huîtres *page 72*
salmon trout terrine with oyster parfait. Filling of salmon trout. Includes oyster forcemeat with carrot sticks and green beans.

Terrine de turbot au basilic frais *page 72*
turbot terrine with fresh basil.

Terrine de veaux aux champignons de couche *page 64*
veal and mushroom terrine.

Thrush pâté
(pâté de grives), a delicate pâté from Languedoc. The boned birds are stuffed with truffled foie gras and baked in a forcemeat of pork, pork fat and game liver, flavoured with Armagnac.

Tim sum
Singapore name for titbits known as dim sum in China.

Timbale de brochet aux crevettes en sauce à l'anèth *page 138*
pike timbale with prawns in dill sauce.

Timbale de brocoli à la sauce aux noix *page 139*
broccoli timbale with walnut sauce. Filling of puréed steamed broccoli, eggs, cream and seasoning.

Timbale de carottes à la sauce aux herbes *page 139*
carrot timbale with herb sauce. Filling of carrots braised in butter, stock and seasoning and whisked with egg and cream. Cooked in moulds.

Timbale de chou-fleur à la sauce d'épinards *page 139*
cauliflower timbale with spinach sauce. Stuffing of cauliflower braised in butter and chicken stock, puréed with eggs and cream.

Timbale de perdreaux aux morilles à la crème *page 136*
partridge timbale with morels in cream.

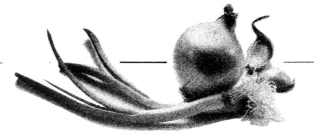

Timbale de pistaches au sauté de faisan *page 137*
pistachio timbale with stewed pheasant, with pork stuffing.

Timbale de saumon au sauté de cuisses de grenouilles *page 137*
salmon timbale with frogs' legs. Served on steamed spinach.

Timbale de saumon fumé au moules *page 138*
smoked salmon timbale with mussels.

Timbales *page 136*
small metal moulds also known as darioles. Originally pâté cases baked blind in cup moulds. Still made in this way occasionally but usually cooked in water without the pastry case.

Tomato mousse *page 135*
mousse made with sieved tomatoes and ketchup.

Tongue
one of the best parts of animals and also game. Particularly popular is smoked ox tongue used in pieces.

Torta pasqualina
Italian Easter pie. Light pastry is filled with seasoned artichoke purée, spinach, possibly winter endive in light ricotta cheese and milk sauce with hard-boiled eggs, and baked

Tourte de brocoli *page 132*
broccoli flan. Broccoli mousse with venison fillets on puff pastry base.

Tourte de ris de veau *page 64*
sweetbread flan, a speciality made from a pork fillet filling and sweetbreads.

Tourte de saumon *page 83*
salmon mould with pike filling.

Trout
large salmon trout in particular are popular for pâté fillings or using whole.

Truffles *page 109*
an expensive fungus. The best of the truffle family are the black Périgord winter truffles. Only in the winter do they develop their full flavour. Périgord truffle is the botanical name; they have the same name when found outside Périgord, for example in Provence or Spain.

Turbot medallion tarts *page 143*

V

Varenyky
Ukrainian patties; cheese, sauerkraut or plum filling. Cooked in salted water and served with melted butter and soured cream.

Vatrushki *page 166*
Russian curd tarts. Pastry filled with curd mixture.

Veal
together with pork the most popular domesticated meat for pâtés. For fine forcemeats the loin is best.

Veal and ham pie *page 159*
traditional English pie. Typical of this pie is the dicing of the veal and ham and not as a puréed forcemeat. Filled with hard-boiled eggs and baked in pastry in a loaf tin.

Veal tarts *page 142*

Velouté *page 148*
velvety white sauce (*velours* = velvet) made with flour cooked in butter and strongly-flavoured light veal stock. Boil 30 minutes, skim, strain in thick reduced cream. Strain through muslin. Depending on the recipe can be made with chicken, veal or game stock.

Venison pasties *page 160*
English. Diced venison is marinated in groundnut oil and port with root vegetables. Pastry rolled into large rounds, filled and covered with second round.

Vintner's pie
chopped snails are mixed with snail juice and chestnut purée and flavoured with brandy. Served in puff pastry cases.

Visishki
Russian fish pies. The chopped sea or freshwater fish is bound in a basic fish sauce, filled into small half-moons of yeast dough and deep-fried.

Vol-au-vent *page 151*
large puff pastry, dome-shaped pastry case baked blind, then filled with fine forcemeat. Attributed to Carême. Requires about 575 g/1¼ lb puff pastry.

Vol-au-vent cardinal
filling of lobster, mushrooms, truffles in white wine, pike balls, brandy and cream. All mixed separately in béchamel sauce mixed with lobster juice and Hollandaise sauce and arranged in layers in the pie crust.

Vol-au-vent president-style
fried sole fillets, sprinkled with lemon juice and parsley. Top with pike balls cooked in fish stock. Then prawns and béchamel sauce with truffle purée.

Vol-au-vent Toulouse-style
a filling of sweetbreads and veal meatballs boiled with root vegetables. Placed in pie case with diced sweetbreads and mushrooms braised in butter, covered with velouté and topped with a slice of sweetbread.

W

White bread *page 34*
one of the best ways of lightening fine

forcemeats without affecting the flavour, especially those made from fish and vegetables. Must be high quality and fresh and of light, airy consistency. Usually moistened in cream and egg white.

Wild boar
the tender meat of a young boar is particularly good for forcemeats.

Wild boar pie with venison fillet *page 51*
Pâté de marcassin au filet de chevreuil.

Wild boar
has an ideal flavour (particularly the back) for stuffings. Combines the advantages of the meat of domestic pigs with a delicate game flavour.

Wine
any wine used for cooking should always be best quality. This alone has the fine flavour necessary for aspic jellies and marinades.

Won-tons
Chinese dish. Meat or seafood filling wrapped in pasta-type pastry. Can be cooked in *congée* (a rice mixture) for breakfast, in the soup for supper but can also be served as a snack – fried or steamed.

Y

Yeast pastry *page 15*
made from 500 g/18 oz flour, 25 g/1 oz yeast, 250 ml/8 fl oz lukewarm milk, 50 g/2 oz butter, 2 eggs, 1 teaspoon salt. Can be used for both hot and cold dishes.

Yorkshire pie
diced onion and beef are fried, then braised with carrot, tomato and leek, seasoned with salt and pepper, transferred to a pie dish and baked, covered with suet pastry.

Z

Zamponi *page 126*
Italian stuffed pig's trotters. Scalded pig's trotters are hollowed out to the toes and soaked. Stuffing: pork loin, fat, seasoning, thyme, marjoram, smoked tongue and diced veal fillet, pistachios. Stuff trotters and sew up. Wrap in strips of linen and cook in beef stock. Particularly good smoked.

Moulds and Other Utensils

The would-be pâté maker should not be put off by the number of implements and tins available. You can make fillings for pies or terrines in any kitchen with the normal range of utensils, but an efficient mincer with a sharp blade and a cutting disc with the smallest possible perforations is essential, or an electric food processor with a sharp blade. It is important to have some experience of your oven and its temperature variations before starting on pâté making. Other utensils are by no means essential, but there are a variety of minor technical aids which will make your work much easier. A thermometer, for instance, to allow you to regulate the temperature of poaching stocks or a meat thermometer which can help determine exactly when a pâté is cooked. The same is true of the many different dishes and tins. You could make do with an ordinary cake tin, but a pie tin which folds open guarantees that the pie will come out of the tin with the pastry intact.

1 Wood-frame sieve with metal mesh for sieving minced meats. A metal mesh is essential to cut through the meat fibres.

2 Conical sieve for straining stocks and sauces.

3 Set of metal bowls for mixing forcemeats.

4 Plastic pastry scraper.

5 Metal pastry scraper, also useful when sieving forcemeats.

6 Rubber spatula, an essential aid for scraping out bowls with hot contents.

7 Rectangular pastry cutters. A set of two different sized cutters (as for round cutters) for cutting out croustades.

8 Small cutters for making funnel openings and decorations.

9 Pastry cutters for tarts and decorations. Plain and fluted round cutters allow for a variety of different decorations.

10 Tartlet tins, plain or fluted. With diameters of 8–12 cm/3–5 in.

11 Open gutter mould.

12 Gutter mould with lid. Used for cooking dishes standing in a water bath and also for mousses (pâtés with aspic). Pâtés made in a tin of this shape are easy to slice.

13 Pastry brush, for brushing pâtés with egg yolk. Choose a wide brush with natural bristles.

14 Plain pastry wheel.

15 Fluted pastry wheel.

16 Pastry crimper for decorating pâtés.

17 Fluted oval pâté mould. This traditional French mould consists of two side pieces, held together with clips, and a base. The mould comes apart, making it very easy to remove the pâté.

18 Collapsible pâté moulds. They consist of two side pieces and a base. The hinged joints make it very easy to remove the pâté.

19 Long loaf tin. The tapered sides make it easy to line with pastry and help the pâté to turn out cleanly.

20 English pudding basin in porcelain. The rim at the top allows for tying the cloth with which the filled basin is covered.

21 Ovenproof bowls for terrines baked without a lid.

22 Terrine dishes of enamelled cast iron with lid. Guaranteed to produce good results.

23 Timbale moulds. Range from 100–200 ml//4–7 fl oz volume, round or oval, but always slightly tapering to make for ease of turning out timbales or mousses.

24 Earthenware terrine dish, in heavy glazed pottery for country-style terrines.

25 White glazed earthenware dishes, oval or rectangular for terrines.

26 Earthenware dishes, open and with lids for terrines. The particularly thick walls guarantee that the filling will cook evenly.

27 Decorative game terrine dishes. The shape of these terrines echoes the classic piecrust and the lid illustrates the possible contents.

28 Round terrine dish, quite deep, intended for spreads.

Technical Terms Explained

A

aiguillettes, long thin strips of meat or poultry.

allumettes, matchstick-sized pieces.

à part, served separately, e.g. a sauce.

à point, at the right time, just right (of cooking time).

B

Bain marie, or water bath, a container partially filled with hot water in which delicate dishes such as sauces are cooked, kept warm or warmed through.

barding, partially or fully covering meat, vegetables, fish, poultry with rashers of fat bacon. Meat fillets used whole in pâtés or pies are often barded.

bateau, boat-shaped tart with savoury filling.

batterie de cuisine, kitchen equipment.

best end of neck, joint between shoulder and neck, used for stewed fillings, or braised.

blanching, pouring over, or briefly immersing in, boiling water. Vegetables or fungi are often blanched to remove unpleasant flavours and impurities. Place vegetables in simmering salted water, boil for a few minutes and refresh in cold water. Some meats, e.g. sweetbreads, are also blanched.

blind baking, baking pastry cases without filling. To help keep their shape they are first lined with greaseproof paper or foil and filled with dried peas or beans. Remove after baking.

boil to clarify, to cook sauces and soups slowly, continually removing foam and fat until completely clear.

boning, removing all bones from meat, poultry or game, without damaging the skin, so as to preserve the original shape and leave the skin intact.

bouquet garni, bunch of flavourings composed of various herbs, vegetables and seasonings. Used to improve flavour of stocks or sauces.

braise, cooking method between frying and boiling.

braisière, cooking pan with tight-fitting lid for braising and steaming.

braising, cooking in a little liquid, fat and the food's own juices.

brioche, yeast cake. Applied to pastry refers to unsweetened yeast pastry.

browning (flour), flour cooked in butter, diluted with stock or water and stirred smooth.

brunoise, finely diced vegetables.

burning off, beating a dough with a wooden spoon over a fierce heat until it comes away from the sides of the pan. The process evaporates any excess moisture in the dough.

C

cannelated, fluted, e.g. tins.

cannelons, stuffed rolls of pastry.

carcass, bird's rib cage.

carrée, front end of back (rib) of veal, lamb and pork.

charcutier, pork butcher.

charlotte, round, cylindrical tin or mould.

chaudfroid, meat dishes in savoury aspic sauce, served cold.

chemise, outside coating.

chemising, lining a tin evenly with aspic jelly or with some other mixture before adding the filling.

cimier, back section of loin of game.

clarify, to remove anything that makes a stock or jelly cloudy. Adding egg white and finely chopped meat binds and removes impurities.

cocottes, small, ovenproof, porcelain or earthenware cooking dishes, in which food is both cooked and served.

colle, softened, squeezed out and diluted gelatine.

collé(e), mixture containing gelatine.

colour, to brown or give colour to.

consommé, strong, clear meat stock. Heat minced beef, diced root vegetables and a little egg white with cold, defatted meat stock and simmer for about 2 hours, strain, bring back to the boil and season.

contrefilet, rib of beef, roasting beef.

couenne, rind, skin.

couleur, brown sugar colour.

court-bouillon, highly seasoned stock for cooking fish.

crêpes, thin, egg pancakes used, for example, to fill the Franco-Russian pie coulibiac.

crustaceans, shellfish.

cuisse, thigh, leg.

cul, hindpart.

culotte, tailpiece of beef.

cure, to keep meat by salting or covering with pickling liquid. Curing keeps the red colour of the meat and increases its flavour.

custard, egg cream.

D

dariole, small, smooth-sided cup mould.

deep-fry, fry until golden in deep hot fat.

defatting, removing fat from stocks, sauces and soups by skimming from the surface.

dégorger, to soak in water, especially applied to soaking blood from brains, sweetbreads, hearts or liver.

demi-glace, strong brown gravy, basic brown sauce.

dressing = trussing, also arranging, or piping forcemeat or pastry into the required shape.

drying, draining or wiping dry.

E

entrées, warm or cold dishes served as part of a long meal to precede the main course.

entremet, small dish served between the main course and the dessert.

essence, highly reduced stock, concentrated gravy.

F

feuillantines, small puff pastry cakes.

ficeler, to tie up with string.

filet d'eau, few drops of water.

fines herbes, finely chopped herbs in various combinations for sauces or soups; sometimes includes finely chopped shallots.

flavour, to season a dish with an aromatic liquid.

fleurons, small, half-moon-shaped puff pastries used to garnish various dishes.

fond, extract produced by cooking meat, poultry, fish or vegetables. Basis of sauces.

fond d'artichaut, artichoke hearts.

fond blanc, white veal or chicken stock.

fond de gibier, game stock.

fond de volaille, poultry, chicken stock.

forcemeat or farce, filling for pâtés, terrines, meats, poultry, fish or vegetables, consisting of very finely chopped or puréed meat, fish, vegetables, fungi etc, seasoned and bound.

fricandeau, part of leg of veal.

fricassée, white stew of veal, lamb or chicken.

friture, deep fat for frying meat, poultry, fish or vegetables. Food to be fried is placed in a wire basket in hot fat. Also called frying fat.

frivolités, unusual small titbits.

fumet, essence, particularly game.

G

gardemanger, cook specialising in cold dishes (including pâtés and terrines).

garnish, to decorate a dish.

garnishing, something served with the main dish, but also the main ingredient of a sauce or soup. The garnish is often included in the name of a dish.

gelatine, pure, tasteless bone extract in powder or leaf form used for setting liquids and light dishes.

gibier, game (hare and game birds).

glace, highly reduced, unsalted stock of veal, chicken, game or fish, used to improve sauces or glaze meats. Glace is boiled until it will set completely when cold, so that it can be cut.

glaze, to cover food with *glace*.

glazing, frying lightly in fat without allowing the food to colour.

graisse, fat produced by boiling stock.

gratiner, to brown under the grill to produce a crust.

greasing, coating a tin with fat to make it easier to remove the contents at a later stage.

H

hanging, making meat juicier and adding flavour by keeping for a time hanging in the air.

J

jelly, various clarified, solidified liquids.

julienne, fine strips of vegetable or truffle, included in or accompanying dishes.

jus, pure meat juice or roasting juices which jellify when cool.

L

lard, to stick small pieces of fat into meat.

lardon, small strip of pork fat.

lier — to thicken.

lining, covering the inside of a tin or dish with thin slices of pork fat or thinly rolled pastry.

M

macerate, to soak a food in a seasoned liquid, pre-season.

mask, to cover with sauce or jelly.

meat thermometer, instrument for determining precisely when a pâté, terrine or galantine is cooked.

mêler, to mix.

mie de pain, white breadcrumbs without crust.

mijoter, to simmer or braise over a very low heat.

mince, finely chop or pass through mincer.

mirepoix, finely chopped root vegetables, onion and lean streaky bacon lightly fried with thyme and bay.

mirlitons, filled puff pastry flans.

mitonner, to boil slowly in liquid.

monter, to beat butter into a sauce or soup.

mousseline, mousse in small moulds.

N

napper, to mask, or cover foods with jelly or sauce.

P

panada, binding or thickening agent for forcemeats.

paner, to dip first in flour, then in breadcrumbs.

pâte feuilletée, puff pastry.

pickling, putting meat, poultry or game in seasoned acidic liquids to make them more flavoursome and mature, or to help them keep.

pickling liquid, highly seasoned, acidic liquids (vinegar, buttermilk, lemon juice, wine) which preserve or mature pieces of meat.

poach, to cook slowly without allowing to boil.

pound, to reduce meat, fish, seasonings, herbs, etc in a mortar.

primeurs, early or spring vegetables, early fruit, young wine.

purée, thick cream or pulp.

Q

quenelle, dumpling, small ball of meat or fish forcemeat.

R

ragoût, dish of chopped meat, fish or vegetables in a highly seasoned sauce. Used as filling.

râper, to rasp, to scrape meat out of the skin or off gristle.

reducing, boiling liquids such as stocks, soups, sauces to the right consistency, or even until thick. Reduces the liquid content and improves flavour.

refreshing, plunging hot foodstuffs into cold water to reduce temperature.

rémoulade, highly seasoned mayonnaise with chopped herbs, anchovy fillets, capers and gherkins.

rissolé(e), fried or baked until brown and crisp.

rissoling, to cook until brown and crisp.

rolling out, rolling a wooden rolling pin over pastry to make it of even thickness.

roux blanc, lightly cooked flour, basis for many sauces and soups.

S

salmis, brown stew of game bird.

sauce chasseur, huntsman's sauce.

sauce à la creme, cream sauce.

sauce mornay, white cheese sauce.

sauce mousseline, foam sauce.

sauce suprême, fine white chicken sauce.

sauce villeroi, white coating sauce.

saucer, to cover with sauce.

sauter, to quickly fry small pieces of meat, poultry or fish.

sealing, technical term for quick frying of meat fillets, liver, fish.

set, various-sized matching containers, e.g. bowls, saucepans.

sieving, passing through a sieve (hair or conical) or a muslin cloth.

skimming, removing curdled egg white from the surface of stocks, sauces or gravies with a perforated spoon.

soubise, white onion purée with meat or poultry.

spinach juice, spinach leaves used to colour sauces. Squeeze out boiled spinach leaves in a cloth, heat the juice slowly, stirring from time to time and removing any bits of leaf that rise to the surface with a sieve, and then strain through a fine sieve.

supreme, a dish made with the best part of the animal, prepared in a specially fine way.

sprinkling, covering a tin with a thick layer of flour, breadcrumbs, sugar or chopped almonds, for example. The tin is first thoroughly greased with fat.

steaming, cooking in water without the food coming into contact with the liquid. To steam you need a pan with a rack or trivet.

strain, to pour a liquid through a sieve or cloth.

stuff, fill with seasoned mixture (forcemeat).

stuffing balls — dumplings.

T

thicken, to thicken a dish with a binding agent.

tourner, to cut to shape, e.g. garlic cloves or olives, to cut notches in mushroom heads.

tranche, slice.

trim, to remove fat, skin and gristle from meat or fish and cut to shape.

trussing, bringing whole boned poultry back to its original shape with the help of a needle and thread.

turning out, tipping a dish out of the mould in which it has been cooked or left to set.

V

velouté, basic white sauce.

W

water bath, *see* bain marie.

Index